Cinema and Society

General Editor

Jeffrey Richards
*Department of History
University of Lancaster*

Frontispiece

Frank Capra (38th
from right) directing
Spencer Tracy,
Katharine Hepburn and
William Demarest in
State of the Union.

HOLLYWOOD GOES TO WAR
FILMS AND AMERICAN SOCIETY 1939-1952

Colin Shindler

Routledge & Kegan Paul
London, Boston and Henley

First published in 1979
by Routledge & Kegan Paul Ltd
39 Store Street, London WC1E 7DD,
Broadway House, Newtown Road,
Henley-on-Thames, Oxon RG9 1EN and
9 Park Street, Boston, Mass. 02108, USA
Set in Century 9pt by Columns
and printed in Great Britain by
Lowe & Brydone Ltd

British Library Cataloguing in Publication Data

Shindler, Colin

Hollywood goes to war. — (Cinema and society).
1. Moving-pictures — United States —
Social aspects
I. Title   II. Series
791.43'0973   PN1995.9.S6   79-40535

ISBN 0 7100 0290 4

For Nancy Lynn White
from Boys Town to Maine Road

'A trip through Hollywood is like taking a trip
through a sewer in a glass bottom boat.'

Wilson Mizner

Contents

Illustrations

General Editor's Preface

The pre-eminent popular art form of the first half of the twentieth century has been the cinema. Both in Europe and America from the turn of the century to the 1950s cinema-going has been a regular habit and film-making a major industry. The cinema combined all the other art forms — painting, sculpture, music, the word, the dance — and added a new dimension — an illusion of life. Living, breathing people enacted dramas before the gaze of the audience and not, as in the theatre, bounded by the stage, but with the world as their backdrop. Success at the box office was to be obtained by giving the people something to which they could relate and which therefore reflected themselves. Like the other popular art forms, the cinema has much to tell us about people and their beliefs, their assumptions and their attitudes, their hopes and fears and dreams.

This series of books will examine the connection between films and the societies which produced them. Film as straight historical evidence; film as an unconscious reflection of national preoccupations; film as escapist entertainment; film as a weapon of propaganda — these are the aspects of the question that will concern us. We shall seek to examine and delineate individual film *genres*, the cinematic images of particular nations and the work of key directors who have mirrored national concerns and ideals. For we believe that the rich and multifarious products of the cinema constitute a still largely untapped source of knowledge about the ways in which our world and the people in it have changed since the first flickering images were projected on to the silver screen.

Jeffrey Richards

Preface

First of all I feel compelled to issue a word of warning. This book does not pretend to be a complete history of Hollywood during the period under review. I acknowledge willingly that I have wilfully ignored serials, shorts, nearly all 'B' pictures and most documentaries. Fans of Val Lewton will read this book and shake their heads disapprovingly. Those among us fortunate enough to appreciate the finer qualities of *Snuffy Smith* and *Joe Palooka* will note with a resignation bordering on despair the marked absence of their heroes.

The *auteur* fetishists and the *genre* freaks and the students of arcane film theory will find this book a dreadful *mélange* of films that simply happen to be interesting to me. As a working producer in the current British television industry I am only too aware of the sort of imperatives that shape the plays and films that are 'pre-sold' to a cinema or transmission slot. It has been of some pleasure to discover that Hollywood in the 1930s and 1940s was but ATV Network writ large.

Films were not created in an artistic vacuum. Their makers were shaped by and responded to various social, political and ideological stimuli and in their work they helped to intensify those feelings which were transmitted to their audience. This book then is basically a different way of approaching the social history of the time.

Historians are still dubious of the value of works of the imagination. I hope this book will help to dispel some of those doubts.

Acknowledgments

My greatest debt is to Frank Capra whose films rescued me from one of my darkest moments and who, in person and in his work, has given shape to my life. I should like to extend my thanks to Brenda Davies and her admirable assistants in the British Film Institute's Information Department and to Mildred Simpson and Bonnie Rothbart at the Library of the Academy of Motion Picture Arts and Sciences in Beverly Hills.

I am particularly grateful to Ron Haver at the Los Angeles County Museum and to the American Film Institute for screening many vital films for me. My thanks also go to Henry Fonda, Philip Dunne, Mark Robson, the late John Howard Lawson and above all to the late Robert Lord for supplying oral testimony unavailable in any other form.

The stills reproduced in this book first appeared in films distributed by the following companies, to whom thanks are due: Warner Bros, Republic Pictures, Metro-Goldwyn-Mayer, Paramount, Twentieth Century-Fox, United Artists, Columbia and Universal. For additional help in this area I am grateful to John Baxter and Al Reuter. I am particularly happy to acknowledge a great debt to John Baxter in that he taught me to write about films. Dr J.R. Pole of St Catherine's College, Oxford taught me to write about American history and Neil McKendrick of Gonville and Caius College, Cambridge, taught me to write properly.

Alarums and Excursions

(Events leading up to September 1939)

By the mid 1930s the Hollywood studio system had
reached the apogee of its glory. The American film
industry had established a pattern of production
which enabled it not only to weather the worst of
the Depression but to thrive during those difficult
years. Executives were fired and stars changed
partners with frenetic abandon; writers wondered
why none of their dialogue was ever spoken in the
pictures they were working on and directors be-
moaned the witless idiocies of the scripts that the
studio's delivery vans tossed on their front door-
steps. Through it all movies were written, produced,
directed, edited, distributed and exhibited to the
satisfaction of the film companies, their share-
holders and their customers.

It was a devastatingly effective form of imperialism. Trade might have followed the flag in classic
nineteenth-century imperialism but in the 1930s
American influence spread abroad in the wake of
Gable's rough grin and Garbo's mirthless laugh.
Coca-Cola, at a later date was just as economically
aggressive but it left no imprint on the mind or soul
as did Shirley Temple and Gary Cooper. American
manners, American aspirations and, less fortunately,
American speech patterns and syntax became
comfortingly familiar to the countless millions of
moviegoers.

The huge overseas market was, in the normal
course of events, the area where the film companies
picked up their profits as production costs were
traditionally recovered by the North American
rentals. High studio overheads, however, which, in
the case of MGM, Paramount and Fox included the
maintenance of large numbers of cinemas as well as

the huge salaries of stars, producers and top executives, meant that European sales were particularly
crucial to the continuing financial success of the
studio system. Garbo's sound films were nearly all
financial liabilities in the domestic market and, by
the mid 1930s the profitability of her films rested
almost entirely on their performance in Europe.

At the same time foreign countries were developing a sensitivity to Hollywood caricature that forced
the studios unwillingly into the uncertain world
of international diplomacy. When Josef von
Sternberg's *The Devil is a Woman* (1935) depicted
a member of the Spanish Civil Guard as being
drunk, the Spanish government instantly demanded
an apology. The Hays Office, which was ceremon-
ially wheeled out for such occasions, offered to
mediate between the Spanish authorities and the
offending company (Paramount) but the former
insisted that the matter was a political one and
could only be dealt with by a fully accredited representative of the State Department. The *Hollywood
Reporter* revealed

> It is admitted that today, due to the political
> situation throughout Europe, censorship on
> pictures touching on topics considered dangerous
> to those in power is tougher than ever. The
> picture companies are through with their former
> stand, 'We'll make it anyway'. They will now
> listen to foreign departments whose business it is
> to keep closely in touch with problems con-
> fronting the sales departments abroad.[1]

It has long been accepted in Hollywood that certain
countries had particular quirks. Japan slashed every
scene in which there was kissing and in 1937
informed the American film industry that the
country took great exception to a movie which
explicitly showed a policeman unashamedly eating
a banana in full view of the public. England disliked
the use of the word 'bum' to mean 'tramp' and the
British Government thoughtfully provided RKO

with a 'technical adviser' to ensure that *Gunga Din* (1939) did not run contrary to official colonial policy. *The Bitter Tea of General Yen* was one of the few films Frank Capra ever made which was not a commercial success — a fact that can be attributed almost entirely to its being banned in the British Empire because of its treatment of the delicate subject of miscegenation. Egypt once deleted a sequence showing an escape from an orphanage on the grounds that 'it set a bad example for school-girls'. These oddities, however, were all tolerated with reasonable good humour because they did not trouble the studios too greatly.

The uncertain political situation in Europe in the late 1930s was quite another story. Mussolini's motion picture bureau banned *The Charge of the Light Brigade*, *Lives of a Bengal Lancer*, *Lloyds of London* and *Clive of India* on the grounds that they contained 'British propaganda'. Ironically, Holly-wood producers, dedicated as they were to the un-alloyed pursuit of 'entertainment', had succeeded in driving out of the movies almost any considered political thought whatsoever. To have their escapist fantasies criticised as propaganda was most upsetting simply because the charges, even if untrue, were impossible to challenge. The fascist dictator-ships simply refused to judge the Hollywood pictures on the same basis as their producers.

As the territory under the jurisdiction of the dictators grew ever larger, the financial profitability of Hollywood movies lessened proportionately. After the Anschluss, Nazi-occupied Austria impounded the money still remaining there from the proceeds of American film rentals. Hollywood studios had learned very quickly that the masters of the New Germany found their product to be infini-tely resistable. Fox's picture *My Weakness* (1933) was banned because the censor, appropriately enough, thought the lace panties on the girls would contaminate the national morality. *Country Doctor* (1936), the epic Twentieth Century-Fox dramatisa-tion of the birth of the Dionne quins, bit the dust when Jean Hersholt was denied Aryan status. The studio produced every shred of evidence it could find to prove that Jean Hersholt was not then, nor had he ever been, a member of the Chosen People, but it was to no avail and the ban remained in force. The ultimate idiocy came in 1936 when, on the explicit orders of Hitler, the films of Mae West, Johnny Weissmuller, Francis Lederer, Fred Astaire, Ginger Rogers, Warner Oland and George Arliss

were prohibited from exhibition in Germany. Weissmuller was Jewish, Lederer was Czech, Arliss had specialised in the portrayal of historical characters with Jewish overtones (Rothschild, Shylock and Disraeli) and Warner Oland had been responsible for that fiendish Oriental *untermensch* Charlie Chan, but the connection of Mae West, and more particularly, Fred Astaire and Ginger Rogers, with anything remotely kosher was never revealed. The only remaining conclusion is that a man who so revered Wagner was incapable of appreciating the finer delights of *Top Hat* and *Swing Time* and rather than risk admitting his own cultural philis-tinism, he simply decreed that no German worthy of the name should have the chance of sampling those aesthetic delights so cruelly denied to him.

However reluctantly, Hollywood was dragged by force of circumstances into the murky realms of American foreign policy. The mood of the film industry throughout the 1930s, like the mood of the country in general and that of Congress in particular, was overwhelmingly isolationist. The division between 'isolationists' and 'internationalists' cut across traditional political groupings, although the internationalists were normally Democrats who lived in the larger cities. The centre of isolationism was, as ever, in the rural Mid-West.

The cause of the internationalists had been struck a violent blow in 1919 when the Senate refused to ratify the Treaty of Versailles which called for the establishment of the League of Nations. The isolationism of successive Republican administrations in the 1920s was succeeded by Roosevelt's early leaning towards economic nationalism. Roosevelt knew perfectly well that co-operation with the decadent powers of Europe was not going to be a sound basis for a popular foreign policy in the 1930s. Everybody was aware that most of the European countries had defaulted on their war loans and popular mythology also held them responsible for nurturing the germs of the economic contagion which swept over the New World after the Wall Street crash.

Additionally, the pro-European internationalist cause was handicapped by the much publicised findings of a Congressional investigation into the profits and influence of the munitions industry. The chairman, Gerald P. Nye, one of the leaders of the isolationist movement, concluded that the munitions makers, in an unholy alliance with international bankers and businessmen, had been responsible for the entry of the United States into the First World War. His demand, fortified by popular support, that profit be somehow removed from the propagation of war, resulted in Congress passing the Pittman Neutrality Resolution in August 1935, by which the export of munitions from the United States was prohibited, as was the shipment of arms on American vessels to foreign belligerents. There was no doubt that the isolationists had reduced the risk of America becoming involved in an international war. They had also, unfortunately, given palpable encouragement to the aggressor nations of the world to become increasingly more aggressive.

Specific acts of aggression served only to strengthen isolationist tendencies. When Italy invaded Abyssinia Roosevelt, with one eye on the 1936 Presidential election, asked only for a moral embargo of shipments to Mussolini's forces. In fact, after the invasion American trade with Italian Africa increased nearly twentyfold. A public opinion poll taken in November 1935 which examined the desirability of the United States becoming involved in a foreign war for whatever idealistic purposes found that 67 per cent wanted no part of it and only 28 per cent were in favour of taking a positive stand against aggressor nations. Even then two thirds of the latter preferred economic sanctions to any form of military participation.

The invasion of Abyssinia, morally shocking though it undoubtedly was, had no very lasting effect on the conduct of Americans either in Washington or Hollywood. After all, film rentals from Abyssinia were low and the size of the Abyssinian vote in American politics was negligible. The treatment by the Nazis of the Jewish population under their control was a very different matter. Pressure was exerted on Washington by the American Jewish Committee, the American Jewish Congress and the B'nai Brith, while the Jewish vote was just starting to make its presence felt within the Roosevelt coalition of ethnic groups. When the Germans demanded apologies for all anti-Nazi statements made by Jews and pro-Jewish sympathisers in America, the US government tried desperately to ensure that all such comments were unofficial. If, as A.J.P. Taylor suggests, appeasement in Britain was the result of a morally justifiable, carefully conceived policy, in America it was a mixture of wanton disregard of human suffering and spineless submission to the political strength of the isolationists.

The advent of the Spanish Civil War persuaded Hollywood to dip its little toe into the icy waters of foreign affairs. After all, it could hardly be avoided, even in darkest Peoria, Illinois. The faces of homeless refugees and helpless orphans stared out from the pages of the daily newspapers, the weekly news magazines and the newsreel screens. Documentaries made by Loyalist sympathisers such as Ernest Hemingway, Lilian Hellman and Joris Ivens were the first motion picture representations. *The Spanish ABC*, *The Spanish Earth* and *Spain in Flames* quickly fell foul of official wrath. *Spain in Flames* was banned in Ohio and Pennsylvania and was denounced by the Governor of the latter as 'pure Communistic propaganda dressed up as a plea for democracy'. Obviously they couldn't fool him that easily.[2]

In the ranks of the feature film Paramount's *The Last Train from Madrid* (1937) had the dubious distinction of being the first Hollywood production to grapple with the complex moral and political issues of the war. Just so that nobody could accuse them of being political propagandists the studio savants took care to add certain 'entertainment' values which involved turning the film into a sort of *Grand Hotel* on wheels. The *New York Times* pointed out that Paramount's Spain, racked though it was by a civil war of unparalleled horror, bore a strong resemblance to MGM's Ruritania and Selznick's Zenda.[3]

Perhaps it was not surprising that *The Last Train from Madrid* should have been the first film whose story had satisfied the Hays Office. Anything slightly more adventurous got short shrift from the industry's self-censorship body whose fear of public displeasure approached raging paranoia. Twentieth Century-Fox halted preparation on another Spanish Civil War story called *Alcazar* because of 'protests' and Universal's *Delay in the Sun* was postponed indefinitely.

In 1937 Walter Wanger was an independent producer who, as a graduate of Dartmouth College, prided himself on being an intellectual cut above the stereotype of the boorish Hollywood producer. When he first broached the idea of a Spanish Civil War picture to the Hays Office, Joe Breen, the head of the Production Code Authority in Hollywood replied baldly, that any material 'involved with or played against' such a background was, in his opinion, 'highly dangerous'.

Nevertheless, the intrepid Wanger set out to chart

the unknown depths of Hollywood's political nature. His first expedition acquired the distinguished services of Lewis Milestone and Clifford Odets. They, fired by the prospect of doing something excitingly different instantly set to work adapting the Ilya Ehrenburg book *The Love of Jeanne Ney*, cleverly substituting expatriate Spaniards for the novel's expatriate Russians. Since this had formed the basis of G.W. Pabst's successful film of 1927 all Hollywood's logic pointed to another smash hit. Unfortunately, *The River is Blue*, as the new project was enigmatically called, flowed straight into native hostility. Joe Breen helpfully suggested that it would be much better if neither side in the conflict were actually identified as such, a suggestion to which Wanger closely adhered throughout the film. Breen also tactfully pointed out that for everyone's better health and good temper it might be a jolly super idea if this Spanish Civil War picture simply omitted any mention of incidents or locations which 'could possibly be tied in with the actual events that have occured or are occurring in Spain'. By this time Odets and Milestone had moved on to other things but the dogged Wanger and his new tame Radical, John Howard Lawson, both agreed to accept Breen's polite emasculation.

Blockade, as the finished film was entitled, was eventually born in 1938 after a difficult and protracted labour. To the Spanish Loyalists who, no doubt, had waited patiently at their local Odeon to see Hollywood's epic tribute to their cause, it must have come as something of a disappointment. In his defence against any demand for a cash refund, Wanger could justifiably point to the shrill cries of right wing paranoia that had accompanied the exhibition of the picture in America. Lawson recalled that it had been due to open at one of the more prestigious Hollywood cinemas but

> at the last minute, the opening was stopped . . . . The picture had been stopped by political pressure. Copies of the script and the film itself were being sent to Paris and to London for consultation with important political figures there . . . . The picture had not been substantially changed. Only minor cuts and rearrangements were made. The film was not slashed and it was not censored heavily but it was changed to please the reactionary political elements in Paris and London.[4]

Lawson conjures up a marvellous image of the Ministers of State at the Foreign Office slaving away deep into the night over a moviola, while the hot line between Whitehall and the Quai d'Orsay buzzed with suggestions as to whether a long shot of Henry Fonda kissing Madeleine Carroll was more subversive than a medium two shot of them holding hands. At the same time he prompts the question as to why top government officials would choose to screen one of William Dieterle's less successful efforts in preference to *Bringing Up Baby* or *Golddiggers in Paris*, both of which were released at about the same time.

Henry Fonda remembers no such Machiavellian re-editing but concedes that as an actor there was no reason why he should have been told. However, he does recall that,

> Before we went into it anything that might have been controversial was eliminated from the story. There wasn't any suggestion that they were Loyalists . . . . It was not the picture that Walter Wanger had thought of making. It was taken away from him.[5]

Blockade, in its final form opened discreetly at a small theatre in Westwood village, but still the chill winds of controversy whistled round it. The Fox West Coast chain of cinemas, under fierce pressure from Catholic groups, declined to screen it at all. The Catholics, because of their identification with anyone fighting the atheistic Loyalists, were the most resolute of the film's opponents. The Church sent round its faithful to picket those theatres which dared to show *Blockade* and was successful in forcing the film out of various cities in Michigan, Nebraska, Louisiana and Ohio. Despite the furore, however, the majority of people who did see the film still crushed it in their own devastating way. One exhibitor wrote,

> This was the controversial film that was supposed to reek of Communism. Naturally I watched it closely and for the life of me I can't see where the shots of Communism crept in.

and another wondered, 'Who was who? What was what? and why was why?'[6]

Nothing daunted, the triumvirate of Wanger, Lawson and Dieterle set to work on a dramatisation of Vincent Sheean's *Personal History*, which was to be the story of a Jewish doctor and his flight from persecution in Nazi Germany. Lawson has even more rueful memories of this one.

Just before it was to go into production, the sets were built and the actors were all engaged Wanger called us in . . . and he was really deeply troubled. He said, 'The whole thing is off. I have to get my money from banks and I'm told I'll never get another penny if this anti-Nazi film goes into production.'

The banks had obviously been scared by the anger aroused by *Blockade* and decided they could not risk a further loss on another political picture. In fact, *Personal History* re-surfaced two years later with a much changed and considerably more attractive face under the title *Foreign Correspondent*, but that is a story better told in a later chapter.

It is illuminating at this point to notice that the most successful, in artistic and financial terms, of the pictures which 'dealt' with foreign policy were probably the Warner Bros series of biographies of great nineteenth-century figures of progress. Like many successful films, the first one initiated a cycle of formula-based successors but surprisingly enough the limitations of the *genre* did not prove too restrictive.

The Story of Louis Pasteur (1936) starring Paul Muni, won three Academy Awards and started the studio down the road that led via Emile Zola and Benito Juarez to Dr Ehrlich and this man Reuter. The Muni films in particular got steadily bolder as they tried to draw parallels between their heroes' struggle for progress against the forces of reaction and the contemporary European scene.

At the end of *The Life of Emile Zola* (1937), Anatole France delivers a funeral oration that seems in retrospect to be nothing but a series of platitudes and self-evident truths.

> 'You, who are enjoying today's freedom, take to your hearts the words of Zola. Do not forget those who . . . bought your liberty with their genius and their blood. Do not forget them and applaud the lies of fanatical intolerance . . . . He [Zola] knew that there is no serenity save in justice. No repose save in truth.'

The sense of *déjà vu* that this scene may induce in modern audiences is the result of having heard such sentiments expressed less eloquently in a thousand other films. In 1937 *The Life of Emile Zola* was considered to be a daring picture, even if it never so much as mentioned the word 'Jew' and wantonly avoided the crucial anti-semitism of the Dreyfus case.

In September 1938 Neville Chamberlain, armed only with an umbrella, flew off to Munich to prevent the outbreak of what much of Europe feared was an inevitable war. He flew back to a hero's welcome, still clutching his umbrella but also waving a piece of paper proving that there was not going to be a war for as long as he waved the paper. Only the Czechs, who had lost the greater part of their country, unsportingly refused to join in the chorus of thanksgiving. The fervour of the rejoicing was proof of the widespread feeling of the imminence of war.

Six thousand miles away in Hollywood recognition of the fact was slowly becoming more apparent. The Hays Report on the film industry published in March 1938 warned gravely that

> Entertainment is the commodity for which the public pays at the box office. Propaganda disguised as entertainment would be neither honest salesmanship nor honest showmanship.

A year later, however, in the wake of events in Europe the same organ trumpeted,

> The increasing number of pictures produced by the industry which treat honestly and dramatically many current themes proves there is nothing incompatible between the best interests of the box office and the kind of entertainment that raises the level of audience appreciation whatever the subject touched.[7]

When we try to quantify this claim, however, we discover that the 'audience appreciation' in 1939 was raised by an idiotic truncation of *Idiots Delight* starring Gable and Shearer, Frank Capra's *Mr. Smith Goes to Washington*, Ford's *Young Mr. Lincoln* and a disastrous film of Robert Sherwood's stage play *Abe Lincoln in Illinois*. Sherwood sold the film rights quickly because he believed 'the international situation is too serious for Lincoln's sentiments about democracy to be withheld from the screen's vast world audience.' Even though the vast world audience showed scant respect for Sherwood's laudable aims the author at least had the compensation of $225,000 of RKO's money. What RKO got out of the exercise is more debatable.

Only two of the films made in 1939 made abundantly clear their disapproval of what was happening in Europe. The first to be released was *Juarez*, the latest in the Muni-Dieterle line of biographical pictures, although this one too cloaked

1 'All right! You've read the script. Which side are you supposed to be on?' Madeleine Carroll looks as though she might have the answer in her handbag. *Blockade*.

2 Goebbels plots retaliation on Warner Bros. *Confessions of a Nazi Spy*.

3 Paul Lukas is introduced to the philosophy of National Socialism. George Sanders looks on approvingly. *Confessions of a Nazi Spy*.

its pretensions somewhat in the safety of history. However nobody apparently saw fit to tell the Press department and the publicity material which accompanied the release of the picture proclaimed,

> In the year 1939, there are leaders whose principles are those of authority, whose selfish interests demand conquests, opposing heroes whose love of liberty demands equal rights for all . . . . Like Benito Juarez, the lives of Jan Masaryk and Eduard Benes are dominated by the principles of democracy . . . . The theme of the picture, that democracy can make no condescensions to the most benevolent authoritarianism is significant to the present day world.

The original material on which the film screenplay by John Huston and Wolfgang Reinhardt was based was Bertita Harding's novel *The Hollow Crown*, a maliciously anti-clerical work. The purpose of the book was to expose the anachronistic corruption of the Mexican Church and it revelled in its portrayal of Pope Pius IX shuffling through the Quirinal in his carpet slippers, rising from his pontifical breakfast of hot chocolate and butter cakes to proclaim the infallibility of Popes, present and future. The final result then was a film with irreconcilable elements and its poor performance in the domestic market was not surprising.

However, *Juarez* was outstandingly successful in overseas sales where the contemporary political parallels were instantly recognised. *Variety* reported that the film played to packed houses in Bombay where the Indians appreciated the homilies on home rule and national sovereignty. No doubt in the same audience sat English gentlemen nodding sagely and sympathising with the beleaguered territories of Europe, smouldering under Nazi oppression.

The only film to come out of Hollywood in 1939 and deal honestly with the European turmoil was Warners' *Confessions of a Nazi Spy*. It was made even more quickly than most Warner productions because of the topicality of its theme. It was adapted from the experiences of a former FBI agent Leon G. Turrou, who had resigned from the Bureau and published the story of how he had cracked a Nazi spy ring hidden within the ranks of the German-American Bund. Milton Krims wrote the screenplay with an assist from John Wexley with none of the arguments that invariably attended the political writings of members of the Radical fringe. Edward G. Robinson who played the part of Turrou

and who was known to the Warner establishment as 'the thinking actor' was uniquely co-operative as was the temperamental director, Anatole Litvak.

In the winter of 1938, while the picture was still being written, there was already considerable speculation about its nature. When Robert Lord, the producer, sent the Hays Office a copy of the second draft just before Christmas he added,

> It goes without saying that this script must be kept under lock and key when you are not actually reading it, because the German-American Bund, the German consul and all such forces are desperately trying to get a copy of it.

The security arrangements Lord was demanding were by no means unjustified. Jack and Harry Warner both received phone calls that threatened their lives and the former confessed that 'no picture ever aroused so much bigotry and hate as this one. We were bowled over by vicious letters, most of them unsigned and there were dozens of phone calls in a similar vein.' A cinema in the German populated area of Milwaukee that dared to show the film was burned to the ground by an outraged band of pro-Nazi sympathisers. The movie itself gained added verisimilitude by its judicious use of genuine newsreel inserts of the notorious German-American Bund rally in Madison Square Gardens on Washington's Birthday, 22 February 1938, during which opponents who made themselves heard were unceremoniously removed and beaten up by the Bund's uniformed hoodlums.

The general tenor of the picture, in particular the scene in which Goebbels appears and directs the dissemination of Nazi propaganda destined for major American cities, provoked the German chargé d'affaires, Hans Thomsen, into angrily denouncing the film to Cordell Hull, the Secretary of State, as an example of the pernicious defamations that were poisoning German-American relations. German influence prevented the picture's exhibition in Italy, Japan and most of the Danubian and Baltic countries, but within the British Empire it was shown, unusually for a controversial film, without a single cut. Ironically, after all the furore *Confessions of a Nazi Spy* turned in a quiet, unremarkable financial performance in the domestic market. Unmollified, the German film industry informed the State Department in a message overladen with Teutonic significance that it was engaged on a series of documentary films dealing with American unemployment, gangsterism and judicial corruption. If these films were ever made they have had a limited impact on the history of the cinema.

Confessions of a Nazi Spy proved to be the most explicitly anti-Nazi film made in Hollywood before America officially joined the war against Hitler. The film again may appear in hindsight to be rather tame but in the context of contemporary American foreign policy it remains a notable landmark. Few of the other studios saw fit to take heart from Warners' example. Paramount wrote confidentially to the Hays Office that *they* would *never* venture into such controversial territory, adding the sanctimonious rider that any picture uncomplimentary to the Nazis was likely to have disastrous repercussions on the Jews still left in Germany. The Hays Office itself cautioned Warners against injecting such 'unfair' elements into the script as the references to Hitler and the dismemberment of Czechoslovakia.

For Warner Bros, *Confessions* was the logical outcome of their consistent hostility to Nazi Germany, which had first taken positive shape in 1936 — not in response to Hitler's occupation of the de-militarized Rhineland but as the result of the murder by Nazi thugs in a Berlin backstreet of Joe Kaufman, the chief Warner Bros salesman in Germany. Thirty years later Jack Warner wrote with evident bitterness,

> Like many an outnumbered Jew he was trapped in an alley. They hit him with fists and clubs and then kicked the life out of him with their boots and left him dying there.

After Kaufman's murder, Warners closed down their German department. When the 'March of Time' episode called *Nazi Conquest No. 1* was offered for sale Warners refused to touch it.

Harry Warner took some pride in producing a series of unprofitable patriotic shorts dramatizing great moments in American history. The fact that Warners willingly sacrificed money in this way was genuine proof of the sincerity of their feelings. When the war was going badly for the Allies after the fall of France, Jack Warner issued a fascinating order forbidding any employee to speak German for the duration of the war. 'At least one producer and a few department heads,' reported *Variety*, 'have gone back to the old practise of counting to ten before they burst into speech.'

When *Confessions of a Nazi Spy* aroused only official disfavour and public apathy, Warners decided to restrict their comments on foreign policy to the minimum. They concentrated instead on a series of recruiting pictures that called for a strong national defence. *Devil Dogs of the Air*, *Here Comes the Navy*, *Submarine D1* and *Wings of the Navy* all publicised the attractions of various branches of the armed services. All of them were directed by Lloyd Bacon, who was himself a naval officer in the Reserve, and they were financed with money from W.R. Hearst's Cosmopolitan Pictures. The overwhelming attractions offered by a life in the service of one's country were further emphasised by the charms of Glenda Farrell and Joan Blondell in *Miss Pacific Fleet* and Dick Powell and Ruby Keeler (for those of a sufficiently liberal outlook) in *Shipmates Forever* and *Flirtation Walk*. The *reductio ad absurdum* of this type of picture-making came when one day in 1942 the telephone rang in Jack Warner's office and General Arnold got on the line to complain that recruitment of rear gunners in the USAF was sluggish but he was sure that a nice cheery film about rear gunners would solve the problem. 'Give it some romantic interest,' added the General helpfully. Sure enough, within a few months Warner Bros' production *Rear Gunner*, starring James Stewart was in exhibition and recruitment soon reached acceptable levels.[8]

As the 1930s ended events in Europe still exercised very little of the American mind. The decade had been dominated by the Depression, by the desperate need for a job, or by the equally desperate need to hang on to one. In 1935 when Congress passed its Neutrality Laws the assembled powers of the world failed to hinder in any way the invasion of Abyssinia by Italy. In 1937 when the Laws were confirmed, Nazi bombs obliterated Guernica. It would be unfair to condemn America for her failure to take a positive stand against the rise of Fascism, when it was clear that she was by no means out of harmony with official policy among the other Great Powers. As long as Europe was officially at peace any American institution or individual to adopt a militantly anti-fascist stance must clearly be the exception rather than the rule. Hollywood which invariably luxuriated in the warmth of the majority opinion looked on approvingly.

The American film industry found life by no means unpalatable in 1939. Whatever political pressures existed were exerted largely on the side of caution. What Hollywood feared above all else was deep division in the country that would cloud the image of America that the majority of film-makers tried to reflect. It was thus with unerring bad timing that Germany invaded Poland and unfeelingly gave Hollywood more than two years of anguish and indecision.

Over There

(September 1939 — May 1940)

The filming of the titles on *Gone With the Wind*
was, like so much of that picture, a mammoth task.
Each of the 'four greatest words since *Birth of a
Nation*' was framed separately as the camera rolled
past on its dolly. During a pause in the action, the
crew turned on the radio to discover that the British
had declared war on Germany. There was a short
discussion and the filming continued. After all,
there had been wars before, there would undoubtedly
be wars in the future, but Al Lichtman at MGM had
seen a rough cut of *Gone With the Wind* and had
assured David Selznick that the picture would gross
at least nineteen million dollars.

Throughout the following twenty-seven months
that separated the Nazi invasion of Poland from the
Japanese attack on Pearl Harbor, the American
attitude to the war in Europe was partly interested
and partly disinterested but always cautious and
invariably confused. Apart from the outright
isolationists who formed a vociferous, influential
but relatively small minority, most Americans had
mixed feelings towards the prospect of another
war. Few were to be seen advocating American
intervention but most people hoped for an Allied
victory.

Nowhere was this belief held more firmly than
in the White House. Franklin Roosevelt had long
since accepted that, in foreign policy, caution was
the better part of diplomacy. After the Japanese
invasion of North China in 1937, Roosevelt had
made a notorious speech in Chicago in which he
had called for a 'quarantine' of aggressor nations
(or in other words an international embargo against
Japan, Italy and Germany) lest the 'disease' of war

infect the Western Hemisphere. The allegory
instantly outraged a vast spectrum of opinion both
official and unofficial. For years the prevailing doc-
trines of foreign policy had held that the business of
America was America and the problems of the Old
World were simply snares to entrap the unwary
President into a morass of unending and unprofitable petty jealousies. Even Woodrow Wilson, who
had been bitterly denounced as a warmonger even
before America had entered the First World War,
always maintained that America could best aid the
world if she came to the ultimate Peace Treaty with
her hands clean, unbesmirched by the emotional
intensities that followed inevitably in the wake of
military involvement.

After the Chicago débâcle, Roosevelt could
hardly be blamed for keeping his anti-fascist lean-
ings largely to himself and to his immediate political
advisers, such as Harry Hopkins and Secretary of
State, Cordell Hull. Events in Europe in the late
1930s served only to confirm the traditional
American scorn for the Old World powers.

The Nazi-Soviet Pact of August 1939 was the
supreme justification of American neutrality. A
more cold-blooded, cynical arrangement it would
be hard to imagine. To the idealists who had seen
in Russia a new concept of democracy it was a
little demoralising to realise that Soviet diplomacy
was indistinguishable from that of the Tsarist
pattern, apart from the absence of gold braid on
the uniforms. To Roosevelt and those who had
watched the growing might of Germany and Italy
with alarm, it was confirmation that a full-scale
European war was inevitable. To the American
isolationists, the Nazi-Soviet Pact was yet another
warning that all Presidential schemes to manoeuvre
the country into the fray must be firmly resisted.

In the summer of 1939, Roosevelt's attempts to
get the Neutrality Laws repealed were unsuccessful.
The President brought all his considerable powers
of persuasion to bear on key Senators but failed to

move them. 'Well, Captain,' crowed Vice President Garner whose relationship with Roosevelt had disintegrated into one of barely disguised mutual hatred, 'We may as well face the facts. You haven't got the votes and that's all there is to it.'

After the declaration of war in September, Roosevelt called back Congress into special session and managed to push through a clause that permitted foreign powers to buy arms from the United States provided the munitions were paid for in cash and transported on foreign vessels. In addition, however, loans were explicitly forbidden to belligerent powers. The result was a direct hindrance to Great Britain, since she had neither the money nor the ships to conform to such requirements. Senator Vandenberg thought that this 'Cash and Carry' provision was a disaster for America and referred to it darkly as 'the first drink of whisky'.

Congressional fears of being sucked into the European mire manifested themselves in the strangest ways. The need for maintaining a strong national defence had always been recognised, yet, between September 1939 and June 1940, the Senate was busily cutting down appropriations for the armed forces, presumably on the grounds that if American troops had no weapons, they wouldn't be able to fight. On 1 September 1939, when General George C. Marshall was sworn in as Chief of Staff, the American army of 227,000 men contained only enough equipment to arm 75,000 of them. The following year, despite the widespread unpopularity of any move that might be seen to further American involvement in the war, America sent Britain so much material that American troops at home resorted to training with bits of telephone poles instead of rifles.[1]

The contradiction remained until Pearl Harbor, principally because although the majority of Americans wanted peace, they were realistic enough to expect American involvement at some point in the proceedings. Also, unlike the situation in 1914, the overwhelming majority of Americans were sympathetic to one side. Roosevelt seized on the mood of the country when he spoke in a fireside chat after the invasion of Poland. 'There will be no blackout of peace in the United States . . . this country will remain a neutral nation but I cannot ask that every American remain neutral in thought as well.' Dr Gallup announced that 96.5 per cent of Americans felt that the country should stay out of the war but that 84 per cent wanted an Allied victory.

The situation was surprisingly complicated by the absence of any fighting. After the Germans had overrun Poland in a matter of a few weeks an eerie calm settled over Western Europe. Everyone knew they were at war but it was difficult to prove it apart from pointing to the ubiquitous gas masks and air raid shelters. Within minutes of Neville Chamberlain's broadcast the drone of the air raid warning siren was heard over the South of England. Yet no winged messenger of death arrived to mar the perfection of a pleasant late summer's day and everyone shuffled back sheepishly to eat Sunday lunch. The phoney war had begun.[2]

In America, the citizens responded to the war with a burst of enthusiasm that the Europeans, who really were at war, found impossible to match. They rushed out and bought 100lbs of sugar and 50lb bags of flour (whether to consume or to use as sandbags in the event of a misdirected Luftwaffe attack is unclear). They also caused a run on maps of Europe and coloured pins but pretty soon the sleeping giant of American industry was aroused and the country staggered under a flood of maps of Europe and coloured pins.

The lack of armed conflict notwithstanding, the war caused an uneasy stir in the film studios while the front offices tried to determine whether it was good for the Jews of Hollywood or bad for the Jews of Hollywood.

Certainly, Hitler's territorial claims in Europe had long been regarded as bad for profits. Soon after he marched into those parts of Czechoslovakia which had not been handed to him by Chamberlain and Daladier six months earlier at Munich, *Variety* concluded that

> Hitler's reshuffling of Central Europe in the past ten days is an additional blow to the American companies' foreign film income . . . . For these major companies (Paramount, MGM and Twentieth Century-Fox) the German sweep through Central Europe this month represents a loss of 2½%-3% of the total foreign business.[3]

The declaration of war in Europe was little help to worried story editors at the major studios. The uncertainties of the summer of 1939 had led to their postponing decisions on spy, refugee and anti-Nazi stories. Warner Bros shelved *Boycott* and *Underground Road* (eventually released in 1941 as *Underground*), Fox held up production on *I Married a Nazi* and Walter Wanger continued to dither over his dramatisation of Vincent Sheean's *Personal History*. It was felt that a sudden declaration of war or conclusion of peace would ruin the market value of the stories. The events of early September gave the green light to production although there remained the nagging fear, intensified in the wake of the phoney war in the West, that peace would break out and cause the pictures to be shelved yet again. *Escape* was a case in point.

> Metro is rushing into production *Escape* book for which it paid $60,000. Studio's speed is due to the fact that *Escape* is a story tying in with the present war and peace before the picture comes out would take the edge off.[4]

The average gestation period for a major Hollywood feature film at this time was about six months or so. As a result of decisions taken in the first few weeks of the war in Europe a spate of films about the conflict were released in the summer of 1940, but due to the firm feeling that the United States should be seen not to be encouraging the propagation of war the American film industry in early 1940 started to get cold feet about the whole business.

> Stories with European backgrounds are being shunted to the sidings by studios in favor of domestic locales. Inasmuch as it is impossible to tell which way the war wind is blowing, producers don't want to be left out on a limb. Writers have been instructed to steer clear of war-ridden countries in treatments.[5]

Nevertheless, although the number of films set in Europe may have been restricted, interest in the war did not slacken in Hollywood, even if it was motivated principally by self-interest. When Paul Reynaud formed a new administration in France a month before the Germans swept aside the invincible French armies, *Variety* pronounced that the new Government was 'considered generally favourable to American film interests here although the New Ministry of Information is rated as "doubtful" '.[6]

Even if concern about the commercial viability of war pictures remained locked into the hearts of Hollywood producers right up to America's entry into the war, they were too aware of the huge profits gathered during the First World War by such generic masterpieces as *The Kaiser — Beast of Berlin*, *Lest We Forget* and *My Four Years in Germany* to ignore war films entirely.

Universal was first into the field in early October with an 'updated' version of their 1930 success, *All Quiet on the Western Front*. The reissue acquired a prologue and an epilogue in addition to a narrator who broke into the film at various points to emphasise the relation between the picture of the last war as portrayed in the film and the stunning actuality of the present conflict. The narration became, according to *Variety*, 'pretty vengeful when it speaks of Hitler and the Nazis'. The new release was not a success and it was withdrawn from distribution quite swiftly. One reason for its relative failure second time around may well have been the fact that it was originally made as an anti-war film and its reappearance as a piece of anti-Nazi propaganda could well have been confusing.

A government foreign policy that positively encouraged caution found a receptive ear in the studios once it became apparent that huge profits were not necessarily waiting to accompany every picture with a war setting. The feeling had been increased in view of the difficulties attendant on the production and exhibition of *Confessions of a Nazi Spy*. In April 1940 the news filtered back to Hollywood that several Polish exhibitors who had shown *Confessions* had been hanged in their own cinemas.

Warner Bros, although they remained consistently anti-Nazi, were prepared to mute their hostility in deference to official requests. They continued with their series of patriotic Technicolor shorts despite the high losses they incurred because Harry Warner felt his studio had 'a tremendous investment in the future of America, and the technical losses are justified in helping to secure that future'.[7]

The script for their production of *The Sea Hawk* was being written in the first months of 1940 by Howard Koch whose committed anti-fascism was carefully concealed in historical dress. As the picture opens a black-garbed Philip of Spain (played by Montagu Love) sits in front of a map of the world raging,

> 'With our ships carrying our flag to the seven seas, with our arms sweeping over Africa, the Near East and the Far West . . . invincible everywhere but on our own doorstep . . . a puny rockbound island secretly gives aid to our enemies . . . .
> You know as well as I that we will never keep Northern Europe in submission until we have a reckoning with England.'

All through the picture Queen Elizabeth (Flora Robson) resists the entreaties of Errol Flynn and the other Sea Dogs to strike at Spain before the Armada is unleashed on England. Elizabeth constantly counters with the argument that her country has not the armaments to match Spain's vast resources. 'Our safety lies in diplomacy not force.' Only after Flynn has brought her irrefutable evidence of Spain's evil intentions does Elizabeth sanction preparations for war.

> 'We have no quarrel with the people of Spain or of any other country. But when the ruthless ambitions of a man threaten to engulf the world it becomes the solemn obligation of free men, wherever they may be, to affirm that the earth belongs not to any man but to all men and that freedom is the deed and title to the soil on which we exist.'

The Sea Hawk, for all its ringing denunciations of the policies of appeasement and isolation, was nevertheless a reversion to the historical dress biographies of Paul Muni and William Dieterle.

Interestingly enough, in the fall of 1939 Dieterle was loaned to RKO for the making of *The Hunchback of Notre Dame* which owed much in the final cut to his Warner biographies. Once more the champion of free thought and academic knowledge (in this case the King, played by Harry Davenport) is pitted against the forces of superstition and prejudice (led by Cedric Hardwicke) which seek to crush the adventurous spirit of man. Certainly the treatment of the gypsies makes them a parallel of, if not the Jews, then at least the thousands of refugees created by the European turmoil. Although anyone less like a nice Jewish girl than Maureen O'Hara it might be hard to imagine, the manner in which Cedrick Hardwicke stops her praying, snapping, 'Praying cannot help you. You come from an evil race,' must have sounded distressingly familiar to those who had suffered from religious and racial persecution.

Outside Warner Bros the other group in Hollywood where opposition to the Nazis was strongest during the Phoney War was within the influential contingent of British exiles. When war was declared, nearly all the able-bodied men volunteered their services but only David Niven managed to get into the armed forces almost immediately and he succeeded only after having incurred the extreme displeasure of Samuel Goldwyn to whom he was under contract. Most of the younger British stars, Laurence Olivier, Brian Aherne, Ray Milland and others all heard the declaration and were instantly consumed by waves of patriotism garnished with guilt, earning as they were huge sums of money while their countrymen faced the prospect of bombings and invasion. Lord Lothian, the British Ambassador in Washington, assured all British artists living in Hollywood that they would be doing a far greater service to their country by remaining where they were and making films that showed off their native land in the best possible light.

In May 1940 the pent-up disgust and jealousy felt by those members of the profession firmly stuck in England for the duration of the war exploded as Sir Seymour Hicks, an actor-manager of the old school, bitterly attacked the British colony in Hollywood whom he scorned as 'gallantly facing the footlights.' He suggested the making of a new film to be called *Gone With the Wind Up* and denounced Alan Mowbray, Alfred Hitchcock, John Loder, Charles Laughton and Herbert Marshall.[8] The indiscriminate criticism was largely unfounded and unfair, particularly in the case of Herbert Marshall who could hardly be expected to be running full tilt at the Germans with his wooden leg.

Nevertheless, the British public was quick to accuse its film personnel of treason if they decided to work in Hollywood at this time. Elizabeth Bergner who was regarded by 1939 as English by adoption left the location filming on *49th Parallel* in Canada early in 1940 and refused to return to Britain for the interiors. Glynis Johns was cast in her part. The biggest storm was reserved for Gracie Fields, Rochdale's greatest cultural ambassador, who had dominated British show business in the 1930s. After Italy entered the war in 1940, her husband, Monty Banks (born in Italy but raised in America) was declared an alien in Britain and she felt it her duty to accompany him to live in North America. She continued to give concerts, donating the proceeds (estimated at £1½ million) to the British war effort, but her relationship with the British people had been fatally compromised.

The amount of money contributed by British stars living abroad never compensated for their 'desertion.' Cary Grant donated his salary from *The Philadelphia Story* ($125,000) and Charles Laughton gave his radio earnings to Red Cross and war relief but such 'sacrifices' made little impact. It was unfortunate that the genuinely concerned British exiles, such as Basil Rathbone and Cedric Hardwicke, who were constantly active in British related causes should have been tarred with the same brush as those Britons who found the Hollywood Hills a mightily effective shelter from German bombs.

American affection for British stars remained undiminished by these affairs. Indeed it even survived the importation of *The Lion Has Wings*, the first British film to deal with the war, produced by Alexander Korda while his mind was evidently elsewhere. It opens with a dextrous montage, devised by Ian Dalrymple and William Hornbeck who cross cut between an English society that showed its people luxuriating in health clinics and seaside resorts and Germans marching, singing and throwing cold water over each other. The film then lumbers into a fictional story that details the way in which every German plane that crosses the Channel is brought unerringly to earth by the magic of radar and its controllers. Chief among these is Ralph Richardson, who arrives home to see his wife switching off the radio after Chamberlain's broadcast of the declaration of war. 'Was that the Prime Minister?' asks Richardson as if Chamberlain had just walked into the bathroom. 'Yes,' replies Merle Oberon, with equal aplomb. 'Are we at war?' asks Richardson with excessive diffidence. 'Yes,' says Oberon pluckily.

It is rare, however, that the dialogue reaches quite such dizzying heights. *The Lion Has Wings* was apparently inspired by talks held between Korda and certain 'important political friends', whom Korda's latest biographer speculates as being either Churchill or Vansittart.[9] The script certainly seems to bear witness to the dead hand of a politician rather than the dead hand of a practised British screenwriter. The token fees paid to the artists (supposedly £5 to the actors and £50 to each of the three directors) indicate that no financial support for the film was forthcoming from the government and the production suffers greatly from its skimpy budget of £30,000 as well as the rushed schedule that permitted no resolution of the conflict between the factual and fictional parts of the narrative. Nowhere is this clearer than in the brief but startling appearance of Flora Robson as Elizabeth I addressing the troops at Tilbury in an unheralded and quite bizarre extract from Korda's 1937 costume epic *Fire Over England*.

Strangely enough, although *The Lion Has Wings* did not find much favour among the English people for whom it was intended, it made an unexpected impact in America where it had secured over a thousand bookings by December 1940. A Hollywood trade paper reported that the Germans seized a print of the film when they overran Paris and took it back to Berlin, where, after a little redubbing of the narration into German it was released to great acclaim as a sparkling comedy.[10]

Also released in America early in 1940 was an unremarkable documentary called *Lights Out in Europe*. It was written by James Hilton, that architect of MGM's Britain and the man who conceived Mr Chips and assisted at the birth of Mrs Miniver. The narration to *Lights Out in Europe* was spoken by Fredric March and the direction, by Herbert Kline, emphasised the darkness that followed in the wake of Nazi conquest. An astonishing review of the film appeared in the Communist magazine *New Masses*, written by Alvah Bessie who achieved eventual notoriety as one of the Hollywood Ten. *Lights Out in Europe* apparently was

> unable to secure material in Germany and France and blandly deprived by British censorship of important anti-war scenes from England . . . . The murderer of these little [Polish] people was Hitler and the finger man was a great British statesman, now leading the forces of civilisation in another crusade for democracy.[11]

The Phoney War was a confusing time for a lot of people.

4 The Führer after a screening of *The Lion Has Wings*.

5 Philosophy in the barber's shop. Chaplin, Paulette Goddard and Maurice Moscovich.

6 Top level Axis discussions before the spaghetti starts flying. Chaplin, Henry Daniell and Jack Oakie in *The Great Dictator*.

7 James Stewart and Margaret Sullavan tend to yet another victim of Nazi barbarism. *The Mortal Storm*.

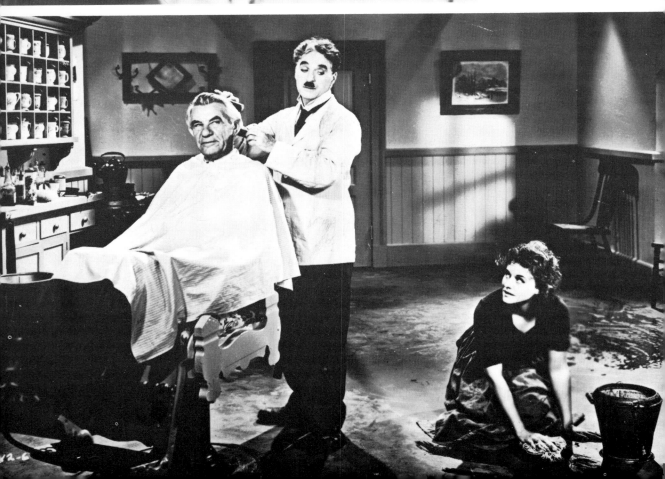

8 Ward Bond as the vicious stormtrooper
learns the intricacies of needlework from
Maria Ouspenskaya and Margaret Sullavan.
The Mortal Storm.

Walking on Eggs

(May 1940 — December 1940)

'I have said it before but I will say it again and again and again — your boys are not going to be sent into any foreign wars.'

Franklin Delano Roosevelt
Campaign Speech, Boston, October 1940

On 10 May German troops struck swiftly at the Low Countries. With deadly ease and efficiency they overran Holland within a week, Belgium in eighteen days and were poised to attack France. After the experiences of 1870 and 1914 when the Germans had made rapid inroads into French territory, France built a series of military forts on her eastern border which were linked by a network of underground railways. The 'Maginot' line as it was known was popularly believed to be impregnable. On 22 June France signed a treaty of capitulation.

The speed and size of the Nazi victories astounded the world. Only one moment had offered relief from the dazzling succession of German triumphs. At the end of May the bedraggled remnants of the British Expeditionary Force had been plucked from seemingly certain annihilation on the beaches of Dunkirk by a flotilla of small British boats. It was a classic reaffirmation that plucky British amateurism was still capable of showing that chap with the Charlie Chaplin moustache where he could get off. The new Prime Minister, Winston Churchill, who had succeeded Neville Chamberlain in one of those silent but murderous coups in which the Conservative Party has always delighted, warned grimly that 'wars are not won by evacuations'. Everybody remembered the words but not their meaning.

The blitzkrieg, like the declaration of war, had the effect in America of pushing people nearer to either the isolationist or the interventionist camp. A coffee shop in Kirkland, Washington followed traditional First World War practice by changing the 'hamburger' on its menus to read 'Liberty steak'. Charles Lindbergh, an excellent pilot but an incom-

petent politician, preached total isolation and stated that American intervention would be a disaster in view of the invincibility of the German armed forces and the inevitability of the German domination of Europe. President Roosevelt dismissed him shortly as a 'Copperhead'. Lindbergh angrily resigned his commission as a colonel in the Air Corps. Roosevelt ignored the petulant retaliation. In Charlotte, North Carolina, the residents of Lindbergh Drive renamed their street 'Avon Terrace'.

Hitler's victories in the West were undoubtedly bad for the Jews of Hollywood. 1400 cinemas in the Low Countries alone were immediately closed, representing a loss of $2½ million in annual revenue to the American film companies. That, added to the losses previously sustained in parts of Scandinavia, Poland, Italy, Spain and the Balkans meant that they had lost over 25 per cent of their annual foreign revenue.[1] By the end of 1940 the whole of Continental Europe was closed to American film imports apart from Sweden, Switzerland and Portugal. The *Film Daily* Yearbook saw nothing but gloom ahead whatever the outcome of the war.

> In the event of an Axis victory, American film companies predict a closed market insofar as American pictures are concerned. 'A British victory would not be worth much in dollar revenue from Europe during the reconstruction period', foreign department officials declare.

War in the Balkans caused particular hardship to Hollywood, as Clay Campbell, the make-up supervisor at Twentieth Century-Fox pointed out. Apparently the bulk of human hair from which the Hollywood wigs were made originated in that troubled part of the world. Now that the difficulties attendant upon sea transportation were so great, there was an appalling shortage of decent hairpieces. Why there was a need to import hair at all was never disclosed, but it undoubtedly accounted for the high incidence of bald-headed Serbo-Croats.

The war, however, meant more than just a lack of wigs and an outbreak of brooches set in the shape of the V for Victory sign which Tiffanys were selling, set in diamonds, for $5,000. One film made in Hollywood during 1940 bore the hallmarks of lengthy if not particularly deep thought. Chaplin had begun writing *The Great Dictator* in January 1939. It was a measure of the success of his approach to the subject that he never shared the fears of other film-makers similarly engaged that a crucial shift in events in Europe would render his film outdated. Chaplin did halt production after the declaration of war but decided to continue after a week in which he had been inundated by tidings of imminent disaster emanating from the Hays Office and United Artists.

Paradoxically, *The Great Dictator* succeeds best when it is at its farthest remove from the political parallel. The nose-thumbing works well enough on its own obvious level — the substitution of Garbitsch for Goebbels and Herring for Herman Goering, and Chaplin's mimicry of Hitler's speaking performances is superb, as each ringing rhetorical statement splutters into a hacking cough. The highlights of the film are those moments of pure Chaplin imagination. Adenoid Hynkel, suddenly frightened by Garbitsch's prediction that he will rule the world whispers, 'Don't say that. You make me afraid of myself.' and he scuttles up the curtain like a mouse. Later, after Garbitsch has left the room he toys thoughtfully with a giant globe, leaping gracefully with it on and off the table in time to the music of Wagner before the balloon bursts and Hynkel is left with nothing but the deflated skin. This sequence is executed with such style that it recalls W.C. Fields's appreciation of Chaplin as 'nothing but a god-damned ballet dancer and if I get the chance I'll strangle him with my bare hands'.

The film works least successfully whenever Chaplin tosses restraint aside and indulges himself in an orgy of moral sentimentality. The most famous example is the six minute closing speech to camera, delivered to the audience with only the most rudimentary attempts by Chaplin as the director to integrate it into the story. The air is heavy with the scent of cascading platitudes.

We want to live by each other's happiness — not by each other's misery. Greed has poisoned men's souls — has barricaded the world with hate — has goose-stepped us into misery and blood-shed . . . . More than machinery we need humanity. More than cleverness we need kindness and gentleness.

The message of the picture was not so much timely as timeless, not so much political as it was religious.

In the seventeenth Chapter of St. Luke it is written 'The kingdom of God is within man'. Not in one man or a group of men but in all men. In you! You, the people, have the power to make this life free and beautiful.

In other words, *The Great Dictator*, despite its predictable blacklisting by countries sympathetic to Nazi Germany, is as much an echo of *Mr Deeds Goes to Town* or any of the other great Capra moral tales of the 1930s as it is an echo of Europe under the dictators.

What distinguished *The Great Dictator* from the other American films made in 1940 was the outright admission of its elements of fantasy and caricature. MGM's two contributions to the anti Nazi 'genre', *Escape* and *The Mortal Storm*, were perhaps equally laudable but equally, if unintentionally, riddled with fantasy. In *Escape*, the name 'Germany' is never explicitly stated, rather in the manner that the word 'Jew' is never mentioned in *The Life of Emile Zola*, as if the mere omission of the name would allow Metro's lawyers to claim that the film dealt with another country whose officials wore black uniforms and worked in concentration camps.

The plot, such as it is, concerns Robert Taylor's arrival in this nameless country and his search for his actress-mother (Nazimova). In his efforts to smuggle her out of a concentration camp and back to America, he is aided by a courageous Nazi doctor (Philip Dorn), a 'countess' who lives in a mansion on the hill (Norma Shearer) and his mother's old retainer (Felix Bressart) who happens, purely by chance, to know a man who forges passports. Shearer is somewhat compromised by her 'friendship' with the courteous Conrad Veidt who, as the highest ranking army officer in the film is pursuing Robert Taylor. Fortunately, Veidt has a heart attack at the crucial time and Shearer nobly stays with him as they hear overhead the sound of the aeroplane carrying Taylor and his mom back to the land of the free. No doubt Taylor and Mervyn LeRoy, who directed this piece of nonsense, regretted ever having left the safer confines of *Waterloo Bridge*.

The Mortal Storm was given a sense of urgency by its release during the week of Hitler's triumphant entry into Paris. It recounts the misfortunes that attend the family of a quiet, well-liked professor at a small university at the foot of the Alps. The professor's two stepsons renounce the old man because of his liberal views and do nothing to prevent his being incarcerated in a concentration camp where he dies of a 'heart attack'. The professor's daughter Freya (played by Margaret Sullavan) breaks off her engagement to a fervent young Nazi (Robert Young), having fallen in love with her father's star pupil, a neighbouring farmer of healthy anti-Fascist convictions. After the news of the professor's death the two ski towards the safety of the Austrian border. Both are shot at and hit by a detachment of Robert Young's SA troops on skis, but although they crawl over the border together, Freya dies in the arms of her lover.

Two elements combine to rob the story of its claims to authenticity. The casting of Frank Morgan as the professor and James Stewart as the farmer introduce such positive strains of Americana into the production as to make the Central European pretence almost pointless. The art direction of Cedric Gibbons destroys it utterly. The final ski-chase is conducted against the crudest of back projections and the pictorial representation of the Alpine villages seems to have sprung from a child's story book. As Stewart and Sullavan ski towards the border, Austria becomes a sunlit valley in a fabled land, as if the Joads's view of California had been suddenly transported to Ruritania.

Nevertheless, for all its caution, MGM had taken some kind of a risk in simply producing a picture in which Germany was mentioned by name and in which the controversial political questions aroused by Nazi persecution of liberals, intellectuals and non-Aryans were clearly stated. The conservative exhibitor's journal *Motion Picture Herald* wrote after the preview

> A few months or weeks ago this Hollywood press audience would have used the word 'propaganda' to describe the film and speculated on the policy prompting its manufacture. The word was not heard in the auditorium or the foyer on June 10th.[2]

Strangely enough, Warner Bros, the most fiercely anti-Nazi studio of them all, failed to contribute at this time, apart from the capers of *The Sea Hawk*.

They did take the story of *Underground* off the shelf and put it into production but Vincent Sherman's film was still not released until the middle of 1941 and then it made little impression, being neither distinguished nor original.

Instead, Warner Bros redoubled their anti-Nazi activities on other fronts. In September 1940 during the Battle of Britain, when the small number of serviceable British fighters appeared likely to have a direct bearing on the outcome of the war, the studio sent Britain two Spitfires (named 'President Roosevelt' and 'Cordell Hull'). When an undercover agent discovered a Nazi film in California on its way to South America the entire Warners editing department was set to work to make a duplicate and replace it before the Germans had realised it was missing.

Both Harry and Jack Warner (who adored public speaking) continued to make their personal views publicly known. Harry Warner addressed his employees in June 1940 shortly after his brother had forbidden the sound of the German language on the lot and stated that there was no place in the country for the fifth columnists. Anyone suspected of fomenting sabotage or indicating disloyalty to the American flag on the Burbank lot would be turned over to the tender mercies of the US Department of Justice.

As Universal had turned instinctively to *All Quiet on the Western Front*, so Twentieth Century-Fox too turned initially to a past success for its first war picture. *Four Sons* had originally been made by the old Fox company in 1928 as a bitter indictment of the way in which war destroys families both emotionally and physically. (Or as a quick exploitation of the market opened up by the success of that studio's *What Price Glory?* and its sequel.) *Four Sons* was now re-written by John Howard Lawson who was dutifully following the Communist Party line as closely as possible and it was produced by Darryl Zanuck who was as anti-Nazi as the next stockholder. The result was a predictable mess and an exhibitor in upstate New York complained that he couldn't make any money on the picture 'even when doubled with *Blondie Has Servant Trouble*'.[3]

When the initial public reaction to these anti-Nazi pictures proved to be only lukewarm the studios had to consider carefully what to do with others of the same ilk already in production. The first port of safety was to change the title — a traditional Hollywood means of pretending that the subject matter changed with it. *I Married a Nazi*, the story of an American wife (Joan Bennett) and her German-American husband (Francis Lederer) and their different emotions on visiting the new Germany, eventually surfaced from the Twentieth Century-Fox studios as *The Man I Married*. Republic altered *The Refugee* to *Three Faces West* and then announced that it had decided not to make another war picture as planned but would do instead *Hit Parade of 1940*.

The sales executives sought safety also in the vagaries of the European situation. They pointed out that business was likely to reflect directly the public's reaction to the war news. It was certainly to be expected that under the influence of each morning's headlines box office recepts would vary sharply from day to day during the national release of these films.

However, to judge from the list of box office champions in 1940 the public seems not to have shied away from the anti-Nazi pictures as such but to have preferred, simply, entertainment in the traditional manner as provided by *Strike Up the Band*, *Boom Town*, *Rebecca*, and *Kitty Foyle*, while *Gone With the Wind* had barely drawn its second breath. The following year *Sergeant York* came top of the poll — an indication that the mass audience recognised quality whatever the theme of the picture.

This conclusion is surely borne out by the relative success of Alfred Hitchcock's *Foreign Correspondent*. This splendid thriller had originally started life as we saw in the first chapter, as an anti-Nazi picture written by John Howard Lawson for Walter Wanger back in 1938. Although Wanger postponed its intended production after the *Blockade* fiasco he never relinquished his hold on the idea entirely. Announcements concerning the writing of a dramatization of Vincent Sheean's *Personal History* appeared in the trade press throughout 1938 and 1939. After Lawson came John Meehan, James Hilton, Charles Bennett, Joan Harrison and eventually Hitchcock himself and costs on the script alone rose to over $200,000.[4]

Although no copies of the various drafts are available, it seems reasonable to conclude that, in view of the writers Wanger employed, a transition was made from the political hard-edge of Lawson through the pro-British feelings of Hilton to Hitchcock's own distinctive obsessions. The story concerns the exposure of a master spy (Herbert Marshall) who masquerades as the leader of an international peace organisation but what one remembers from the film is invariably the Hitchcock set pieces — the assassination of the Dutch diplomat by a press photographer with a gun hidden in his camera and the moment when Joel McCrea realises that the windmill is turning the wrong way. The casting of McCrea as the naïve foreign correspondent who learns the truth behind the Fascist conspiracy never fully satisfied Hitchcock. The director always believed that McCrea was too lightweight but his first choice, Gary Cooper, had rejected the script as too much of a thriller (whatever that may mean). Certainly Cooper would have given greater strength to the finale of the picture as the foreign correspondent broadcasts a report from bomb-torn London to listeners in America.

'The lights have gone out in Europe! Hang on to your lights, America — they're the only lights still on in the world! Ring yourself around with steel, America!'

The factual radio reports of Ed Murrow, broadcast as German bombs exploded near him, had the effect of driving home to listening Americans the grim reality of the new civilian war. The Blitz which followed the Battle of Britain intensified the pressure on America to make a positive stand against the encroaching tide of Nazism.

For President Roosevelt the options were closing fast. Angrily he denounced Italy's cowardly entry into the war to claim a share of the spoils. 'On this tenth day of June 1940 the hand that held the dagger has struck it into the back of its neighbour', he told an audience at Charlottesville, Virginia and went on to declare that America would not only proceed to rearm herself but would 'extend to the opponents of force the material resources of this nation.'

Unfortunately, certain armaments were not within his gift. The Battle of Britain had prevented the Germans from winning the air space over Britain but the danger of invasion remained constant, owing to the loss of nearly fifty British destroyers, a cumulative disaster that was likely to deprive the Royal Navy of its crucial command of the seas. In desperation Churchill asked Roosevelt for fifty 'overage' First World War destroyers but the President knew that this was a matter for Congress, and Congress, unlike the country as a whole, was unsym-

9 Joan Bennett learns from Lloyd Nolan
the awful truth behind the swastika
embroidered on her husband's pyjamas.
The Man I Married.

10 Claudette Colbert trying to remember
which version of *Arise My Love* she is about
to shoot.

11 Gary Cooper, winner of distinguished service medals and Best Performance by an Actor for 1941. *Sergeant York.*

12 Vivien Leigh contemplating life as the Red Army's pin-up girl; Laurence Olivier contemplating making *Henry V. Lady Hamilton.*

pathetic to the request. Senator Key Pittman of Nevada, the Chairman of the influential Senate Foreign Relations Committee, suggested in all seriousness that it was futile for Britain to fight on and that it would be much more sensible if her population simply emigrated en masse to Canada and left the British Isles neat and tidy for the new Nazi owner. Even the pro-British members of Congress were reluctant to accept the President's request for fear that the leasing of ships to a belligerent power was a violation of international law.

Boldly Roosevelt decided to bypass Congress and negotiate a deal with Churchill on his own. On 3 September 1940 America transferred the fifty old destroyers in return for the lease of naval bases on British Western Hemisphere possessions. Roosevelt claimed that the destroyers were not essential to national security and in any case the swap he had completed was in fact the most astute deal 'in the reinforcement of our national defense . . . since the Louisiana Purchase'.

Roosevelt's audacious stroke of policy nearly cost him his job. In addition to all the other considerations the President was running for re-election for a third and unique term of office. He had carefully avoided declaring his explicit intention of breaking the longstanding two term tradition in American politics but he had clearly encouraged a cynical stage-managing of the Democratic Convention in Chicago to ensure his drafting and nomination. The Republicans too had drafted a candidate at their convention in Philadelphia but the remarkable emergence of Wendell Willkie on the sixth ballot, roared on by the packed vociferous galleries chanting 'WE WANT WILLKIE', was in spite rather than because of the influence of the Old Guard.

Willkie called Roosevelt's transfer of the destroyers 'the most dictatorial and arbitrary' Presidential act in American history but his campaign was sorely compromised by the candidate's basic agreement with Roosevelt on the crucial issue of support for the anti-Nazi forces in Europe and the establishment of a strong national defence. Robert Taft and the powerful isolationist elements in the Republican party would have been quite content to have attacked Roosevelt as a warmonger but Willkie never had the stomach for it. (Or the voice either — he contracted dreadful laryngitis at the start of the campaign and never shook it off until after the election.)

Crucially, the two candidates agreed on the other political controversy of the campaign, as Roosevelt lent his support to the Selective Service Act. The Burke-Wadsworth Bill which had been languishing in Congress was revived by the White House interest and became law in the fall of 1940, thus permitting the first peacetime draft in American history. The Bill was long overdue from the army's point of view. Just weeks before it was passed grand scale manoeuvres had been conducted in which pieces of drainpipe had been used in place of mortars and beer cans were substituted for hand grenades. These variations on ammunition were deployed against 'enemy tanks' which were represented by lorries with the word 'Tank' painted in large letters on the sides.

Nevertheless the Bill was not carried without Congressional fireworks. Senator Wheeler pronounced that the passage of the Bill would 'slit the throat of the last Democracy still living' and that Hitler would inscribe on its headstone 'Here Lies The Foremost Victim of The War Of Nerves'.

Hollywood's contribution to the Selective Service debate was to step up production of its service comedies and dramas. The dramatic moment when the Secretary of War, Henry Stimson, reached into a fishbowl and drew the first number to determine the order in which the eligible men would be called up was captured by newsreel cameras and quickly tacked on to the front of the hugely popular Abbott and Costello comedy, *Buck Privates*.

If one picture may be said to typify this period in the war it is probably Mitchell Leisen's *Arise My Love*, starring Claudette Colbert and Ray Milland. Colbert manages to secure the release of Milland from one of Franco's jails in which he has been awaiting the death sentence for his part in the Spanish Civil War. Together they escape to Paris, whence they are compelled to flee before the arriving Nazis. Their return to America is postponed indefinitely as their ship is torpedoed and they are washed back to Europe where she becomes a dedicated reporter and he joins the RAF. Bosley Crowther of The *New York Times* was less than enchanted with the film, describing it as

simply a synthetic picture which attempts to give consequence to a pleasant April in Paris romance by involving it in the realities of war, but a war that has been patently conceived by someone reading headlines in California.[5]

As far as the last assertion goes he was probably right. Claudette Colbert revealed in an interview after the war that

> often during the filming . . . we had to make quick revisions to keep up with the swift progress of events in Europe. We all had the feeling that we were doing something more than just making another picture.[6]

She was probably right too because what the interview failed to reveal was that these 'revisions' were being made not by the writers Charles Brackett and Billy Wilder but at the request of the Paramount front office who wanted to avoid censorship in countries which maintained 'a neutral or complacent attitude to Nazism.' Apparently, the original anti-Nazi script by Wilder and Brackett was shot as written but then the actors returned to the cameras for dialogue takes that toned down the passages that might have been offensive to Nazi sympathisers. It is not recorded whether Paramount screened the Churchill version or the Hitler version for Mr Crowther.[7]

No Way In

(January 1941 — December 1941)

'Approval of this legislation means war. . . . We will be . . . repaid those dollars wrung from the sweat of labor and the toil of farmers with cries of "Uncle Shylock". Our boys will be returned in caskets; returned with bodies maimed; returned with minds warped and twisted by sights of horrors and the scream and shriek of high powered shells.'

Senator Burton K. Wheeler on Lend Lease Bill
12 January 1941

Roosevelt won the Presidential Election easily enough in the end even though Willkie cut his majority in the popular vote to five million — the narrowest margin in any election since 1916. Once it was over Roosevelt was committed to the defence of Britain even if it meant war. In this resolve he was joined by the majority of his cabinet including the two Republican members Henry Stimson, the Secretary of War and Frank Knox, the Secretary of the Navy. Throughout 1941 Roosevelt's policy appeared to be a blatant provocation of the Germans in the hope that Hitler would retaliate with one major outrage that would enable the President to lead a united country into war.

Churchill's message of congratulation on Roosevelt's victory was accompanied by further urgent requests for aid. The occasional bold stroke of diplomacy like the sale of the destroyers was now no longer sufficient to stave off the danger of imminent collapse. A master plan of full scale open aid to Britain was vital if America were not to be confronted by the total Nazi domination of Europe.

At the end of the Christmas holiday 1940 Roosevelt emerged with the basic idea of Lend-Lease which he first expounded on 29 December in a radio fireside chat. To clarify the issues he resorted to one of his classic metaphors, comparing the current European imbroglio to a fire in a neighbour's house. 'Obviously', he said, 'if I've got a hose which my neighbour needs, I simply connect it up to his

hydrant and when the fire is out my neighbour returns my hose or buys me another if it has been damaged.'

There was a basic flaw in the metaphor of course. The likelihood of Britain either returning spent ammunition or, in view of the crippling debts she was then incurring, being in a position to repay America at the conclusion of hostilities was remote. Nevertheless, the tide of fortune on Capitol Hill was running in the President's favour. The Lend-Lease Bill was given the roll number of 1776 and, secure in its patriotic wrapping, it became law on 11 March 1941. Having won the major point Roosevelt immediately caused another sharp intake of breath when he made his first requisition under the law for $9 billion.

The debate over Lend-Lease drew the final battle lines between the interventionists and the isolationists. The former included General Pershing, Harold Ickes, John Dewey and Harry Hopkins among their most outspoken number, the bulk of whom was composed of Democrats, Jews and liberal and conservative anti-Fascists. The isolationists led by Herbert Hoover and the diehard anti-New Dealers found strong support coming from La Follette and the Mid-Western Progressives, the Irish and other Anglophobes, committed anti-Semites like Father Coughlin, Gerald L.K. Smith and Lindbergh, pacifists, Communists and assorted paid-up members of the lunatic fringe.

The two camps formed organisations to express their views. Back in May 1940 William Allen White had founded the Committee to Defend America by Aiding the Allies but within a month the Committee to Defend America First had made its appearance. The latter was largely administered by a group of Mid-Western businessmen led by Robert Wood of Sears, Roebuck. Within six months America First was claiming 60,000 members and an enormous financial chest. Certainly the organisation was rich enough to run a series of full-page advertisements in

140 newspapers. It may well be that the bulk of the membership believed passionately in a remarkable British-Jewish-Capitalist conspiracy to drag America into war. One Mid-Western leader stated categorically, 'Roosevelt and his wife are Jewish and this goes for 90 per cent of his Administration', a fact that would have surprised the thousands of unfortunate Jewish refugees whom the rigid immigration controls barred from entering America at this time.[1] It would also have confused the Nazi propagandists who had been hinting darkly at Eleanor Roosevelt's negroid appearance. Nevertheless America First could not be dismissed as a collection of insignificant crackpots as the membership of Joseph Kennedy, Alice Longworth and John Foster Dulles made clear.

Just before the Senate passed HR1776 the annual jamboree of the Academy Awards ceremony was broadcast nationally by radio. Roosevelt, who never believed in scorning an opportunity for effectively publicising his policies, addressed the brightest stars in the cinema firmament. He praised the industry for its favourable newsreel coverage of the Lend-Lease debates and asked for further co-operation in advancing 'the spirit of inter-American solidarity'. This was taken as a direct rebuke to the isolationist Senator Burton Wheeler who, in his wild diatribe against Lend-Lease, had also accused the film industry of war-mongering. After the Washington hook-up had been disconnected Hollywood returned to the serious business of declaring 'When You Wish Upon A Star' the best song of 1940.[2]

In 1940 Hollywood had ventured briefly but unprofitably into the complex field of foreign affairs. In 1941 it returned gladly to the more familiar and more rewarding territory of simply recruiting for the armed forces. High on the list of the year's commercial successes was the Abbott and Costello romp *Buck Privates*. Although principally an excuse for the popular if obvious clowning of the two stars, the obligatory sub-plot (in addition to the guest star appearance of the Secretary of War) is of some interest because of the light it sheds on the changing role of the soldier in American society in 1941. A spoiled millionaire's son and his chauffeur whom he has constantly mistreated are drafted at the same time. The spoiled brat tries all his old tricks and generally makes himself thoroughly unpopular especially with the girl to whom both he and the ex-chauffeur are attracted. Fortunately, in the sixth reel, he realises the error of his undemocra-

tic ways and makes a heroic sacrifice before he and his rival in love set off cheerfully together to the Officers Training School, a new mutual respect for each other as soldiers having bridged the previous social gulf. The additional bonus of the Andrews Sisters singing 'Red, white and blue/Are colours that look good on you' makes *Buck Privates* an effective patriotic celebration of the Selective Service Act.

Its success led directly to other comedies of a similar nature such as Paramount's *Caught in the Draft* starring Bob Hope and *Great Guns* and *Tanks a Million*. Not all such stories were comedies. In fact 1941 saw many dramatic male stars donning uniforms as they advanced towards the cameras. The *New York Times* warmly applauded the cavortings of Ray Milland and William Holden in *I Wanted Wings*.

> This cinematic salute to the Army Air Corps and to the young men who are entering it today is a vastly exciting motion picture and a dependable inspiration to the youth of the land.[3]

Errol Flynn flying a *Dive Bomber*, Robert Taylor on his *Flight Command* and Ann Sheridan singing of her *Navy Blues* all made due acknowledgment of the co-operation they received from their appointed branch of the armed forces. Darryl Zanuck went slightly further when he produced *A Yank in the RAF*, but since Tyrone Power's real reason for being in London is to look at Betty Grable's legs which are on display in a West End show, the fervour of the film's ideological basis is noticeably restrained. *A Yank in the RAF*, *Dive Bomber* and *Caught in the Draft* were all among the year's seven most profitable pictures, a fate denied to the previous year's anti-Nazi efforts although *The Great Dictator* made something of an impact when all its returns had been collated. Hollywood was considerably happier when it could switch rapidly from an emotional plea for patriotic sacrifice to a tuneful song. *A Yank in the RAF* might have been Zanuck's tribute to the gallant Few but he took care to include 'Another Little Dream Won't Do Us Any Harm' and 'Hi-ya Love'. MGM did its best for the Navy, suggesting in one film that the prospective nautical recruit could expect to spend much of his time strumming a guitar on Waikiki Beach while native girls danced seductively close by. Nobody thought to mention the proximity of the Japanese air force.

Nevertheless, these pictures all made money although they were no doubt aided by the fact that

1941 was the start of the financial boom years that took Hollywood to its remarkable peak of 1946. 1940 had been a poor year for the industry so 1941 was appreciated as the start of the much heralded recovery. So well did Hollywood apply itself to the search for new markets that the total 1941 gross for the seven major film companies amounted to an increase of $36 million over the 1939 figure. Columbia had doubled its profits to over $1 million, Warners made $5½ million and MGM led the way with $11½ million. Income from Great Britain increased 25 per cent over the two years but the biggest compensation for the lost markets of Europe came from Latin America which exported Carmen Miranda to Twentieth Century-Fox in 1940. In quick succession Fox returned *Down Argentine Way*, *Weekend in Havana* and *That Night in Rio* which effectively consolidated the Hollywood version of Roosevelt's Good Neighbor policy.[4]

Profitability came too from the upturn in the domestic market. The new policy of national defence entailed relatively lavish government expenditure in the creation of new armament factories which obviously meant jobs for their employees. The employees in turn needed new houses in which to live since the factories were normally built outside the established urban areas and thus the construction trade, a crucial 'trigger' industry in a modern industrial society, began its own boom period. The motion picture industry regarded the economic upturn with eager anticipation.

The increased importance of the domestic market affected the nature as well as the profitability of many pictures. Garbo had long been dependent on her European admirers to maintain her viability at MGM. With the removal of the bulk of her faithful disciples the studio decided to convert their prized queen of costumed suffering into an all-American comedienne. The result, *Two-Faced Woman*, despite a spirited supporting performance from Constance Bennett and the appointment of George Cukor as the director, drove Garbo into retirement. It was an excessive reaction to a weak film but Garbo knew perhaps better than her studio that it was pointless for her to attempt the sort of roles best played by Carole Lombard. She retreated and waited for her former audiences to return. Eventually they did but she never emerged to illuminate them.

One film above all others made in 1941 benefitted from the dual preoccupation with the war in Europe and the need to appeal principally to American audiences. Howard Hawks's production of *Sergeant York* from a script written by John Huston and Howard Koch deservedly won an Oscar for Gary Cooper, general critical acclaim and the much coveted place of the year's top money-making picture. The portrait of the First World War hero who overcomes his Christian scruples to become America's most decorated soldier, lays considerable emphasis on the man's internal mental struggle between his patriotism and his pacifism. His fundamentalist religion complicates issues still further as he declares, 'Aint nothin' written in the Book that aint true', but armed with his bible and the Mayor's book on American history he goes off to the top of a mountain to figure things out. He concludes that in war it is possible to kill in order to save lives and his decision to fight becomes, by implication, America's also. Of course, the ease with which he then proceeds to pick off German soldiers and wipe out a machine gun nest seems to be added proof of God's approval of the decision, as does the popular national acclaim and the return in triumph to his satisfying life on the good soil of Tennessee. Alvin York himself felt so strongly about the issues raised by the film that he allowed a statement in his own name to be displayed in the publicity and advertising of *Sergeant York*.

> By our victory in the last war we won a lease on liberty, not a deed to it. Now, after 23 years, Adolf Hitler tells us that lease is expiring and after the manner of all leases we have the privilege of renewing it or letting it go by default.

British interest in Hollywood and all its films grew appreciably during the war years. In the first three months of the Phoney War fourteen additional film correspondents flew out to California to join the resident press corps. Audiences withstood even those movies which portrayed Britain herself in the most bizarre of images. Chief among these was Twentieth Century-Fox's *Manhunt*, Fritz Lang's film of Geoffrey Household's novel *Rogue Male*. The book had been written by an Englishman as an examination of a certain type of compatriot and his reaction, as a gentleman, to the arbitrary exercise of power by dictators. Fritz Lang and his writer, Dudley Nichols, were clearly concerned with quite different matters. When *Rogue Male* was filmed again in 1976 by BBC-tv,[5] the attendant publicity ignored the very existence of *Manhunt* as if Lang's version had been just an unfortunate aberration.

In many ways it was, and the success of the opening sequence seems to prove it since it was here that Nichols stayed closest to the book. Walter Pidgeon plays Thorndike, a big game hunter who stalks the Nazi leader just to see if he can get him in his sights. He lines up Hitler and gently squeezes the trigger — to no effect as the gun is not loaded. He carefully inserts a bullet and realigns the telescope sights, at which point he is seized by patrolling SS guards. The Gestapo tortures him to try to extract a confession that Thorndike's mission had been ordered by the British government. Pidgeon is flung off the top of a cliff but manages to survive and make his painful way back to England. However the tentacles of Nazi violence pursue him into the very heart of the English countryside. The East End where the ship docks proves to be a complex of foggy archways and cobbled streets which look more like the home of Dr Caligari than Millwall Football Club. The sense of disorientation is greatly increased by Pidgeon's encounter with a quite improbable Cockney prostitute played by Joan Bennett with an accent which seems to begin in Northern Ireland and progress via New York to somewhere in Australia. Her speech abounds in such sophisticated repartee as, 'Lumme! Coo, this is loverly aint it?', 'Are the rozzers arfter 'im?' and 'Ooze them blowkes' as if Nichols had based her dialogue solely on that of the unreformed Eliza Doolittle.

The final confrontation between Walter Pidgeon and his principal antagonist, George Sanders (John Carradine already having been dispatched on the Piccadilly Line outside Holborn tube station) takes place in Pidgeon's lair in the New Forest (which looks more Black than New). Sanders forces Pidgeon to sign the fateful confession incriminating His Majesty's Government but the resourceful hunter outwits him by means of a hastily improvised bow and arrow which fires the gold plated pen back with the nib going straight between the eyes. The expiring Sanders shoots our hero, who, undeterred, doggedly eats his way through the vital document. A quick montage of newsreel clips takes Pidgeon through to his first airborne mission over Germany, where he bails out with his trusty high precision rifle. An admiring voice over concludes, 'It might take months and it might take years' but clearly Hitler might as well come out of the Chancellery kicking a signed copy of *Mein Kampf* in front of him.

Manhunt's political sensibilities were an uneasy combination of Lang's brief experiences under the Nazis and Nichols's moral disgust. Alexander Korda, although Hungarian himself in origin, managed in his films to convey a particular brand of Britishness that was attractive both to the British and the Americans, not because it was a faithful reflection of his adopted nation but because it was how the British liked to see themselves. *Lady Hamilton*, released by United Artists in 1941, married Korda's talents as a producer and director perfectly with the very English writing of R.C. Sherriff. The film, although ostensibly a vehicle for Vivien Leigh and Laurence Olivier, was designed as a blatant piece of British flag-waving, or, as Korda himself defined it, 'propaganda with a very thick coating of sugar indeed.'[6]

Lady Hamilton was shot under the most straitened of circumstances. The production plans were so far in advance of the shooting script that Sherriff and his partner, Walter Reisch, frequently found themselves writing pages of dialogue that were due to be filmed in a matter of hours. Sherriff, in his autobiography, recalls with commendable restraint the sickening occasions when Korda or Olivier dispensed with his efforts and improvised dialogue on the set. The more outrageous patriotic homilies do not bear the imprint of Sherriff's usual polished speeches. The most famous example is Nelson's reaction to the unexpected and desperately needed supplies brought to him by Emma Hamilton. Smacking his fist against his palm, Nelson looks out of his porthole and cries, 'Look out, Bonaparte! By Gad! We shall lick you now.' Similarly, Nelson's warning to the Lords of the Admiralty draws a crude parallel between the Peace of Amiens and the mirage of peace offered by Hitler at Munich, and seized so eagerly by the British and French governments. 'You can't make peace with dictators. You have to destroy them! Wipe them out!' Sherriff's hand is more visible in Emma's husband's explanation of the origin of the war — 'There are always men who, for the sake of their insane ambition want to destroy what others build.'

Despite all the restrictions imposed on the film by the six week shooting schedule and the size of Korda's budget that forced him to represent the Battle of Trafalgar with a dozen model ships, *Lady Hamilton* proved to be a spectacular success, especially in America where sympathy and admiration for Britain was running high in the summer of 1941. Nobody seemed unduly distressed by the manner in which the film had settled for a superficial treatment of the Nelson story. In any case there was much to admire in the performances of an exquisite Vivien Leigh, the cynical Alan Mowbray as her cuckolded husband and Gladys Cooper as the frosty, betrayed Lady Nelson. Olivier himself seemed uneasy with his part as if he resented not having the opportunity to portray the egocentricity of the real Nelson, but audiences welcomed the conventional hero of popular mythology.

Lady Hamilton's success was not confined to Britain and America. In Russia it brought Vivien Leigh the welcome if surprising honour of being adopted as the Red Army's pin-up girl and the film played in Moscow to capacity audiences for months. By far the most distinguished admirer was Winston Churchill, who had shown sufficient interest in the announcement of the production to take time off from the conduct of the Second World War to bombard Korda with a series of helpful cabled suggestions. Korda, with due regard for their author, kept his counsel — much to Churchill's surprise since they had been intended as publicity devices.[7] Whether or not his suggestions influenced the making of the film, *Lady Hamilton* remained Churchill's favourite motion picture, although the loyalty of his closest aides was sometimes strained by the frequency of the Prime Minister's screenings of the film.

The triumphant reception accorded *Lady Hamilton* was directly responsible for the production of Hollywood's most famous pro-British film, *Mrs Miniver*. Sherriff was quickly transferred to the MGM studios to polish the screenplay fashioned by James Hilton, Arthur Wimperis and Claudine West. The full story of *Mrs Miniver* belongs more properly to the war years in which it was released but certain points may still be made with profit here.

While Mr Miniver is on his way back from Dunkirk with a boat full of the BEF, Mrs Miniver captures the German pilot who has crashed in the neighbourhood. At the end of the scene in which she neatly disarms the young savage and speaks glowingly of the virtues of the British health service, she hears overhead a returning RAF plane. When it cuts its engine she knows for sure it is her son and brightly she asks the German pilot whether he similarly signalled his mother of his safe return. The boy shakes his head. 'No', sighs Mrs Miniver, 'I thought not.'

Louis B. Mayer, bearing in mind the relative unprofitability of *Escape* and *The Mortal Storm*, held agitated conferences with the producer Sidney

Franklin and the director William Wyler. Additionally, fear of offending a nation with which America was not at war, neutral countries sympathetic to Germany and, perhaps most important of all, fear of upsetting the still powerful isolationist elements in Congress combined in Mayer to produce dire forebodings which he tried hard to instil into Franklin and Wyler without too much effect. Nevertheless, despite the fact that within a month of the start of principal photography America was at war and Mayer's pressure on Wyler to relax the anti-German emphasis disappeared entirely, Mrs Miniver's snort at the young pilot's failure to acknowledge his mother never appeared in the final cut, although this might well have been due to considerations other than those of L.B. Mayer's tender political, not to say oedipal, sensibilities.[8]

Both *Mrs Miniver* and *Lady Hamilton* found favour in official political circles far beyond the hopes of their creators. Roosevelt was so impressed by *Mrs Miniver* that he had copies of the vicar's inspiring sermon reprinted and dropped by the USAF over Occupied Europe. Similarly, in August 1941, when Churchill arrived at the Newfoundland rendezvous to meet Roosevelt and formulate the Atlantic Charter, to nobody's great surprise the film he had screened after dinner was *Lady Hamilton*.

This meeting of the two leaders edged America still closer to an official declaration of belligerency. They met in an atmosphere of gloom and disbelief. When the Germans invaded Russia on 21 June 1944 it was confidently believed that Hitler had finally overreached himself. Yet by the time of the Atlantic Conference his troops had overrun Yugoslavia and Greece and were penetrating deep into Soviet Russia, throwing the Red Army back before them.

Support for Russia of any kind had always been a sensitive political issue. Distrust of the Bolsheviks had barely been alleviated by official recognition of them in 1933 and the events of 1939-40 had only served to exacerbate matters. The Nazi-Soviet Non-Aggression Pact was the crucial sign that war was likely to break out in the fall of 1939 and the cynical Russian invasion of Finland in 1940 was regarded with as much disgust in America as was reserved for any of the Nazi conquests.

Days before Hitler turned on his ally, the Fourth American Writers Conference was held in New York. Terry Ramsaye, the editor of the *Motion Picture Herald*, attended and was appalled by the naked left wing sentiments expressed. 'There came cheers for

Stalin and the Russian idea, jeers and hisses for Roosevelt and America.' Ramsaye declared categorically that Americans went to the theatre or cinema for entertainment. 'If they want to know what these or any other American writers have to say they will read a book.'[9] Thus the place of the writer in the show business.

The American Communist Party quickly stood on its head a week later but then its life had been full of such ideological contortions and one more moral gyration required no special effort. The bulk of the American people needed time to absorb the new balance of power in Europe. Time, unfortunately, was a precious commodity in the summer of 1941. Roosevelt called once more on his reservoir of diplomatic charm and persuaded Congress to extend the provisions of Lend-Lease to Soviet Russia but, as Churchill was quick to point out, Lend-Lease wasn't proving quite the spectacular success that had been envisaged six months before.

The Nazi U-boats had been creating havoc with the vital British supply lines in the Atlantic. At the Newfoundland conference Churchill persuaded Roosevelt to provide protection for Lend-Lease supplies and US Navy vessels were soon patrolling sea routes in 'neutrality zones' which in practice extended as far East as Iceland. Inevitably closer escort meant greater provocation of the U-boats. Hitler, with a war on three fronts already in progress, was reluctant to extend it still further and instructed Doenitz, the Admiral in charge of the German Navy, not to retaliate. Still Roosevelt remained short of the big explosive incident he was clearly looking for.

On 4 September 1941 the American destroyer *Greer* en route for Iceland tracked a submarine and reported its movements to the British. Irritated, the U-boat commander loosed two torpedoes against the *Greer*, both of which missed. Roosevelt instantly declared that the *Greer* had been attacked and that henceforth American naval vessels would be instructed to 'shoot on sight' if they feared imminent attack by marauding German submarines. The only other step Roosevelt could constitutionally take was to revise the Neutrality Laws to the extent of permitting the arming of American merchant vessels. In November 1941 the appropriate amendment scraped through Congress, passed by 212 votes to 194 in the House and by 50 to 37 in the Senate. Although the shift in opinion since May 1940 had been significant on the Hill, it was obvious that in the last few months of peace many Americans still refused to acknowledge the inevitability of military involvement.

Hollywood was given conclusive proof of this in October 1941 when, despite the caution it had displayed in selecting its war stories and despite the generous measure of compensating entertainment values it had seen fit to provide, the American film industry found its worst fears realised. Senate Resolution 152 proposed that a congressional subcommittee investigate 'any propaganda disseminated by motion pictures . . . to influence public sentiment in the direction of participation by the United States in the . . . European War'.

All the movies that had caused so much heart-searching in the past two years were resurrected and paraded before a collection of hostile unsympathetic politicians. Warner Bros were condemned for making *Confessions of a Nazy Spy*, *Underground*, *Dive Bomber* and *Sergeant York*. MGM was accused of impure thoughts during the production of *Escape* and *The Mortal Storm* and Fox was keel-hauled for producing *The Man I Married* and *Manhunt*. The Senators asked Darryl Zanuck plaintively why he didn't make more pictures like *Brigham Young* which had flopped its way through 1940. Zanuck replied forcefully to the effect that he wasn't in business to make flops of historic proportions. Mary Astor had been ludicrously miscast as a homespun amalgamation of the Mormon leader's many wives, and the story had virtually abandoned Dean Jagger in the title role and gone off in search of a marginally more interesting but totally irrelevant love affair between Tyrone Power and Linda Darnell. The Senators shook their heads and returned to the attack.

Senators Nye and Clark, the authors of Resolution 152, were in the vanguard of the Congressional isolationists. They had constantly opposed the revision of the Neutrality Laws, the passing of Lend-Lease and the Selective Service Bill. They believed passionately that the United States must only fight if she herself were in danger of attack. The investigation into Hollywood's anti-Nazi films was intended to embarrass the interventionists in both the film industry and the Roosevelt administration.

The Hollywood moguls with their paranoid fear of state intervention and anti-Semitic pogroms discovered to their horror that dealing with the American Senate had suddenly become akin to dealing with the Fascist dictators. Their motives were misconstrued, their protestation that making money was all that they were really interested in was not having much effect and the occasional film they had sanctioned which had raised its head out of the California desert sand had brought forth only the wrath of vengeful political and social pressure groups.

The hearings dragged on into December 1941. Eyes closed, head bowed Hollywood braced itself for the inevitable rebuke. Suddenly, out of the pale blue yonder came the sound of a most unlikely rescuer — the drone of 353 planes of Japanese air squadrons as they dived in formation over the drowsy American naval base at Pearl Harbor.

A Date Which Will Live In Infamy

(December 1941)

War between the United States and Japan broke just as it began to look as though the sheet music business would have its biggest year end since 1938.

Variety 10 December 1941

The afternoon of 7 December 1941 was one of intense activity in the newspaper offices of America as they struggled to get a Five Star Final on to the streets. A woman in Chicago, noting the surging crowds round a street vendor, asked a man emerging from the ruck what all the fuss was about. 'We're at war, lady.' 'Well, whaddyer know!' she exclaimed. 'Who with?'[1]

Despite the fixed stare America had been giving Europe for eighteen months and more, war came to America and took everyone by surprise. Nothing could be more in character than the way in which Britain and America committed themselves to years of armed conflict. Britain declared war and found nothing to do for nine months but dig air raid shelters and complain about the irritating increase in red tape. America joined in the fray with a bang that was heard round the world.

Although the American public was disconcerted by the violence of the awakening, politicians and political observers had been increasingly aware of the likely consequences of Japan's expansion in the Pacific. In essence it had begun ten years before when Japanese forces invaded Manchuria. From 1937 onwards only the occasional Russian show of strength prevented Japan from overrunning China without opposition but these hostilities ceased when Japan signed the Tripartite agreement in 1940.

Hollywood too had its suspicions. *Variety* reported in April 1940 that the Education Ministry in Tokyo had banned *Zaza*, *The Cowboy and the Lady* and *Girl Trouble* which it had termed unfit for general consumption. This all sounded suspiciously like the platitudinous comments which emerged from Goebbels's Ministry of Propaganda. If further

evidence of future trouble were needed, it came in the simultaneous disclosure that the German film *Unternehmen Michael*, which glorified German conduct in the Great War, had received official sanction to be released throughout the country.[2]

The Nazi victories over Holland and France in the early summer of 1940 had certainly caused Japanese eyes to turn enviously towards the Dutch and French colonial possessions in South East Asia. With Britain concerned with the prospect of imminent invasion only the United States remained as a counter-weight to Japanese intentions in the Pacific.

The crucial weapon in the American armoury was an economic one. Japan was incapable of producing many vital raw materials herself and this irritating dependence on imports gave America a bargaining lever she did not hesitate to pull. In July 1940 an embargo was placed on shipments of aviation gasoline and scrap metal to Japan but because the Russians were occupied with the Nazi invasion on their Western front, many Japanese were clamouring for a decisive move into French Indochina, the Dutch East Indies (possession of which would have given them access to vital oil, rubber and tin supplies) and possibly Burma. The moderates, led by the Prime Minister, Fumimaro Konoye, were worried by the prospect of a war with the United States that they felt could not be won.

The Konoye government offered Roosevelt a compromise. If America would simply call off its embargo, stop the aid flowing to Chiang Kai Shek and recognise the Japanese conquest of China, Japan would undertake not to violate the independent existence of the Philippines and French Indochina. However, Konoye's hand was forced by the increasing militancy of the army leaders and in July 1941 Japanese forces occupied the military bases of French Indochina anyway.

Konoye tried desperately to bring Roosevelt to some sort of agreement, a policy Roosevelt was personally inclined to support. However, under urging from Cordell Hull and the State Department who were convinced that Japan was bluffing, Roosevelt refused to attend any conference until an agreement was reached with regard to the Japanese occupation of China. Hull had pushed Konoye backwards off the cliff. On 18 October 1941 his government toppled with him and was replaced by the die-hard militarists headed by Hideki Tojo.

Negotiations with Washington were continued but the die was cast. The Emperor gave his wooden acceptance of plans to attack the United States. On 25 November aircraft carriers left Kuriles and sailed eastwards. Japanese thumbnails sped over their maps towards Hawaii.

On the evening of 6 December, Roosevelt received the first thirteen intercepted and decoded parts of the Japanese reply to his latest request. He looked at his closest aide, Harry Hopkins, and stated emphatically that war was inevitable. Hopkins mused thoughtfully, 'It's too bad we can't strike the first blow and prevent a surprise.' 'No', replied the President firmly, 'We can't do that. We are a democracy of peaceful people. We have a good record. We must stand on it.'

The following day at 1.50 p.m. Washington time Roosevelt's lunch with Hopkins was interrupted by a phone call from Frank Knox, the Secretary of the Navy, who read out a wireless message, 'AIR RAID ON PEARL HARBOR THIS IS NOT DRILL'. When Ed Murrow came away from dinner that night at the White House he reported that there had been

> ample opportunity to observe at close range the bearing and expression of Mr Stimson, Colonel Knox and Secretary Hull. If they were not surprised by the news from Pearl Harbor then that group of elderly men were putting on a performance which would excite the admiration of any experienced actor.

As he was leaving, Roosevelt asked Murrow whether he had been surprised by the attack. 'Yes, Mr President', replied the reporter. Roosevelt shook his head. 'Maybe you think it didn't surprise us!'[3]

The surprise lay not in the likelihood of a Japanese attack but in its location. Nobody of any political or military importance thought it likely that the Japanese would have the temerity to strike at the very heart of the American naval defence. The Administration was convinced that the blow would land on Guam and the Philippines. Shortly after Roosevelt received news of the Japanese reply to

his latest proposal, that last day of peace, General Walter Short, the Army commander in Hawaii, was handed a warning message from Army intelligence. JAPANESE NEGOTIATIONS HAVE COME TO PRACTICAL STALEMATE. HOSTILITIES MAY ENSUE. General Short felt that to put his men on a constant alert would be to exhaust them. Fortunately for the author of *From Here to Eternity*, and Frank Sinatra whose career the film version in no small measure revived, Saturday night leave was granted as usual.[4]

The attack came just before 8 a.m. local time. Within ninety minutes 8 battleships, 3 light cruisers and 4 miscellaneous vessels had been sunk or badly damaged; important shore batteries were knocked out and 188 aeroplanes, over 50 per cent of American air power on the island, had been destroyed, ignominiously, on the ground. It was a devastating opening blow, comparable only with the pre-emptive strike made by Israeli pilots on the first morning of the Six Day War, when they too wiped out the bulk of the enemy's air power. In addition, 2,400 Americans were killed and 1,178 injured. So great were the casualties that full reports were not released until much later to prevent a national panic. The Japanese lost 29 planes, 5 midget submarines and less than a hundred men.

It was like Agincourt with Japanese names replacing Davy Gam Esquire. It was also perhaps a little less heroic in that the attack had occurred without official warning. It transpired later that the Japanese had attempted to send a declaration of war before they bombed Pearl Harbor but the decoders in the Japanese Embassy in Washington had stopped work early on Saturday night. The attempt to present Hull with the declaration next day was abandoned. The Japanese diplomats felt the sharp edge of the old man's tongue and retreated at an undiplomatic sprint down the corridors of the State Department. They returned to the embassy where the rest of the afternoon was spent in burning official documents. Outside the gates a small crowd gathered, ominously quiet, craning their necks as if to see into the hearts of the building's occupants.

The general reaction throughout the country was a mixture of anger, confusion and sheer disbelief. Many Americans heard the news on the radio, the announcement coming in the middle of some wildly inappropriate programme. Sunday afternoon was no time for serious programming, apart from the traditional relay of the New York Philharmonic concert from Carnegie Hall. Len Stirling, a staff announcer for Mutual Broadcasting System, broke into the commentary on the Dodgers *v* the Giants football game at the Polo Grounds.

> We interrupt this program to bring you a special news bulletin. The Japanese have attacked Pearl Harbor, Hawaii, by air, President Roosevelt has just announced. The attack also was made on all naval and military activities in the principal island of Oahu.

The switchboard was immediately flooded by calls from fans objecting to their game being interrupted. Many others, recalling the famous Orson Welles hoax broadcast waited for the network to announce the title of the new drama.

The anger and confusion was felt just as deeply in Congress. When Franklin Roosevelt addressed a joint session of Senators and Representatives the following day he was cheered wildly, even by those who had been his sworn enemies twenty-four hours before. Once more, as had happened on his first inauguration day over eight years previously, the country looked to the President to give them courage, hope and strength. He began without ceremony.

> 'Yesterday, December 7th 1941, a date which will live in infamy, the United States of America was suddenly and deliberately attacked by naval and air forces of the Empire of Japan. . . . With confidence in our armed forces, with the unfloundering determination of our people we will gain the inevitable triumph, so help us God!'

Once the initial ferocity and terrifying reality of the attack had worn off, people looked around to see how they could justify the President's faith in them. The town of Mikado, Michigan, which had named itself after the tuneful Gilbert and Sullivan comic opera, suffered six weeks of communal embarrassment before it found an acceptable replacement. The idea of naming itself Pearl Harbor, Michigan was abandoned and the town settled for MacArthur, Michigan, after the expected hero of future victory in the Pacific.[5]

The predictable wave of anti-Japanese feelings swept over the country. Within a month of Pearl Harbor a seemingly never-ending set of variations on a theme were emerging from Tin Pan Alley. 'Slap the Japs', 'A Jap is a Sap'. 'They're Gonna Be Playin' Taps on the Japs', 'The Japs Haven't Got a Chinaman's Chance' and 'To Be Specific It's Our Pacific' were just a few of the instantly forgettable titles and songs.[6] Meanwhile *Variety* breathlessly confessed in an article headed 'Japs notorious show biz gyps',

> Now that the US and Japan are at war it may be revealed that American showmen, authors, dramatists, composers and copyright owners have long conceded to Japan the world-wide undisputed championship in chiselling. The Japs have been the most bare-faced thieves in the world of ideas.[7]

Certain anti-Japanese tendencies, however, were not quite so amusing. On the West Coast an unpleasant persecution of Japanese immigrants and Americans born of Japanese parents resulted in internment for most and harassment for all. Poised somewhere between the sensible and the absurd was the instruction to band leaders to note carefully the reactions of the audience when the national anthem was played.[8] Anyone who sneered was to be reported to the police. While this seems to be particularly harsh on those who were about to sneeze or simply had involuntary facial expressions that falsely indicated dislike of 'The Star Spangled Banner', the danger of fifth columnists, especially in a strongly pro-German area like Milwaukee, was correctly realised.

Eddie Cantor achieved a level of political comment occupied by no other human being. *Variety* printed his letter on the front page but whether it was designed to arouse laughter or allied solidarity it is difficult to be sure. Cantor makes the perfectly sound point that the pictures of German, Italian and Japanese faces seen in America never showed anyone laughing. The comedian then went on to castigate the Fascist dictators because they were incapable of timing a laugh in their speeches and Cantor compared them most unfavourably to Winston Churchill, who, he claimed,

> has become the envy of every comic within earshot. What a comedian! What laughs! Our own FDR. . . . Newsmen in Washington flock to his Press Conferences not only for news but for laughs. Even the gallant Russians are showing previously unappreciated healthy humor as they blitz the Fritz.[9]

Hollywood, as was to be expected, arrived immediately after Pearl Harbor in a burst of patriotic enthusiasm and economic shrewdness. Paramount changed the title of their picture *Midnight Angel* to

13 'Darling, there seem to be a lot of little yellow men up here!' Donald
Barry realises the awful implications of his heinous act. *Remember Pearl
Harbor*.

Pacific Blackout but it failed to rescue the pedestrian script, wooden acting and incompetent direction and the picture was quickly laid to a merciful rest under its new headstone. Warner Bros announced the making of *Spy Swatter* starring Jimmy Durante and Phil Silvers, Monogram the forthcoming production of *She's in the Army Now* and the East Side Kids looked destined to join the remnants of the US Navy in *I'm an American*. Republic registered the title *Remember Pearl Harbor* and David Selznick *V For Victory*.

Government regulations, which emerged almost immediately after Pearl Harbor, had a significant effect on the workings of the American film industry. On 9 December army officials moved into all the studios and commandeered the firearms used in production which were then turned over to civil defense units. At this time there was still a very real fear on the West Coast that the attack on Pearl Harbor was only the prelude to a Japanese invasion of the West Coast. In view of the hundreds of miles of unprotected coastline from San Diego to San Francisco the fear was understandable. No promise was made by the army as to when the guns might be returned.

The Hollywood studios were ordered on to a daylight shift from 8 a.m. to 5 p.m. so that employees could get home before dark and the subsequent blackout. All night filming which had enabled the studios to function so efficiently was halted. Further regulations would hit the industry in the coming months but this was enough to test the depth of its patriotism. What concerned the executives most of all was the worrying drop in movie theatre attendances in the first few weeks after Pearl Harbor. Fortunately, audiences soon returned when the immediate panic was over, and indeed, they increased hugely in a very short space of time.

As for the movie personnel, reaction was as varied as was likely to be found in any other profession. Men who were already in the Reserve, like the Warner Bros producer Robert Lord, were called up immediately, although Lord's induction was postponed while he completed principal photography on *Wings for the Eagle*. Lord later remarked that he preferred the hazards of hand to hand jungle fighting with the Japanese to producing another picture with Errol Flynn. There was the usual hard core of hedonists who regarded the war as a grossly unfair imposition on their enjoyment and who shouted loudly about the infringement of personal liberty when their private planes were grounded. In the wake of Carole Lombard's tragic death early in 1942 her husband, Clark Gable, wrote to President Roosevelt asking for action in Hawaii or the Philippines. Roosevelt, with other matters on his mind, replied gently asking Gable to remain in Hollywood making pictures for civilian morale. The request was denied.

Republic's *Remember Pearl Harbor* was first past the post in the sprint for topicality. Donald Barry stars as an undisciplined American soldier in the Philippines who deserts his post and falls in with a disreputable crowd of Fifth Columnists working for the Japanese. However, when he realises the full implications of this devil's work he reaches GHQ with warnings (alas fractionally too late) of the attack on Pearl Harbor. Luckily he is in time to lead the action in the Philippines (also attacked shortly after Pearl Harbor) where another chapter in Japanese treachery is defeated by American troops in a short but fierce engagement.

The film is notable for its singular omission of Pearl Harbor and indicates how difficult Hollywood writers found the concept of defeat. For the British defeat has invariably been glorious and audiences have been positively obsessed by films about Dunkirk and other military disasters. Americans do not take readily to the idea of losing and John Wayne's loving tribute to the defenders of the Alamo left the country significantly unmoved. *Remember Pearl Harbor* was unmemorable for reasons other than this. Joseph Santley was not the director to turn a mundane script into anything exciting and Donald Barry who had been a reliable Western star for Republic under the name of 'Red' Barry found acting without a horse to be a task that was beyond him.

Remember Pearl Harbor should be seen more as a symbol than as a propaganda weapon in its own right. The Japanese had done more than they realised when they bombed Pearl Harbor. Waiting in the wings was not only *Stage Door Canteen* and *God Is My Co-Pilot* but *The Purple Heart* and *Since You Went Away*. The emotional heavy artillery was being drawn up. Hollywood had not waited to be drafted. It was enlisting right now.

All Through The Night

(December 1941 — October 1942)

There was one little problem still unsolved. The anger felt by all Americans on 7 December was directed almost exclusively against the cowardly little yellow men. There could be no doubt that Congress would support a declaration of war on Japan but taking the initiative against Germany was a different and, for the President, worrying matter. Predictably, following Roosevelt's address to the Joint Session of Congress the vote in favour of war was 388-1. (The single dissenting vote was registered by an elderly Congresswoman by the name of Jeanette Rankin who, even at that stage, refused to modify her pacifist principles.) But not a word was mentioned about the war in the Atlantic.

Help came from the least expected quarter. Hitler's crushing drive into the heart of Russia had at last been halted by the onset of winter and the resolution of the native defenders. Frustrated on the Eastern Front, Hitler found the behaviour of the American destroyers in the Atlantic particularly irritating. A few months before he had made an emotional and fateful decision to postpone Operation Barbarossa for a month in order to invade Yugoslavia, in retaliation for an internal *coup d'état* which had removed Hitler's puppet government there. A man who would jeopardise such a momentous event for the assuaging of his own hurt pride was clearly going to be sensitive to the actions of a non-belligerent country that insisted on firing on his submarines.

German strategists had been haunted by the spectre of a protracted war on two fronts since the days of General Schlieffen. Now the Japanese invoked the Tripartite Agreement and asked for German support in the fight against America. The Nazi chiefs wanted Hitler to resist temptation and pleaded that they were simply incapable of fighting a war on such epic scale. Hitler had heard these arguments before, had ignored them and had been proved right. After three anxious days, on Thursday 11 December, Germany declared war on the United States. Mussolini, now more than ever Hitler's lapdog, followed suit immediately and Congress reciprocated that same day. By now even the redoubtable Ms Rankin was persuaded to change her mind.

Doubts about the origins of the Pearl Harbor débâcle still lingered and a Congressional investigation was in progress after the end of the war. The traditional charge, that Roosevelt and Churchill had 'conspired' to drag the United States into a 'Jewish' war was once more aired and rejected for lack of evidence. If there was the slightest lack of total commitment to the fight against Japan and Germany the events of the first few months of 1942 quickly removed it.

By 1 January 1942 the Japanese had made successful landings on Guam, Hong Kong, Borneo, Wake Island and the Philippines. More important strategically was the campaign being waged on the Malayan peninsula. The Royal Navy was outfought and outmanoeuvred and its newest and most prized battleship, the *Prince of Wales* along with the heavy battle cruiser *Repulse* was sunk by torpedo bombers. Worse was to follow. In February Singapore fell before the relentless yellow tide, its big guns still pointing uselessly out to sea, unable to turn and deal with the land attack.

MacArthur was forced to retreat on to the fatal Bataan peninsula from which he was removed while his troops died bravely and helplessly. The names of Bataan and Corregidor became synonymous with death and despair. On 6 May, to prevent even more pointless slaughter, General Wainwright was compelled to surrender the rock together with its 11,000 American defenders. There had not been a similar capitulation since Appomattox and since Americans won as well as lost at the conclusion of the Civil War it became safe to say that there had been no real parallel in American history.

Even surrender brought no relief. The captured men were then led on a 65-mile 'death march' at the end of which the weak and the wounded lay dead from exhaustion. The Japanese controlled the entire Pacific west of the Midway and north of the Coral Sea. In North Africa Rommel was approaching the gates of Cairo and it was becoming increasingly clear that the Germans and the Japanese were likely to shake hands fairly soon in India, the brightest jewel in the British imperial crown. American seamen were being torpedoed off the East Coast and a flotilla of Japanese U-boats slipped easily into the unprotected waters off Santa Barbara.

It was in this unaccustomed atmosphere of military disaster that the American film industry addressed itself to the task of restoring shattered morale. To a certain extent Hollywood had been responsible for the creation of a totally false mental image of the Pacific islands now the scene of so much carnage. The picture was invariably one of rum and balmy nights, winds gently stirring the palm fronds, native boys shinning up trees for coconuts and dusky maidens in fitted sarongs diving into sleepy lagoons. The obvious inhabitants of these parts were Dorothy Lamour, Jon Hall and Maria Montez and the presence of the US Marines there was upsetting rather than comforting.

The confusion was considerably intensified by the bewildering procession of islands such as New Britain, New Ireland, New Hebrides and New Guinea between which Americans were unable to distinguish and yet all of which produced death lists that made their names as infamous as Ypres or Paschendaele. To most of the Occidental world the islands of the South Seas had remained unchanged since the days of Captain Cook and Clark Gable. It was perhaps appropriate that the US Navy started the war with obsolete charts first fashioned in the eighteenth century. On the Eastern Front in the First World War the armies of Russia and the Austro-Hungarian empire had warily circled round each other for weeks, each totally unaware of the location of the enemy. For the first few months of the Pacific War the US forces pirouetted in similar bewilderment.

One of Hollywood's basic problems during the war years was the same one that had bedevilled the industry in the two years before Pearl Harbor. The fastest production schedule was unable to produce an 'A' film for exhibition in less than four months.

The fear of being outdated by military events remained constant until VE Day. After the initial deluge of war pictures in 1942, such production slackened considerably. *Variety* reported in September 1942 that Twentieth Century-Fox was dating most of the stories for its musical pictures before Pearl Harbor on the grounds that the situation was changing so quickly that it would be unwise to take any chances on the inclusion of topical sequences.[1]

In the middle of March 1942 the production plans of the studios indicated that more musicals would be made that year than at any time in cinema history, topping the bonanza of the halcyon early 1930s. Before the end of the year though story editors faced a new and agonising dilemma. In purchasing likely material for the 1944 season should they assume that the war would be over? If it was, their studio would find themselves with unsaleable material and it would be awkward to shift the blame on to the efficiency of the Allied forces.[2]

The difficulties attending feature films did not apply to documentaries which responded readily to the new circumstances. Naturally the desertion of many of its crucial creative talents (Capra, Wyler, Huston, Ford) to this new field disturbed the Hollywood studios but they were at least partly appeased by the announcement that the Office of War Information, which was assuming far too much power for their liking, would let Hollywood dramatise the war as such and would restrict itself to the production of factual films only.

At its best the OWI turned out charming essays like Josef von Sternberg's *The Town* which set out to portray the opposite side of American life to the one traditionally seen in the staple action movies. No gangsters were to be seen in this unpretentious little town, filled with people of non-American descent, who were in turn homely, boring and appallingly complacent.

More representative of the durable documentary film was John Ford's *The Battle of Midway*. The battle itself on 4 June 1942 was the first defeat inflicted by the Americans on the brilliant Japanese admiral Yamamoto. Ford supervised Robert Parrish's editing of the picture and shot some of it himself, despite being injured in the process. Because of the nature of the director's previous films the facts were quickly absorbed into a new legend. The *Hollywood Reporter* had no qualms about printing it.

> Commander Ford shot the story of the battle
> of the Midway perched on top of one of the
> main targets of the raiders . . . one arm almost
> useless as the result of a Jap machine gun bullet
> sprayed down from one of the raiding planes.[3]

Hollywood was clearly unable to reproduce this kind of tangible heroic immediate reflection of the war even if it had so desired. Although there were to be excursions into the territory of propaganda, Hollywood mainly contented itself during the war years with pictures of heightened reality and pictures of no reality whatever — both of which it was extremely good at. Indeed it was revealed at the end of the war that the Japanese had resorted to the propagation of outrageous lies in the attempt to stem the flow of inspiration emerging from Hollywood. One story which caused riotous rejoicing in Japan told of the deaths by bombing of Shirley Temple and Deanna Durbin.

The government too recognised the important strategic position occupied by the American film industry. Although it was primarily concerned with the non-fiction film, developments in its feature film's treatment of war themes indicated that Washington was keeping a watchful eye on West Coast production. As early as May 1942 *Variety* divulged that top level discussions had resulted in a decision not to portray Hitler and Hirohito as personal symbols of German and Japanese evil. The American public was to be taught that the German and Japanese people were equally to blame for tolerating and co-operating with such leaders.[4] This was a significant step forward from Flora Robson's speech at the end of *The Sea Hawk* in which she claimed that England had no quarrel with the people of Spain whom she neatly divorced from the mad insatiable tyrant Philip II.

It was the government who outlined for Hollywood the six basic patterns for pictures related to the war after Roosevelt in an address to Congress had called for public information on certain vital issues. The first was the issues of the war itself into which category fell such diverse movies as *Watch on the Rhine*, *Wilson* and *This Above All*. The second was the Nature of the Enemy as seen in *Hitler's Children*, and *This Land Is Mine*. Third came the United Nations and its Peoples by which was meant everything from *Mrs Miniver* to *Mission to Moscow* and *Dragon Seed*. The fourth category was the pressing need for increased production and despite the unglamourous surface, the portrayals ranged from *Wings for the Eagle* to *Swing Shift Maisie*. The Home Front was self-explanatory, as indeed was the final section of the Fighting Forces, a genre in which Hollywood had long splashed happily. Even films which were simply composed of military heroics invariably made obeisance to at least one of the categories mentioned. This traditionally took the form of a final panegyric recited by the 'tough' Sergeant over the dead body of the 'baby' of the platoon.

For America one of the biggest single problems of the war was the fusion of its ethnic minorities into a cohesive disciplined united fighting force. In Britain the problem was always one of class differences, as illustrated by Carol Reed's film *The Way Ahead* in which the tough Sergeant (William Hartnell) under the command of the educated officer (David Niven) performs wonders with assorted members of the middle and lower classes. The hugely popular *In Which We Serve* positively revelled in the clarity of the distinction between the Captain and his wife (Noel Coward, his pipe and Celia Johnson) and the lower middle class Chief Petty Officer (Bernard Miles and his pipe) and the faithful but somewhat unreliable working class (John Mills, Richard Attenborough and not a pipe between them).

One of the difficulties that would confront any attempt to plead the cause of ethnic integration in America was that unquestioning obedience had never been a strong national characteristic. The majority of Americans have always looked more favourably on the exhortations of advertisers than those of politicians or Pentagon officials. (The discovery of the advertisers by the politicans was a black day in American history.) Consequently it became Hollywood's task to take the place of the latter by donning the disguise of the former. It needed a few trial runs to get things right. Bruce Humberstone's film *To the Shores of Tripoli* was seemingly dedicated to the self-willed young tearaway who joins the Marines for all the wrong reasons and flouts all the rules. The *New York Times* complained angrily that if this indeed were the case Congress had better be rapidly informed of the real state of affairs.[5]

Gradually, a winning formula began to emerge from these war films. It was based on the coincidental but fortuitous composition of the typical platoon which inevitably comprised the tough Sergeant, the rich kid, the ex-con, a Jew, a Polish-American, an Italian-American and a Black.

The Blacks in particular seemed to benefit from the move from the glorification of rugged individualism to the salutation of ethnic unity. Ernest Anderson in *In This Our Life*, Kenneth Spencer in *Bataan*, Ben Carter in *Crash Dive* and of course Dooley Wilson in *Casablanca* are a long way removed from Stepin Fetchit and Bill 'Bojangles' Robinson. It would be premature to suggest that this indicated a major philosophical leap forward by Hollywood. It really was little more than a recognition of the advances American Blacks were making anyway.

In 1940 pressure exerted by the National Association for the Advancement of Coloured People (NAACP) in threatening a march of 100,000 Blacks on Washington was rewarded when Roosevelt issued an Executive Order which, if it did not solve all the problems overnight was at least tangible recognition that a discriminatory problem did exist and needed government intervention. During the war, Black soldiers were integrated into army units and the economic boom eventually percolated down to the solid 20 per cent hard core of unemployed Blacks. Just as the Civil Rights movement can be seen as a logical successor to the March on Washington movement so Dooley Wilson may be properly regarded as the cinematic parent of Sidney Poitier.

The one minority group to get it in the neck both in real life and on the screen were the Japanese-Americans. The Issei (first generation Japanese-Americans) and the Nisei (their offspring) were instantly recognisable as such and thus subject to immediate retaliation by angry Americans. In the aftermath of Pearl Harbor they found that their insurance policies were arbitrarily cancelled, their cheques bounced, the milkman refused to deliver and shopkeepers declined to serve them.

The Attorney-General of California, Earl Warren, later to become one of the great liberal Supreme Court Chief Justices, issued a warrant authorising the rounding up of such 'aliens' and their transportation to camps in other states. To all this the Federal government was deafeningly silent and the American Civil Liberties Union ineffective in its opposition. Like most recent immigrants the patriotism of the Nisei traditionally exceeded that of long-standing American citizens and if positive proof were needed it came in the increasingly lengthy and spectacular roll of deeds performed

by those of their number in the armed forces. It is without question that many of the acts were inspired by the passionate desire of the Nisei to achieve sympathetic recognition for their families in the internment camps.

No such sympathy was forthcoming during wartime, however, and Japanese-Americans on the screen became synonymous with treachery. The first film to make such an explicit connection was *Secret Agent of Japan*, directed by Irving Pichel very quickly for Twentieth Century-Fox. By March 1942 Hollywood had not really had the time to distinguish between the new anti-Japanese formula that was required and the old Charlie Chan formula that had been a staple product for many years. 'Miss Lynn Bari', wrote one reviewer disdainfully, 'in a gown that clings like adhesive tape slinks about as if wearing a sandwich sign labelled "Don't look now but I'm a spy." '[6] Scarcely better as a contribution to the 'stab in the back' school of movie history was *Little Tokyo USA*, released by Columbia in April 1942 and deserving of no further comment.

Somewhat better cobbled together was John Huston's *Across the Pacific* which made its appearance a few weeks later. Although the evil Japanese-Americans are to be found lurking in shadows and peering through keyholes, the real villain is Sydney Greenstreet who is matched opposite Bogart and Mary Astor in another version of the winning formula introduced by *The Maltese Falcon*. This time Greenstreet's avarice leads him into treason and his epigrammatic conversation with Bogart includes the admission, 'The oriental way of life holds great appeal for me. You probably don't share my enthusiasm for the Japanese — wonderful people.' Like Donald Barry before and many good men thereafter Bogart just fails to warn the United States Air Force of the attack on Pearl Harbor and has to content himself with an exchange with a Japanese Prince whose arrival has precipitated much undemocratic bowing and scraping. 'You guys have been looking for war', accuses Bogart. 'That's right', concedes the Jap, 'That's why we started it.' 'You may start it, Joe', comes the unarguable reply, 'but we'll finish it.'

Such bluster was the only possible Hollywood response in 1942 to a war that the Americans were coming uncomfortably close to losing. In an attempt to finish *Wake Island* on a rousing note Paramount took the costly step of halting production just before shooting was due to take place on

14 Rosamund John and Michael Redgrave with upper lips specially prepared by the make-up department. *Way to the Stars*, like *Mrs Miniver*, was a triumphant portrayal of the British at war.

15 Dooley Wilson is an integral part of the Bogart-Bergman romance. *Casablanca*.

16 Lee Tracy is told by his agent that the studio isn't taking up his option.

17 The Union preserved again. Humphrey Bogart in *Across the Pacific*.

ROBERT
TAYLOR
IN
"BATAAN"

with GEORGE MURPHY
THOMAS MITCHELL
LLOYD NOLAN
ROBERT WALKER
DEZI ARNAZ

18 Waiting for Nippon. The patrol before decimation. *Bataan*.

19 Jack Benny (alias Professor Siletsky) makes one more attempt to upstage his wife (Carole Lombard). *To Be or Not To Be*.

20 'Jude! Jude! Jude!' Cary Grant dupes Walter Slezak in *Once Upon a Honeymoon*.

SILENCE PENDANT L'EMI

the closing sequence. 'The completion', it was explained in May, 'will await developments in the war and it will be written to conform to the situation possibly as late as July 15.'[7] The situation proved no more comforting in July than it had been in May.

MGM's *Bataan* was acclaimed on its release (May 1943) as being, along with *Wake Island*, one of the first realistic accounts of the Pacific War. In retrospect, however, it appears to be composed largely of impossible heroics, its realism presumably lying in the ultimate deaths of the protagonists. Robert Taylor plays the sergeant whose platoon is commanded to blow up the bridge over a ravine and generally delay the approaching Japanese while MacArthur regroups his forces. The various conflicts between the individual members of the patrol are progessively submerged as Japanese snipers pick them off one by one and the rest come to the full realisation of the nature of their mission. Robert Walker's letter to his mother is eventually dictated by Taylor who states simply, 'It don't matter where a man dies so long as he dies for freedom.'

The film is ultimately compromised by the staging of a pitched battle between the patrol and what appears to be the entire armed strength of the Japanese Empire. The Americans, reduced to five in number, mow down line after line of glinting yellow faces, crawling and charging through the dry ice like so many vermin. They abandon their machine guns and resort to hand-to-hand combat in their seemingly successful repulsion of the Japanese army for the loss of just two of their own men. The final shot of Robert Taylor firing ferociously into the tidal wave of advancing Japanese is as near to a glorious exit as was possible, given the comprehensive military defeat sustained on Bataan. Even then all is not lost as the roller caption points out that those 'heroes of Bataan made possible the victory of the Midway'.

Bataan at least overcame one problem successfully. The demand for extras to play the Japanese soldiers greatly exceeded the supply provided by Central Casting. The traditional sources, Chinese and Filipino actors, had more work than they could handle so Tay Garnett, the director of *Bataan*, appointed what he called a 'Nip Scout' whose job was to tour the Western states looking for suitable extras. The only condition demanded was that they should 'know how to simulate bayonet attacks'.[8]

The defeat on Bataan proved a better setting for *So Proudly We Hail*, a rousing tribute to the sterling work done by the nurses on the island. The coincidental presence there of Claudette Colbert, Paulette Goddard and Veronica Lake might have detracted from the 'realism' of the action scenes but in a sense the film, as a woman's picture, benefits precisely from its incorporation of certain glutinous strains of durable sentimental fiction.

Since American soldiers were not fighting in Europe in 1942 Hollywood films which dealt with the Nazi enemy were usually a mixture of warnings against fifth columnists at home, paeans of praise for the occupied peoples of Europe or stories of daredevil Americans behind enemy lines. *All Through the Night* was a link between the pre-war pussy footing and post Pearl Harbor conviction. The film was a blend of dire finger-wagging, comedy and a last minute single-handed rescue of the country by Humphrey Bogart. The Nazi spy ring once uncovered has to face the most effective opposition Warner Bros could assemble at the time — Bogart, Phil Silvers, James Gleason and Frank McHugh, 'their own stock company of tough guys, Broadway sharpies and muggs'. No wonder Conrad Veidt retired in confusion.

Veidt reappeared shortly afterwards in Jules Dassin's *Nazi Agent* which was built around his playing of identical twins — one a good German (i.e. a naturalised American) and the other a bad German. The good German has a budgie in his flat above the bookshop while the bad German wears a monocle and drinks heavily. The good German kills the evil twin but sacrifices his share in the American dream in so doing. As he boards the ship that will take him back to hate-filled Germany a crowd of extras jeer him mercilessly. As the general rhubarbing dies away, one extra ad libs enthusiastically, 'Get out and and and stay out', thus justifying his six-week correspondence acting course.

To Be or Not To Be was released in March 1942 to a barrage of hostile notices which found the film to be in the grossest of bad taste. One critic went so far as to call Lubitsch's comedy propaganda for Goebbels. Both Lubitsch and Alexander Korda, who was also involved in the commissioning of the screenplay, were shocked by the reaction.[9]

As expatriate Central Europeans their portrait of the Poles were clearly suffused with an affection for their obstinacy and idiocy. One would have thought that the casting of Jack Benny and Carole Lombard as the married acting team of Joseph and Maria Tura would have established the film's credentials as a comedy with a few political overtones. The dialogue crackles in the way one would expect from two of America's leading comic performers. Lombard rages at Benny's constant upstaging of her, 'If I catch a cold, you sneeze, if I go on a diet, you lose the weight and if I were to have a baby I'm not so sure I'd be the mother.' 'I'd be happy if I were sure I was the father,' returns Benny whose manic egotism and suspicion of his wife's infidelity lead him into feats of patriotic action.

The accusations levelled at *To Be or Not to Be* were principally that it reduced the issues of the war in Europe to a bad joke. Hitler was to be outwitted by a group of incompetent actors and the Gestapo was peopled by idiots. There was something to the latter charge. Sig Ruman who was cast as the redoubtable 'Concentration Camp' Erhardt ('I do the concentrating they do the camping') had made a living for nearly ten years out of the screen portrayal of Teutonic idiots and this part was no exception. Benny, in disguise, asks his opinion of Tura as an actor. 'Ah yes,' recalls Ruman, 'I saw him once before the war. Believe me, what he did to Shakespeare we are now doing to Poland.'

Herman Weinberg, in his book *The Lubitsch Touch*, tries to answer contemporary criticism by pointing to the film's brilliant analysis of the hierarchical nature of the Nazi creed. In the final analysis the film is really only justifiable on the grounds of comedy. Thirty-seven years on it appears as fresh and certainly funnier than when it was first made.

Once Upon a Honeymoon, on the other hand, though it was made at the same time and in similar circumstances, has dated badly. Like Lubitsch, Leo McCarey, in his own right a master of film comedy, was over six thousand miles away from the events he was depicting. Lubitsch, although personally involved in aiding victims of Nazi aggression in Europe, refrains from any mention of serious political matters in his film. McCarey blunders into a political minefield wearing the boots and philosophical deftness of a circus clown. Frank Capra, with whom McCarey shared a common Catholic immigrant background, was often labelled a political naïf, but McCarey makes him look in comparison like a philosopher of some originality. At least Capra returned constantly to the same area of political thought and had the integrity to put ideas developed in the 1930s to practical use in the *Why We Fight* series. McCarey remained in Hollywood as chief public relations officer for the Catholic Church.

The problem with *Once Upon a Honeymoon* is that McCarey is not content to make either a straightforward political statement or a comedy film but deliberately chooses to marry the two with disastrous results. One recalls fondly various pieces of McCarey business which so distinguished his 1930s comedies. Cary Grant having inveigled his way into Ginger Rogers's presence by pretending to be her dress designer has to take her measurements with an unco-operative steel ruler. Albert Dekker tells Ginger of his three-country 'allegiance' — spying for America in France and being paid by Germany — and, 'best of all', he concludes, 'No income tax!'

What one resents is less what Robin Wood has called the film's 'decline into solemnity' than McCarey's positively enraging superficial appreciation of the issues. Lubitsch makes a 'cheap', certainly funny, joke out of concentration camps. McCarey goes further and plays a scene inside one of them after Ginger Rogers has nobly changed places with a Jewish chambermaid (Natasha Lytess) and she and Cary have been arrested. The two heroes protest that they are Katie O'Hara and Pat O'Toole but the Gestapo is unimpressed. Cary inquires and discovers that of the two doors facing them one leads to a room where Jews are sterilised. Not surprisingly he becomes extremely agitated until they are ushered through the other door and meet the American consul who looks like Cordell Hull. 'I guess you're glad to see me', he grins and they exit happily, their laughter drowning the sound of the involuntary vasectomies being carried out in the adjoining room.

Inevitably and rightly America is regarded as the last outpost of safety and democracy but McCarey's 'oath of allegiance' scene is as flippant and callous as the rest of the film. James Stewart looking at the Capitol in *Mr. Smith Goes to Washington* or Gary Cooper articulating what he sees in Grant's Tomb in *Mr. Deeds Goes to Town* made their patriotism emotional and sincere. McCarey plays out a scene with Ginger Rogers and Albert Dekker imitating various American regional accents as proof of their American authenticity that is as embarrassing as it is unfunny. Clearly *Ruggles of Red Gap* had been left far behind and McCarey was travelling at high speed via Bing Crosby and the fantasy world of *Going My Way* to *My Son John* and the outer edges of paranoia.

In comparison to the foregoing, Twentieth Century-Fox's *This Above All* assumes the hallmark of political integrity. The novel by Eric Knight was something of an oddity in that it appears to belong more properly to the writing that so characterised English literature in the mid 1950s. The story of Briggs, the aggressive working-class soldier who deserts because he feels the war is being waged to preserve the stagnant and repressive British class system, made for a powerful and daring novel in 1941. His 'rescue' at the hands of a middle-class young nurse is terminated by death and what remains are his tirades against the smugness of traditional British institutions.

The casting of Tyrone Power as the disillusioned soldier was the first step in Darryl Zanuck's 'cleansing' of the property. The commissioning of R.C. Sherriff to write the screenplay ensured that English patriotism would emerge largely unscathed and between the two of them it was no great surprise to find the hero still alive at the end of the film. Quite what was the contribution made by the director, Anatole Litvak, remains unclear. Litvak had many qualities, not the least of which was first-hand knowledge of certain European countries, but his knowledge of England was to say the least limited.

This Above All made its own claim to a place in film history when Joan Fontaine as the nurse delivered a speech in praise of England that was proudly pronounced as the longest speech ever made by a woman in the movies. Having refused to define what England means to her, she proceeds to contradict herself.

> 'England, it's Monty and the boys coming up the road from Douai . . . helping the weaker men into the boats instead of getting in themselves. . . . That's England too; knowing that we'll never give in, knowing that we won't be beaten. We won't. We just won't.'

Hollywood's vision of England reached its roseate summit of glory with William Wyler's film, *Mrs Miniver*, a universally popular, finely wrought piece of work which has undeservedly fallen into critical disrepute. This aesthetic sniffing has been caused by the picture's lack of 'realism' (as evidenced by such contemporary documentaries as *Listen to Britain* and *London Can Take It* which had been released to great acclaim in America). *Mrs Miniver* did for England what *Casablanca* did for European refugees and what *Since You Went Away* did for the American family at home — it took a fictional group of people in the middle of a very real situation and treated their problems with drama and yet with compassion. One doesn't complain of *Casablanca* that it looks more like a Burbank studio than the location of the Churchill-Roosevelt conference in January 1943. Bogart's epigrammatic Rick or Paul Henried's heroic Victor Laszlo are no more 'real' than Mrs Miniver or Lady Beldon.

The problem with *Mrs Miniver* is that everyone is terribly nice. Apart from the German flyer who has been encountered earlier and a spy whose scene was removed in the final cut (for dramatic rather than political purposes) there is nobody on whom one can vent one's spleen. Mrs Miniver splurges extravagantly on a silly hat and Mr Miniver on a new car while the Vicar admits to sneakily purchasing a box of his favourite cigars. Even Lady Beldon (played by the inevitable Dame May Whitty), who appears to stand in the way of a marriage between her granddaughter (Teresa Wright) and Mrs Miniver's son (Richard Ney), is revealed as an old crab apple with a core of solid gold when she reverses the decision of the cowed judges in the Flower Show and awards the coveted first prize to the dogged Station Master, Mr Ballard. Ballard is killed in an air raid within the hour, which only increases Lady Beldon's stature.

The one speech of any real venom given to Lady Beldon was lost during the editing. 'Middle class government', she spits,

> 'That's the whole thing in a nutshell. We've had middle class government so long it has turned us into a nation of wet hens. No traditions, no authority and no discipline.'

That speech is effectively replaced by Lady Beldon's more generalised complaints at being pushed around by 'middle class women buying things they can't possibly afford . . . I don't know what this country's coming to — everyone trying to be better than their betters.' Since this is delivered straight at Greer Garson the direction makes it into a joke; the original political statement was more serious and would have been much more difficult to contradict.

The stereotyped middle-class existence is greatly emphasised by the presence of Ada the cook and Gladys the serving maid. Ada complains bitterly to Mrs Miniver that Gladys is in such a state because her young man has been called up by his regiment that 'she's not fit to wait, mum, she's not reely.' 'Never mind, Ada', replies Mrs Miniver bravely, 'We'll manage somehow.'

Ada herself is nobly sacrificed to the Tank Corps Canteen as Vin Miniver enlists in the RAF. Clem, although too old for active duty, is roused at the dead of night and ordered to the landing stage where, fortified by his wife's freshly made sandwiches and Thermos flask, he meets up with his crew and fellow small-boat owners — Nobby and Joe the barman. 'Mac' arrives wearing top hat and overcoat over his full evening dress having left the Savoy in something of a hurry. 'Good man', says Mr Miniver absently. 'Any idea what we're up to?' 'Who cares? Their's not to reason why — gallant 600' comes the cheerful if convoluted reply and the ranks are immediately swollen by the dentist, a farmer and good old Sir Henry, the retired Indian Army colonel.

The general restraint shown by the writers, actors and director in the making of *Mrs Miniver* was a major reason for its success. One remembers with affection that underplayed scene of Clem going off to Dunkirk, Mrs Miniver hiding the German pilot's gun behind some crockery and responding to the torrent of Nazi invective with a bright 'How about a nice cup of tea?' and the sudden twist as Teresa Wright is killed when one has been awaiting with increasing certainty the death of her young husband.

The final scene is a sermon in a ruined church in which words and pictures combine to present movingly and simply the portrait of a nation united in and by war. Henry Wilcoxon, who plays the vicar, apparently rewrote the speech with Wyler to emphasise the democratic aspect of the new warfare.

'Why in all conscience should these be the ones to suffer? Children, old people, a young girl at the height of her loveliness. . . . Because this is not only a war of soldiers in uniform, it is a war of the people — of all the people — and it must be fought not only on the battlefield but in . . . the heart of every man, woman and child who loves freedom.'

During the service Richard Ney slips quietly into the pew traditionally occupied only by the Beldon family and places a comforting arm on Lady Beldon's shoulder. As the old lady herself finally admits, 'War's brought us to our senses in more ways than one.'

Mrs Miniver opened at Radio City Music Hall in New York City on 4 June 1942. Within ten weeks it had attracted a million and a half spectators. In all it grossed $6 million in North America alone and swept the board at the Academy Awards where it took four of the top five prizes.[10] It may well be that a few of the admissions had been prompted by

the curious spectacle of Greer Garson playing the mother of Richard Ney whom she had just married in that other world outside the sound stage but it was the political significance of the film's success that really distinguished it. Roosevelt told Wyler that *Mrs Miniver* had appreciably lessened the problems attendant upon increased aid for Britain. Frank Knox, the Secretary of the Navy, saw the picture with Billy Wilkerson, the editor of The *Hollywood Reporter*, and remarked dramatically afterwards, 'God Bless the men and women who made this film; its effect in these trying days will be miraculous.'[11]

Mrs Miniver may not have been quite the divine gift Knox had proclaimed it, but it certainly aroused in America feelings for Britain that were never to be quite so fervent again. The English may have grumbled that the film was quite unlike any part of the country they had ever seen but that didn't stop them turning out in their millions to see it.

MGM were so delighted that they speeded up the release of *Journey for Margaret*, again set in war-torn England but this time pleading specifically for the adoption of endangered British children. The story of two young children who are unable to settle happily in an extremely pleasant foster home and who are taken back to America by a journalist (Robert Young) has so many obvious moments of pathos that it is surprising to find it quite so deftly handled by 'One Shot Woody' Van Dyke. As the two children discover that the city lights are still on when they arrive in New York harbour their admiration for America knows no bounds.

Margaret O'Brien's performance as one of the children in question was so glutinously compelling[12] that there was an instant demand for the adoption of little English girls with blonde hair, preferably about six years old. It came as a considerable surprise to Americans when they were confronted with the offspring of Cleckheaton and Wapping. Nevertheless evacuations continued throughout the war years. Noel Coward and Gertrude Lawrence made themselves responsible for the organisation of the evacuation of the children of British actors to America. The youngsters themselves were shepherded into performing in a concert on Broadway to give thanks to their benefactors and to raise money for more of their fellows to follow in their privileged footsteps. The concert opened with the children singing 'There'll Always Be An England' and included sketches by Miss Lawrence herself and Constance

21 Greer Garson, May Whitty and Henry Wilcoxson affirming that as there's MGM, there'll always be an England.

22 The Secretary of the Navy thought *Mrs Miniver* was worth a flotilla of destroyers. Greer Garson and Walter Pidgeon are sure of it.

23 Government rationing regulations served only to exaggerate Wallace Beery's natural truculence. *Rationing*.

Collier entitled 'Gratefully Yours'.[13]

What the children found in America during the war was only a superficial similarity to life in Britain. There was one fundamental difference. By mid-1942 it was fairly clear that there were going to be no enemy attacks made on the American mainland. Americans joined in the war on the home front with much fervour because arguments over rationing were not overshadowed by the very real fear of German occupation. Also, a nation which was geared to high consumption found it difficult to adjust to the scarcity of long-accepted items particularly when for perhaps the first time in more than a decade there was actually surplus cash in the household budget.

The rationing of petrol in America in 1942 (the normal 'A' allowance was three gallons per week) created one of the more bizarre phenomena of the war years. Cars would lie in wait for petrol delivery lorries and then follow them through the streets to the petrol stations where they would fill their tanks with as much petrol as they were allowed so they could follow more delivery lorries to more filling stations. Rationing affected more than supplies of sugar or tyres. The War Production Board came down heavily on the use of metal for asparagus tongs, spittoons, bird cages, cocktail shakers, hair curlers and lobster forks. Rationing inevitably led to hoarding, although one old lady who had stored over a thousand tins of food in her cellar was presumably made to see the error of her ways when unexpected floods removed the labels off every single tin.[14]

Shortages were subject to rapid changes. Sugar, butter, alcohol, meat and cigarettes were expected to be in short supply, but there seemed to be no logical explanation for the capricious disappearances of book matches, bicycles, paper, nappies, girdles and beer mugs. Everyone, though, was temporarily amused by the enforced closure of the Philadelphia ration office which had forgotten to ration fuel for itself.

The entertainment industry addressed itself to the home front with commendable, if sometimes misplaced, enthusiasm. The popular song 'Deep in the Heart of Texas' had to be removed from radio broadcasts to factories when it was discovered that workers banged their hammers, or whatever they happened to be holding at the time, in the hand-clapping phrases. Smashed machines and chaotic conveyor belts bore witness to the seductive rhythm of the song. Girls who copied the Veronica Lake peek-a-boo hairstyle which was the rage of 1942 found that its dangers near factory machinery outweighed the advantages of its allure. They were less than gratified to discover that they were also forbidden to wear Lana Turner-style sweaters, halters or other revealing garments because their fellow male workers were walking wide-eyed into a variety of unpleasant industrial accidents.

Joe Smith, American gave the home front workers an entertaining little homily while reminding them of the importance of their essentially boring jobs. The foreword states simply

This is a story about a man who defended his country. His name is Joe Smith. He is an American.

Robert Young plays Joe, a $1 an hour worker in an aircraft factory who, on answering questions regarding his loyalty satisfactorily (his parents were European immigrants), is promoted to a more important job on a new prototype plane. Soon after dropping off his son at school, where he watches the children pledging their allegiance to the flag of the USA, he is captured by enemy agents and tortured for vital information on the new plane. To offset the pain he recalls all the trivial treasured moments of family life which are the source of his ties to democracy. Although blindfolded he remembers the sensations of his journey and manages to help the police retrace the path by means of an ingenious map scribbled on the pavement. The film looks distinctly simplistic today, but the unanimity of the critical delight with which it was acclaimed on its release in April 1942 argues strongly for its contemporary effectiveness.

Hollywood by and large knuckled down well to the problems facing home front industries in general and propaganda media in particular. Lowell Mellett of the Office of War Information (OWI) told producers how to insert important war propaganda into even the most traditional of pictures. 'For instance, suppose there was a love scene in a cafe', Mellett argued, 'The girl could say to the boy, "I only want half a spoonful of sugar. It's not only patriotic — it's good for my figure too." And Judy Garland could point to Mickey Rooney's refusal to wear trousers with turn-ups and say, "I admire him for it." '[15] The producers' replies went unrecorded, but one has only to recall the moment in *Since You Went Away* when Claudette Colbert stops shovelling the coffee into the pot, pauses and returns the spoonful in question back into the canister, to see that Mellett was not without influence.

The Hays Office found this sort of bandwagon a most congenial one. The Hays officials requested the film companies to eliminate all scenes of destruction, such as automobile wrecks, furniture breaking and endorsed the prohibition on food wasting down to a ban on pie throwing. Such scenes, they declared sternly, were not in keeping with the national mood of strict economy and the salvage of usable objects. The films of 1942 were notable in the eyes of the Hays Office for the satisfactory use of stock shots of screeching tyres and car chases.[16]

Ammunition, even with blank cartridges, was severely restricted. This wrought havoc with the cowboy film as a credible *genre*. *Variety* remembered fondly a time when

> Used to be a cowpoke would shoot off half a case of cartridges while pursuing his guilty quarry lickety split over rocky gullies when any honesta-gawsh real waddy wouldn't dream of proceeding at a pace faster than a slow walk for fear of an injury to his nag's legs. Now he's allowed to take aim only once and his man's gotta drop. It makes for better shootin', pardner.[17]

War regulations were perhaps an explanation, though hardly a justification, to disappointed fans of Hopalong Cassidy who found their hero in his latest adventure coming upon his girl friend, 'Sunbonnet Sue', out hoeing the vegetables in her victory garden.

The studios were certainly happy enough to float Lew Ayres off down the river in the passionate days of March 1942. Ayres explained very carefully that even though he was a pacifist he was more than willing to serve in the front line but he did not want to carry a rifle. The declaration of Ayres's pacifism was the cue for an immediate self-righteous outcry. The manager of the Fox Theater in Hackensack New Jersey reported that he received 135 phone calls within twenty-four hours of the announcement protesting that his cinema was showing *Dr Kildare's Victory*.[18] MGM sanctimoniously declared they were withdrawing all the Kildare films from distribution but their action was only the traditional Hollywood response to box office pressure. Hollywood never forgave Ayres the embarrassment he had caused them by not only having principles but also daring to admit them publicly. Although he returned after the war, he never regained his former popularity even though his performances in *Johnny*

Belinda and *Advise and Consent* suggest that his craft had not suffered.

The studio executives and their publicists could point proudly to their physical contribution to the war effort and to their record of compliance with the most irritating of government rules. Nevertheless they were eager to accept Brigadier-General Hershey's proposal that the film industry be categorised a restricted occupation and its members be exempt from military service. However, the Screen Actors Guild, perhaps even more sensitive to possible public criticism, led the film unions into a recognition of their responsibilities. The Guild sent over 1,200 extras from film work to the Southern Californian war production industries. Extras particularly in demand were those who had had engineering or carpentry experience.

There was, however, one issue which united the guilds even more solidly, this time in opposition to a 'patriotic' proposal. Because celluloid stock contained inflammable chemicals Hollywood found its supply of raw film also subject to rationing. Various means of saving film were tried. William Wyler's enlistment in the armed forces was of great benefit in itself, but on Friday 12 June 1942 The *Hollywood Reporter* announced to an ashen-faced industry 'FILM CREDITS SLATED TO GO'. The long arm of the Second World War was indeed threatening the removal of screen credits on the grounds that by just displaying the title and the names of the stars over 20 million feet of film a year would be saved. Over the weekend the town rocked with violent discussion. On Monday morning The *Hollywood Reporter* headlined the decision — 'DIREC—TORS NIX CREDIT BAN'. At a meeting of one hundred directors the voting had eventually resolved into a 97 to 3 victory for the restoration of sanity. The Screen Writers Guild announced a week later that it would be happy to consider a proposal whereby screen credit would be replaced by printed programmes or even larger advertising space on posters for its members but by then the danger had passed and no further nonsense was entertained for the duration.

Hollywood was altogether happier exhorting the masses to buy war bonds. This was their kind of war. At the end of each film, where the Blue Eagle of the NRA had once flapped proudly, stood the message AMERICA NEEDS YOUR MONEY. BUY DEFENSE BONDS AND STAMPS EVERY DAY. In the foyer of each cinema was a stand where the converted

24 The press release for this picture reads: 'Mickey, a three year old wire-haired terrier belonging to film actress Louise Allbritton, became Hollywood's first canine donor recruiter enlisting volunteers for the Mobile Blood Bank at Universal Studios where his mistress is playing in *Angela*.'

25 Anne Baxter and Franchot Tone discover what war is really like at Paramount Studios. *Five Graves to Cairo*.

26 The sanitised version of the Stalin purges. Victor Francen in *Mission to Moscow*.

could fulfill such requests. Stars gave their services willingly to expeditions designed to sell war bonds. Carole Lombard indeed gave her life, for it was on her return from such a sales drive that the plane carrying her crashed, killing all on board.

The incentive to buy bonds or subscribe a percentage of the weekly pay checks to one of the various Payroll Savings Plans was so great during 1942 because products were in such short supply and war work of one description or another claimed nearly all the people for a greater part of their time. The result was a slowly accumulating mass of wealth that looked to economists, industrialists and politicians in 1945 like nothing so much as a loudly ticking bomb that was liable to explode the minute wartime restrictions were lifted.

For the American film industry and for the average wage earner, 1942 was the first year of the unexpected but no less welcome boom. The opening months of the war sent individual picture earnings heading towards their highest for fifteen years. The average 'star' movie was grossing nearly $1,250,000, which represented something like a gross profit of $600,000 and a 'hit' would soar into the $4 million category. In the days of petrol rationing, when a new tyre cost $100 on the black market and a retread at least $50, a 35 cent visit to the movies was an attractive investment. In 1942 an average of 90 million admissions were recorded at the box office in America each week. Presumably that figure does not count the many thousands of children who climbed in through the window, under the turnstile or up the fire escape.

Costs rose proportionately of course. The making of a feature film cost approximately 15 per cent more in 1942 than it had in 1941. However, since in 1942 101 pictures grossed a total of $182·5 million, the profits of the individual studios were not greatly affected. The returns for Loews Inc. (the parent company of MGM) for the twelve months ending 31 August 1942 showed a profit of $12,133,294, after taxes had been paid.[19]

The massive stimulus given to the economy by the war finally solved the lingering problems of the Depression. At the end of 1941 there were still nine million men unemployed and three million on relief rolls. Half of the draftees in 1942 were rejected on the grounds of unfitness caused by malnutrition. By the end of the year the problem was not depression but inflation, which, during 1942, was running at something approaching 25 per cent. The hastily constituted Office of Price Administration froze the prices of rents in defence areas and certain consumer goods at their March 1942 levels but the large rise in farm costs fuelled a 50 per cent average increase in food prices. The OPA prevented runaway inflation, though certain die-hard industrialists grumbled that such government interference with market controls was going to sap the moral fibre of Americans nourished by twelve years of character-forming privation.

The awakening of the slumbering giant of American industry was the principal reason for the Allied victory in the Second World War. The munitions that poured off the assembly lines permitted American troops the luxury of spraying the trees with bullets in their search for enemy snipers. The German soldiers were appalled at such profligacy. At the end of 1942, trapped in the terrifying cold of the infamous Russian winter, huddled in summer clothing issue, they had cause to regret their leader's brazen challenge to the 'soft' democracy of the New World. On all fronts the Allies had stemmed the tide of the enemy advance and had begun the long-awaited counter-attack. The Germans had been stopped within sight of Moscow and at the very gates of Stalingrad. On 23 October Montgomery's Eighth Army opened the battle of El Alamein, the successful conclusion of which enabled the landing of new Allied armies and the invasion of North Africa. In August the US Marines had landed on the notorious island of Guadalcanal. It would take six gruelling months but the conceited, insolent Japanese were soon to learn that shooting peas at the American eagle could be a very unrewarding experience.

7

Here Is Your War

(November 1942 — May 1944)

In America, Republic is releasing a British made film titled *At Dawn We Die*. In England the same feature is playing under the title *Tomorrow We Live*.

Hollywood Reporter
23 March 1943

When the Germans invaded Russia in June 1941 there was a good deal of controlled smirking going on in certain Washington circles. There had long been a secret hope that the twin bogies of American capitalism, Nazi Germany and Soviet Russia, would scratch each other's eyes out and leave the world for America to bustle in. The events of Operation Barbarossa seemed to be offering renewed cause for optimism after the unfortunate hiatus of the 1939 Non-Aggression Pact. Yet within months, the American government was thinking seriously of sending troops on to the European continent in a direct response to an appeal from Stalin, and Russia had pledged her commitment to the principles enshrined in the Atlantic Charter. Total war made impossible demands on political ideology.

In May 1942, with his country suffering casualties at a rate impossible for America and Britain even to comprehend, Molotov made his plea for the opening of a second front to draw German land and air forces away from Eastern Europe. The United States toyed with the idea of a limited invasion of France but under pressure from the British finally agreed that their best strategy was to invade North Africa and draw off Rommel's strength.

On 8 November, aided by air and sea cover, Anglo-American forces landed successfully at Oran, Algiers and Casablanca and began to drive east. Montgomery's Eighth Army, following the brilliant victory at El Alamein, advanced westward to join up with the new forces and together they trapped 275,000 German and Italian troops who surrendered helplessly with their backs to the sea, squeezed into a bottleneck on the Tunisian coast. For Germany it was, as Churchill remarked, 'The end of the beginning', but the Russians remained convinced that the immediate opening of a second front in Occupied Europe was a military imperative.

The Russians, nevertheless, began 1943 on a brighter note than they had ended 1942. In the wake of the renewed hope in Moscow, Leningrad and Stalingrad, relations between the major Allied powers steadily improved even if this was simply a recognition of their military interdependence. Churchill visited Moscow in August 1942 to explain to Stalin that the Second Front was being postponed in favour of the North African campaign. Stalin accepted the necessity but did not cease to press for the adoption of his tactics on the Western Front at the earliest possible date.

Ironically, Stalin found tactical support among the American Joint Chiefs of Staff who felt that the North African campaign followed by an invasion of Sicily would be pecking at the outer shell of the Axis and not seriously troubling its defences. Roosevelt, however, accepted Churchill's submission that an invasion of France in 1942/3 would be impossible without overwhelming air superiority and confidence in the ability of industry to supply such a mammoth undertaking.

The opening of the Second Front and relations with the Soviet Union were subjects of constant debate in America during 1943 and, marching loudly along in the rear, Hollywood tossed in its own inimicable two cents' worth. *Comrade X*, MGM's gentle anti-Communist satire starring Clark Gable and Hedy Lamarr was instantly provided with introductory titles explaining that no offence was intended to the good citizens of the Soviet Union who, it was felt, would take the jokes in good faith.

Warner Bros became involved in the controversy by direct order of the White House. According to Jack Warner, he received a telephone call from his old friend the President of the United States who asked him to make a film from the book *Mission to*

Moscow, written by the former American Ambassador to Russia, Jospeh E. Davies. 'We have to keep Stalin fighting', explained Roosevelt, 'and this picture of yours can make a case for him with the American people.' Warner was duly flattered and pledged his studio to the making of the film.

Davies himself became increasingly involved with the movie and the finished product reflects his own political feelings. While shooting was underway the part of Molotov was recast, this time with Gene Lockhart, and all the previous Molotov footage was scrapped and reshot. The official explanation was that Davies was unhappy with the original interpretation and felt it was 'unacceptable to the American and Russian governments'.[1] What the producer, Robert Buckner, thought was not mentioned. Davies's supervision of the casting was supplemented by a filmed prologue starring himself (before he reluctantly handed over to Walter Huston who impersonated Davies in the film) in which he explains that his motivation for writing the book was an unquenchable desire to 'tell the truth about the Soviet Union'. He affirms his belief in the American system and also in the honesty and integrity of the Soviet leaders, who are devoted to the cause of world peace. His final dedication is to 'that patriotic organisation, the Warner Bros'.

The essence of *Mission to Moscow* is the conviction that Russians are just like Americans with fur hats and the ideological divisions are more imagined than real. Litvinov quotes the words of Woodrow Wilson as he defends Haile Selassie at the League of Nations in 1936. Molotov declares his deep respect for Franklin Roosevelt — 'a great man with a profound sympathy for mankind'. Best of all is a memorably platitudinous tea party given by Mrs Litvinov, Commissar of Cosmetics, for Mrs Davies in which they reach the inescapable conclusion, 'I guess women are much the same the world over.'

In general, the film is brilliantly directed by Michael Curtiz, skilfully blending in newsreel footage with dramatic reconstruction but it is riddled with such political bias as to make *Triumph of the Will* look like an objective current affairs programme. Schacht and von Ribbentrop are portrayed as cackling conspirators and the casting of Henry Daniell in the latter role stereotypes the man's villainy. Trotsky, Nazi Germany and Japan are all linked to outbreaks of sabotage in Russia. Germany and Japan are shown to be planning the partition of the country between them and a Trotskyite group is apparently all ready to capture the Kremlin by force and exterminate all opposition. Davies asks Chinese victims of Japanese aggression why they came to Russia and is told in no uncertain terms, 'Russia is our friend, Mr Davies.'

The Stalin purges of 1937 and 1938 are thus justified on the grounds that they were little more than minor matters of national security. Even the Non-Aggression Pact of August 1939 is easily explained as a reaction to misguided British and French appeasement of Hitler at Munich which had left Russia defenceless should the might of Nazi Germany be directed against her. The cynical invasion of Finland is simply all part of the master strategy that is only becoming apparent in 1943. The inevitable ending of the film is a utopian picture of Americans and Russians yet unborn who will march together down the road to freedom.

Most of *Mission to Moscow* still takes the breath away with its grandiose political assumptions. However, restrained wonder at this audacity was not a luxury to be indulged in 1943 and the picture aroused more violent controversy than almost any film ever made by the studio, including *Confessions of a Nazi Spy*. What particularly upset Americans was the portrait of the Senate as a hotbed of profiteering isolationists. 'And I say, gentlemen', remarks one member of that august body, 'not only can we do business with Hitler but we can make a nice profit doing so.' 'It's going to be Hitler's Europe', says another, 'and I say, what of it?'

Warners felt sure they were making a momentous contribution to screen history. The $250,000 that was originally to be spent on advertising was eventually doubled. Of this, 87.5 per cent went on space bought in daily newspapers, with particular emphasis to be laid on 'Catholic, Protestant, Jewish and other religious publications'. The public image of the Russian leaders in America was undergoing a marked change. The Comintern, the instrument of worldwide Communist revolution, was dissolved in May 1943. Stalin suddenly appeared a lovable shaggy dog instead of the moody grizzly bear of former times. Davies spoke eloquently of these heroes at a lunch given by Warner Bros just before *Mission to Moscow* was released.

> There is no man in the world I would trust more fully than Joe Stalin or Maxim Litvinov or Vyacheslav Molotov or Marshall Clementi Voroshilov.[2]

The trade press received the film with a deathly

explosion of superlatives and phrases that testified to their admiration for Michael Curtiz's direction and their own absorption in the philosophy of show business.

> Never in the history of motion pictures has a film faced so severe a test as the one undertaken by *Mission to Moscow* and never has a film earned so magnificent a tribute as that paid it . . . a magnificent, informative and truly epochal screen document.

Elsewhere, however, it made some powerful enemies. The Hearst Press predictably threw up its hands in horror at the prospect of a film which had seemingly been written, shot and edited by key figures of the Soviet Praesidium. In Illinois, the State Attorney General accused Warner Bros of 'falsifying through distortion' and the Republican National Committee tore viciously at it as detestable New Deal propaganda. In October 1943 Congressman Walter Ploeser from Missouri cited *Mission to Moscow* as evidence of subversion that clearly demanded a thorough investigation into the workings of Hollywood. Unfortunately for Mr Ploeser he was unable to endure for another four years to see the House UnAmerican Activities Committee respond to his call and the dream of interrogating Betty Grable's legs in a glamorous Hollywood nightclub remained another unkept campaign promise.

Bad notices on the Right were not unexpected. Vitriolic attacks from the Left were slightly more surprising. Traditional liberals like La Follette and Professor John Dewey came out in support of the Trotskyites who complained bitterly of Stalin's 'whitewash'. A pamphlet published by the Socialists Workers Party left no doubt of the writer's political convictions.

> No book and no number of films can whitewash Stalin's crimes against the world working class. *Mission to Moscow* [has] become a conveyor belt in the mechanism of Stalin's frame-up and murder system against his political opponents in labor's ranks.

To their credit, neither Jack nor Harry Warner shifted their ground, although Jack Warner simply reiterated that the film was made at the direct request of the President and bewailed the fact that despite his good intentions and the thumping losses he was incurring he seemed incapable of pleasing anyone. Harry Warner hit back angrily at his isola-

tionist attackers and sneered

> We would hate to be known as the company that made the most successful musical film of this great war for freedom.[3]

MGM certainly succeeded in making the best musical picture of the war set in Russia, which was a reasonable compromise. *Song of Russia* starring Robert Taylor as a conductor on tour in Russia in 1941 fought its way grimly into that special category reserved for uniquely idiotic motion pictures. The start of the picture which shows Taylor conducting his orchestra in 'The Star Spangled Banner' as if it were the climax of Ravel's 'Bolero' suggests strongly that *Song of Russia* should have been shown to the Nazis instead of the Allies. The performance of Susan Peters as the brilliant young Russian pianist with whom Taylor falls in love and of Robert Benchley as Taylor's manager are both good enough to make one embarrassed for their being caught up in such horrendous activities.

Once again the similarities between the Americans and the Russians are pointed up. Peters shows Taylor the sights of Moscow at which he enthuses, 'I can't get over it. Everyone seems to be having such a good time . . . You could be an American girl.' Taylor returns with her to her village, Tschaikowskoye, and recalls fondly that he too was raised on a wheat farm and even had a tractor which he called 'Big John'.

The music is supplied almost entirely by the first few bars of Tchaikovsky's B flat piano concerto although the incidental music wanders farther afield. As *Variety* put it

> Tschaikowsky's cleffings are particularly prominent and additional music has been supplied by modern Russian composers none of whom is billed. The Jerome Kern-E.Y. Harburg combination has contributed the tuneful 'And Russia Is Her Name'.[4]

Goldwyn's *The North Star* also enlisted top musical talent, this time Aaron Copland and Ira Gershwin, in an attempt to produce a popular film about Soviet Russia. The original idea had been that of William Wyler who, along with the writer, Lillian Hellman, went to see whether the film could be shot on location. Litvinov reminded them that there was enough shooting going on in Russia already and by the time studio arrangements had been made in Hollywood, Wyler had joined the Signal Corps and

27 Neither the Stalin purges nor the imminence of the German panzer divisions can distract these Russian peasants from their customary behaviour. The smiling faces of *Song of Russia* were later to be used as evidence of Communist subversion in MGM.

28 Erich Von Stroheim in *North Star* (or *Armored Attack*).

29 Dana Andrews in *Armored Attack* (or *North Star*).

30 If Darryl Zanuck had known what a box office egg *The Moon is Down* was to lay he might have been tempted to join Henry Hull on the scaffold.

Anne
BAXTER
Dana
ANDREWS
Farley
GRANGER

"ARMOURED
ATTACK" "A"

(Formerly "NORTH STAR")

Lewis Milestone had assumed control of the project.

Like *Mission to Moscow* and *Song of Russia*, *The North Star* strove hard to draw parallels between American and Russian society. Perhaps the striving was too hard because the first half of the film looks suspiciously as though a group of well known Hollywood actors have adopted Russian names for a short holiday on a farm in Oklahoma. The confusion aroused by the invasion of Nazi panzer divisions in the second half is dreadful. The men and women who were simple peasants are transformed by the attack into heroic defenders and liberators of their village.

Hellman's writing is at its best in its portrayal of the 'good' German (Erich von Stroheim), whom Walter Huston sees as being significantly worse than the 'bad' German (Martin Kosleck)

> 'To me *you* are the real filth. Men who do the work of Fascists and pretend to themselves they are better than those for whom they work.'

Once again the intrusion of 'politics' (despite Sam Goldwyn's earnest disavowals) stirred fierce resistance on the editorial pages. The Hearst Press on instructions from San Simeon condemned it as 'Bolshevist propaganda'. The *Daily News* remarked acidly that native Russian films would do a better 'propaganda-entertainment job'. Unfortunately, one million copies of The *Sunday Mirror* had already gone to press with a favourable notice of *The North Star* by the film critic when the editorial commandment was issued. The presses were stopped, the offending notice was removed and the editor wrote a bitter condemnation (without the advantage of having seen the film) which concluded with the defiant claim that it could not have been worse 'if Stalin had made it'.

Ironically, *The North Star* was a great success in Russia itself, presumably on account of its novelty value. The Soviet Embassy in Washington reported happily that it had gone down particularly well in Siberia, playing to capacity audiences in Novosibirsk, Tomsk and Stalinsk.

Goldwyn always regarded his films, much as he regarded his employees (especially the actors) as his children. *The North Star* was the ugly duckling of the family. In the 1950s he obstinately clung to his children in the face of the large cheques being waved by television distribution companies. *The North Star*, however, was tossed unceremoniously out of the nest.

Miraculously the ugly duckling, with no help from Danny Kaye, turned into a swan of anti-communism. In 1958 it reappeared under the title *Armored Attack*, considerably shortened from its original running time and sporting a wondrous set of new ideological feathers. All references to Russia were deleted and after Anne Baxter's final panegyric in which she prophesies the coming of a free world for all men and asserts that the earth belongs to the people, new material is added, including newsreel footage of the Hungarian uprising of 1956. The March of Time commentator reminds the audience that the Communists are carrying on in the tradition of the Nazis. The distinct impression is left that the little Russian village originally under attack by the Nazis has now become a little East European village apparently under attack by the Russians. Such technical virtuosity leaves one in no doubt why Hollywood was for so long the Mecca of film artists.

For the purposes of Hollywood, Russia in the Second World War was the land of Tchaikovsky and Cossack dances, whose people, like all others in Occupied Europe, suffered the privations of the invaded. The Communists were replaced by freedom fighters, ideological dogmatism by idealistic humanitarianism. In practice, the villagers from *The North Star* became indistinguishable from the Norwegian villagers in *The Moon is Down*, the Resistance in *The North Star* flowed in the memory into the Resistance in *Commandos Strike at Dawn*. All the pictures set in Occupied Europe dealing with the Resistance followed a fairly strict formula, sacrificing national individuality to the stereotyped needs of the hour.

In the light of the Allied decision to postpone the invasion of France until 1944 the importance of native patriotic movements increased proportionately. In every occupied country men were needed to sabotage industrial works and construct methods of aiding escaped prisoners of war and others wanted by the Nazis. The spate of Hollywood films made American audiences aware of the problems and the vital nature of such work. Sometimes producers tended to hedge their bets somewhat as in the making of *Edge of Darkness*, Warner Bros' picture about Norway's Resistance. Robert Rossen's script was an unhappy amalgam of Hollywoodiana and Ibsen, while Lewis Milestone's casting of Morris Carnovsky and Roman Bohnen mixed uneasily with the mandatory Errol Flynn and Ann Sheridan. Paul Muni's mission as the leader of a Norwegian resistance movement in *Commandos Strike at Dawn* is punctuated by an incidental and embarrassing romance, while Humphrey Bogart is motivated in his Free French flying activities in *Passage to Marseilles* by the prospect of dropping notes to his young child in Vichy.

France was certainly the one European country (apart from Great Britain, whose links with Europe are the result of pure geographical mischance) most likely to stir Americans to an emotional sympathy. The rousing strains of 'La Marseillaise' and the chant of 'Vive La France!' somehow combined with dim memories of Lafayette and French aid during the Revolutionary Wars to produce a feeling of regret that Paris was under the heel of the Nazi conqueror. Perhaps the best remembered moment of all such war films was in *Casablanca* when, in the unlikely setting of Rick's Café Americain, the 'Wacht am Rhein' is drowned by the fervent singing of 'La Marseillaise'. Victor Laszlo gives the order to the orchestra which Rick endorses. France, more than any other country, symbolised the civilisation that was temporarily lost to the forces of barbarism. However, the real France never reached the Hollywood screen. Jean Renoir's *This Land is Mine* never emerges from the suffocating cloak of Dudley Nichols' convictions and *The Cross of Lorraine*, despite the presence of Jean-Pierre Aumont, is still a vehicle for Gene Kelly to display his versatility. The latter though makes no concessions to flippancy in the story of the escaped prisoner of war who rediscovered his courage in time to inspire the town where he is hiding to retaliate against the enemy oppression. As the sun of a new dawn rises in the background the picture dissolves to the Cross of Lorraine, the symbol of Joan of Arc, flying proudly on the flagpole.

Hollywood's contribution towards unity in the Allied cause should in no way be underestimated. It made palatable the wooden and almost meaningless official declarations and frequently calmed the feelings of suspicion that inevitably existed whenever national self-interest and egotistical arrogance clashed with the demands of overall strategy. In particular, the American view of traditional imperialism jarred with Britain and France. Twenty-six nations had agreed on 1 January 1942 that the war was being waged for the principle of national self-determination as set down in the Atlantic Charter,

but Stalin rarely took his eyes off the attractive outlines of Eastern Europe and De Gaulle's ambition was to restore France to her former (imperial) glory. Roosevelt's periodic niggling of Churchill as to what he proposed to do about granting independence to British colonies after the war stung the latter into retorting sharply, 'I have not become the King's First Minister in order to preside over the liquidation of the British Empire.' The matter was postponed until the conclusion of hostilities.

Apart from this disagreement, relations between the two men remained excellent. Eisenhower turned SHAEF (Supreme Headquarters, Allied Expeditionary Force) into a truly united organisation, although the reaction of the British men to the stockpiling of American troops in their country, as they saw their women being seduced by packets of chewing gum and cigarettes, was that they were 'overpaid, oversexed and over here'. Under no such reciprocal strain the American public continued to bundle for Britain and to welcome the best British films and films made about Britain.

The cordial glow kindled by *Mrs Miniver* remained alive for some years and induced MGM to repeat their success of 1942. The producer of *Mrs Miniver* Sidney Franklin, eventually emerged late in 1943 with the thought of adapting Alice Duer Miller's poem *The White Cliffs of Dover*, to which end he again turned to Claudine West to write the script with Irene Dunne replacing Greer Garson as Metro's compulsory matronly heart-throb. The emphasis this time is on the historical ties that unite Britain and America, personified by Miss Dunne as the average American girl who came to Britain for a two week stay in 1914, married into a run of the mill aristocratic family and sacrificed her husband and then, seemingly, her son in two world wars. Franklin even attempts another *Mrs Miniver* twist as the audience is prepared to learn of the death of her husband in the trenches when the bad news turns out to be the death of her brother-in-law, a much happier event.

Despite the stalwart presence of C. Aubrey Smith and the precocious charms of the young Elizabeth Taylor, *The White Cliffs of Dover* is as glutinous a piece of schmaltz as ever went into the making of Louis Mayer's favourite chicken soup. At the end of the picture Irene Dunne talks to her son of the grand alliance. 'I see your people and my people. Only their uniforms are different. How well they march, John. Together. They'll help bring peace again. A peace that will stick.' Poor Aubrey Smith

ROSAMUND JOHN · MICHAEL REDGR
DOUGLAS MONTGOMERY · JOHN MI

WAY TO THE STAR

G.F.D. RELEASE   CERTIFICAT

31 German bombers sighted over
Denham. Asquith's budget for *Way to
the Stars* clearly didn't stretch to the
provision of four separate pairs of
binoculars.

32 Irene Dunne counts the cost of the
struggle to preserve democracy. Peter
Lawford anticipates an MGM seven-year
contract. *The White Cliffs of Dover*.

33 The war career of Alan Marshal:
(above) Leaving Irene Dunne for the
First World War in *The White Cliffs
of Dover*.

34 (below) leaving Larraine Day for
the Second World War in *Bride by
Mistake*.

is made to stand on a balcony next to Miss Dunne and her offspring watching the arrival of the American Expeditionary Force in 1917 and, as she exclaims 'They'll bring peace, they'll bring Daddy home again' (they don't), he ceremoniously presents his prized chessboard, affirming it a small return for the benefits the Americans are about to bestow on the British. For a man who was once captain of Sussex and a brilliant forcing right hand batsman in the style of Archie MacLaren the humiliation was complete.

He was much better served by his appearance in *Forever and a Day*, a remarkable picture about the emotional life of a London house. The film was the product of the combined labours of virtually the whole of the British colony extant in Hollywood in 1943. Cedric Hardwicke was the organising brain behind the effort which persuaded RKO to provide the facilities for the making and distribution of the picture. Neither the directors nor the cast which included such redoubtable names as Gladys Cooper, Herbert Marshall, Anna Neagle, Dame May Whitty, Donald Crisp and Charles Laughton charged fees for their services. Hardwicke, in his function as producer, sensibly kept for himself the best part in the film as the plumber who installs the first iron bath in the house although Buster Keaton as his mate makes a surprising but welcome appearance. Over it all hangs the presence of Aubrey Smith, his craggy features framed over the mantelpiece seeming to adopt a particularly frosty glare when he spies some of the more immoral or unpatriotic scenes played out in front of him. Even the Blitz fails to remove him and the reassurance of his presence persuades his young female descendant and her American admirer to promise to rebuild the house after the war. 'A house is more than just bricks and mortar,' she tells him. He nods understandingly. 'After all', he declares looking at Sir Aubrey, 'It's what *he* would have wanted.'

To facilitate a better understanding of the British reality, George Archibald, the director of the Films Division of the British Information Service, was sent to America in 1943 to supply factual information about Britain and her people in wartime. Fortunately, his mission seems to have been largely a waste of time, although he did leave a certain Miss Russell ensconced in an office in Hollywood.[5] It seems unlikely that the lady had a profound effect on the production plans of the major studios.

Hollywood rarely looked beyond the stereotype when portraying foreigners whether they were allies or enemies. The Germans were depicted as swine whether of the cultured variety (like Conrad Veidt and Erich von Stroheim) or the barbaric (everyone else). It was a coincidence that the average Nazi who was painted with such bold black stripes in propaganda films happened to be every bit as unpleasant as the imagination of the average Hollywood scriptwriter had envisaged him. It was hardly surprising then that the films which centred on the behaviour of the Nazis should have emphasised their sickening brutality and sensual enjoyment of human pain, misery and degradation.

Chief among the most successful demonstrations of this art was *Hitler's Children*, an independent production which became notorious for the profit it returned its enterprising investors. Edward Golden paid out $10,000 for the film rights to Gregor Ziemer's book *Education for Death* and obtained $75,000 from a bank for financing the production. Unfortunately the bank's board of directors disapproved of their manager's enthusiastic plunge into show business and withdrew what had not yet been spent of their money. Golden then went to RKO who reluctantly agreed to provide the missing bridging finance for the picture whose total negative cost was $172,000. RKO had no great faith in the drawing power of their unplanned offspring and deliberately refrained from advertising it too heavily. Without warning, the word of mouth spread so quickly that within months the film had grossed $5 million.

The film itself was fairly undistinguished, being simply a superficial ramble over the familiar territory of Nazi methods of enslavement. There was nothing very exceptional either in the casting of Bonita Granville as the attractive American girl who had been born in Germany and was hence, albeit protestingly, subject to German authority. The master stroke was probably the advertising still showing Miss Granville in a state of undress being publicly flogged by the Nazi officials for her refusal to submit to their licentious suggestions.

Unwittingly perhaps, Golden and the director, Edward Dmytryk, had stumbled on a staggeringly successful formula for profitable picture-making. The juxtaposition of explicitly sadistic scenes (at least by 1943 standards) and a high moral indignation satisfied both the latent (and not so latent) sado-masochistic inclinations of the audience and the obligatory outrage of the censors. As the film garnered its increasing financial and critical success, the advertising campaign in the most respectable of press outlets unashamedly pressed home its advantages. Apart from the ubiquitous picture of Bonita Granville's flogging, lurid accounts of forcible sterilisation and Nazi methods of potty training for prospective Hitler Jugend members began to seep into the American consciousness.

Inevitably *Hitler's Children* begat Hitler's grandchildren. Monogram's advertising campaign for *I Escaped from the Gestapo* starring Dean Jagger and John Carradine screamed,

> 'He felt the Lash of Nazi Terror! When they torture you for hours and then sneer that your mother is held hostage . . . you think you'll go mad!'

Unfortunately, the effect of such purple copy was somewhat dissipated by the tag line which proclaimed *I Escaped from the Gestapo* to be 'Monogram's follow-up hit to *Silver Skates*'.

John Carradine found the war years to be a busy time. His distinctive brand of cold-eyed, supercilious villainy was much in demand, although even he could do little with Douglas Sirk's nonsensical tribute to the martyrs of Lidice, in which he was required to impersonate the Nazi 'Hangman' Heydrich. *Hitler's Madman* seems to have been written, shot and edited by lesser MGM employees who, for some kind of wager, did the whole thing from start to finish wearing blindfolds. Only something quite extraordinary could account for the plethora of elementary errors.

The opening minutes are portents of doom as we pass in quick succession a signpost which shows 1 km to Lidice and 18 km to Prague and then one which suggests 1 km to Lidice and 30 km to Prague. There is no suggestion that this is either a clever trick to fool the Boche or that the Czech civil service is in desperate need of an overhaul. A rousing dramatic scene follows whose effectiveness is curtailed by the riveting appearance and disappearance of the studio microphone.

Finally, Heydrich lies on his deathbed talking with Himmler who symbolically turns out the Hangman's bedside light. Again, the worthiness of Sirk's aim in this confrontation is undercut by the inescapable conclusion that he has confused Himmler with Goering. So the evil, menacing figure of the head of the Gestapo is in fact played by a fat, jolly actor who might have wandered in from Dingley

Dell (where his costume may have occasioned some comment). *Hangmen Also Die*, although it never married the talents of Bertolt Brecht and Fritz Lang entirely successfully, was a considerable improvement on the telling of this tale.

Ironically, the images of *Hitler's Madman* have a greater potency than those of *Hangmen Also Die* precisely because of their memorable idiocy. Similarly, *Above Suspicion*, although well constructed as a thriller in its own right is immeasurably strengthened by the wildly inappropriate casting of Joan Crawford and Fred MacMurray as an Oxford don and his excitable bride. Taken on a tour of medieval torture instruments Crawford dubs the fingernail remover 'a totalitarian manicure' and Conrad Veidt tells them that the terrifying 'Iron Maiden' is know as 'the German Statue of Liberty'. Again, what one recalls is not so much the brilliantly orchestrated murder during a concert performance of the Liszt E minor piano concerto (the shot drowned by a drumbeat in a recognisable tribute to *The Man Who Knew Too Much*) but the daft conversations between MacMurray and Basil Rathbone, who apparently knew each other at Oxford.

After the murder, Rathbone invites MacMurray, Crawford and another Englishman called Thornlea back to his castle for what one anticipates is going to be either coffee and doughnuts or tea and crumpets. The strained conversation between the three Oxford men ('Trinity actually, sir', clarifies Thornlea) is wonderfully concluded by Joan Crawford who sits smartly at the piano and announcing, 'You remember this, Count. You went to Oxford', launches into a spirited rendition of the Eton boating song.

Above Suspicion has only an incidental connection with the war in that its principal story could have been told equally well had the enemy been one of John Buchan's 'certain foreign powers' instead of the Gestapo. The same argument may be applied strictly to *Casablanca*, although those who revere it, those who misquote it, those who laugh uproariously in the cinema at its every 'joke' and ruin everyone else's enjoyment, would probably disagree violently. Nevertheless, the fact remains that *Casablanca* is largely a conventional romance tinged with the overtones of war. The end is like many another romantic film (*Another Dawn*, *Cynara*) and the deft way in which Woody Allen works around it in *Play It Again Sam* proves conclusively that it has little to do with the war.

Der Führer's faces

35 (above) After a particularly deadly blast of special effects.

36 (below) 'And I say we're here!' The German General Staff looks unconvinced by Richard Basehart's portrayal. Although made in 1961, *Hitler* captured perfectly the attitudes and ethos of its 1940s counterparts.

37 The cast of *Casablanca* about to be presented with more script changes.

38 It all proves too much for Conrad Veidt.

Whether or not Paul Henried will get to America to continue his great work as the leader of the Resistance is totally subservient to the romance between Bogart and Ingrid Bergman. Once the propellers start to turn on the Lisbon plane it really doesn't matter as one is simply carried along on the emotional tide.

Warner Bros originally saw *Casablanca* as a sequel to their successful *Kings Row* and announced Ronald Reagan and Ann Sheridan as the two stars. The story was loosely based on a stage play called *Everybody Comes to Rick's*, written by Murray Burnett and Jean Allison, which closed before it reached Broadway. The script was so long in preparation that Reagan and Sheridan moved on to finer things (in this case *Juke Girl*, a saga of the problems of migrant fruit workers in Florida). The Epstein brothers, who had little enthusiasm for the project, wriggled out of it with the calm assurance of seasoned Hollywood writers. Howard Koch, on whom the task devolved, managed to finish 65 pages by the first day of shooting, after which the gap between the production's requirements and the completed shooting script narrowed rapidly. It is likely that Koch's concentration was not aided by the memo from Jack Warner which observed that the cost to the company if the gap disappeared entirely was $30,000 a day.

Despite all the attendant complications, *Casablanca* remains a remarkable achievement, an enduring testament to the creative resourcefulness of the system which also produced *Brother Rat and a Baby* and *Shipmates Forever*. Over it all hangs the promise of America, the ultimate refuge for the persecuted and the homeless. When Bogart lets the unwitting Bulgarian win enough at the roulette wheel to pay for their exit visas, his wife exclaims, 'He is an American, Jan. You see, America must be a wonderful place.'

America is the sleeping giant, who, once stirred, will surely crush the impudent enemy. Conrad Veidt scorns Bogart as 'just another blundering American' but Claude Rains reminds him wryly, 'We mustn't underestimate American blundering. I was with them when they blundered into Berlin in 1918!' Koch even manages a dig at the isolationists when Bogart muses, 'If it's December 1941 in Casablanca, what time is it in New York? I bet they're asleep in New York. I bet they're asleep all over America.'

Enough hints are dropped to suggest that Bogart has a history of anti-Fascism, but the picture is left deliberately murky. Claude Rains recalls that he ran guns to Ethiopia in 1935 and fought for the Loyalists in Spain. Yet Bogart himself retorts that he was well paid for doing so and in any case he is not prepared to stick his neck out for anybody — 'a wise foreign policy' concedes the Vichy Prefect of Police.

Inevitably, since one remembers principally the tartness of Bogart's dialogue, his commitment to the Allied cause is bound up with his relationship with Ingrid Bergman rather than a separate issue in its own right. Conrad Veidt reads out the list of his anti-Fascist activities but Bogart simply takes hold of the book and wonders aloud, 'Are my eyes really brown?' When the Germans marched into Paris Bogart remembers only certain features of the day he had spent with Bergman. 'The Germans wore grey. You wore blue', he says shortly. The nearest he comes to a positive statement is in his urgent persuasion of Bergman to get on the plane with her husband. (Would the Hays Office have allowed her to stay with the man who was not her husband?)

> 'Ilsa, I'm no good at being noble. But it doesn't take much to see that the problems of three little people don't amount to a hill of beans in this crazy world.'

Yet there is more of the eternal triangle than the Tripartite Agreement about this scene.

Casablanca was so successful that Warners remade it in various disguises at least five more times before the end of the war. It was a most felicitous mating of the talents of Koch, Curtiz, the cameraman, Arthur Edeson and the assortment of *émigrés* and draft rejects who made up the cast. The ultimate seal of approval was granted to the picture by Franklin Roosevelt who, at the moment of the film's release, met with Churchill in Casablanca to discuss future war plans. Jack Warner abandoned plans to get one of his press agents on to the Joint Chiefs of Staff.

The abundance of war-related films began to take its toll in 1943 leading to a desire for more escapist entertainment, particularly musicals. It occurred to certain clever motion picture executives that if both war films and musicals were popular, then a musical war film would be sensational. To a certain extent they were right. Irving Berlin's *This is the Army* was a huge success, 'the kind of entertainment', wrote the *New York Times*, 'as American as hot dogs or the Bill of Rights. It is in its way a warmly reassuring document on the state of the Nation.'

Warner Bros struck again when they produced *Yankee Doodle Dandy*, a hagiographical account of the life of George M. Cohan. The film waves the flag so fiercely that on occasions the audience is less likely to be captivated than concussed. Cohan, born on the Fourth of July, clearly sprang from the womb dressed in red, white and blue nappies. His aggressive personality and remarkable versatility were frequently mistaken for talent even when he insisted on writing the same song over and over again and passing it off as new. Cagney delivers it with precisely the required zest and conviction and even manages to elevate the line 'When we get too sophisticated and high hat for flag waving some nation thinks we're a push-over' into an unobjectionable statement.

However, his final deathly conversation with Franklin Roosevelt on the occasion of his award of the Congressional Medal of Honor defeats even Cagney's manifold talents. 'A man may give his life to his country in many different ways,' declares the President. ' "Over There" is as powerful as a cannon. We need more songs to express America.' 'Where else', wonders Cagney in awe, 'could a simple guy like me come in and talk things over with the top man?' 'Well, that's about as good a definition of America as I ever heard', intones the President and the conversation seems destined to end up in one of those Marx Brothers cul-de-sacs of non-sequiturs of 'Well I haven't said anything worth hearing' and 'Well that's why I haven't heard anything' to the total impasse of 'Well that's why I haven't said anything.'

Occasionally the desire of the musical film to expose its topicality led it into the realms of the absurd as this review of *When Johnny Comes Marching Home Again* makes clear.

The presence of a heroic marine [Allan Jones] gives [it] a topical flavor . . . but the presence of Phil Spitalny's all-girl orchestra plus that of Gloria Jean . . . more than offset any military tone that a single marine, especially a singing one, might provide.[6]

Star Spangled Rhythm, ostensibly about the shore leave of a group of sailors in Hollywood is only an excuse for a series of flag-waving and eyebrow raising numbers. The latter is represented by the appearance of Paulette Goddard, Dorothy Lamour and Veronica Lake in a song entitled 'A Sweater, A Sarong and A Peek-a-boo Bang'.

In due course the entire resources of Hollywood were drafted into the war effort. Basil Rathbone returned as the lead in *Sherlock Holmes and the Secret Weapon*, chasing Nazi villains in contemporary London, discovering, to nobody's great surprise, that the head of the Nazi spy ring was Professor Moriarty. The Nazis turned up in the most unlikely places. They tried hard to get their hands on the treasures of Maria Montez's temple in *White Savage* and in *Northern Pursuit* even attacked Errol Flynn in a coonskin in the wilds of Canada. Their greatest achievement was undoubtedly their appearance in the 1943 version of *The Desert Song*, where they were constructing a North African railway in the Moroccan desert. Fortunately they were not aware that Dennis Morgan, who was to be found most evenings playing the piano in a night club, was also the redoubtable Red Shadow who, with Irene Manning, was principally responsible for the destruction of their evil plans.

It should not, however, be presumed that Hollywood's reaction to the war was entirely superficial. One of the real benefits to the industry in the long run was that so many of its personnel and so many of its basic audience were suddenly confronted with political problems of a complexity never previously encountered. This gave new opportunities to men like Dore Schary who really felt he had something to say. After the success of *John Smith, American* he set to work with Sinclair Lewis on a complicated political allegory in the form of a Western. *Storm in the West* tried to use the conventions of the Western to explain world events since 1938. The death of Chuck Slattery (Czechoslovakia) at the hands of outlaws Hygatt, Gribble, Gerrel and Mullison (Hitler, Goebbels, Goering and Mussolini) sparks off more fighting. Eventually, Joel Slavin (Stalin), a Civil War veteran from Georgia (sic) who has taken over the 'old Nicholas place' (the Winter Palace?) joins Ulysses Saunders (the United States) and Walter Chancel (Winston Churchill, Walter Cronkite?) in a successful alliance to capture the outlaws. MGM rejected the idea as 'too political'.[7] It seems a shame even though a glance at the script would appear to indicate tht the film could only have been understood if seen in conjunction with the reading of at least two comprehensive works of historical reference.

39 'Warner Bros this way.' James Cagney as George M. Cohan — the USA personified. *Yankee Doodle Dandy*.

40 Washington, Jefferson, Roosevelt and Lincoln betray no emotion as they watch Bing Crosby make off with their legacy. *Star Spangled Rhythm*.

41 'Don't turn round Heinrich but there's a man with a bald head staring at the back of my neck.' Suspicion and paranoia run riot in the upper reaches of the Nazi party. *Hitler*.

42 Humphrey Bogart thinking hard about the attractions of the Merchant Marine. *Action in the North Atlantic*.

43 Incest at Twentieth Century-Fox. William Bendix in *Guadalcanal Diary*. Special guest star — Betty Grable.

Nevertheless MGM went ahead with Cukor's *Keeper of the Flame* which, despite its superficial similarity to *Citizen Kane* renounced Welles's flamboyance in favour of a serious examination of the roots of a possible American fascist movement. Unfortunately the solemnity of their mission induced in Cukor, Tracy, Hepburn and the scriptwriter, Donald Ogden Stewart, a ponderous style that conveyed little more than a worthy dullness.

Hitchcock explored further the nature of the enemy in *Lifeboat*, but he fell foul of the critics who saw in Walter Slezak's portrait of the sole Nazi member of the boat a more eloquent advocate of his political system than the inept, quarrelsome products of democracy were of theirs. Lillian Hellman's play *Watch on the Rhine* did not transfer as well to film as *Tomorrow the World* in which a Nazi boy of twelve creates havoc when brought to live in an American household. Nevertheless, the fact that they were made in 1943 is an indication of the slow maturing of the film audience. *Variety* defined just how far audiences and film-makers had progressed together.

> No longer . . . is it necessary to cloak the more serious thoughts and aspects behind a melodramatic yarn or sugarcoat the messages to the public. . . . Such terms as 'Fascists' and 'appeasers' can be used without offence.[8]

Much of the credit for this new state of affairs lay with the documentaries to which audiences were being constantly introduced. To Frank Capra, as to most self-respecting Hollywood artists, 'documentaries were ash-can films made by kooks with long hair'. His own brilliant series of orientation films called *Why We Fight* were all indelibly stamped with the unmistakable Capra touch even though he gave directorial credit to Anatole Litvak and others. The first in the series, *Prelude to War*, was so favourably received by both the Army High Command and the White House that pressure was exerted on film distributors and exhibitors to release the film in commercial theatres. Cinema owners and the War Activities Committee of Hollywood resented the creation of a dangerous precedent but in the event *Prelude to War* was not a great success on commercial release and the rest of the series was shown as originally intended only to personnel in training.

In retrospect the series looks something less than startling. *The Negro Soldier* is particularly embarrassing in the wake of subsequent Civil Rights activities and *The Battle of China* diplomatically omits any mention of the Communists. There are also reconstructed scenes of enemy schoolchildren singing hymns to their respective dictators. The important points to remember about *Why We Fight* are that there had previously existed no native documentary tradition and that Capra was to a great extent hampered by the automatic restraints imposed on any political commentator in wartime.

Capra and Darryl Zanuck in particular provoked severe personal criticism both from the Press and certain politicians because of what was felt to be their privileged entry into the armed forces. It appears likely however, that 'the Hollywood Colonels' would have met with similar hostility whatever their performance while in uniform. The mid-term Congressional elections of 1942 had given increasing power to those sections who had not forgotten either the 'scandal' of *Mr Smith Goes to Washington* or Zanuck's role in the Senate investigation of Hollywood's anti-Nazi films.

Zanuck flung himself into his work as a colonel in the Signal Corps with his customary zeal, although his film of the North African campaign *At the Front* was noticeable principally for the multitude of shots of Colonel Zanuck armed with a tommy gun and smoking the inevitable cigar. Owing to political pressure, Zanuck was eventually removed from active duty and instructed to sit twiddling his thumbs in Washington until he got bored and returned to Twentieth Century-Fox. The Hollywood press muttered darkly of sinister Washington threats to frame innocent movie moguls and use them as pawns in a political power game.

The best of the single wartime documentaries, such as Wyler's *Memphis Belle* or Huston's *Report from the Aleutians*, although superb films in their own right, had considerably less immediate effect on the film-going public than their fictional feature-length brethren. Nobody questioned whether they were realistic. Many people questioned whether they should pay 35 cents to look at them when the same outlay would bring a long stare at Betty Grable's legs. There is no comparison between Wyler's *Memphis Belle* and Victor Fleming's *A Guy Named Joe* as films, but in terms of shaping the attitude of the public during the war, the latter was much more important. Its purpose was to emphasise the need for self discipline. To this end Tracy, as a daredevil pilot is killed off early on so he can go to the USAF version of heaven, which is ruled over by Lionel Barrymore who is carrying so many medals on his chest it is a miracle he doesn't fall over every time he stands up.

Each of the services in turn was given its very own Hollywood blessing. *Ladies Courageous* proudly announced that it had been sanctioned as 'the official motion picture story of the Women's Auxiliary Flying Squadron — now known as the WASPS', after which it launched into a silly tale of a lady pilot who takes up a P40 and commits suicide because her husband has been flirting with Diana Barrymore. *Action in the North Atlantic* did its bit for the Merchant Marine, although its scriptwriter, John Howard Lawson, made sure that it included due acknowledgment of the sacrifices of the Russians for whom the cargo was destined.

The war against the Japanese was fought more slowly than the war in Europe in that the fighting was restricted to less territory. The battle of Guadalcanal lasted from August 1942 until February 1943 and saw some of the bloodiest and most futile action of the war. *Guadalcanal Diary*, although like *Wake Island* much praised on its release as a forthright realistic account of the battle, was only more of the same Hollywood version. The film opens with the marines on board ship 'somewhere in the Pacific' singing 'Rock of Ages'. Sammy Kline is bellowing as lustily as anyone, justifying himself with, 'Why not? My father was a cantor in the synagogue' which sounds like nothing so much as the classic First World War announcement that the Chief Rabbi had sanctioned for Jewish soldiers the eating of pork in the trenches.

The Marines are just plain folks, like William Bendix, boasting of their girls and writing to their mothers, waiting desperately for the mail truck and confessing during a particularly heavy Japanese bombardment, 'I aint no hero. I'm just a guy. I'm here 'cause someone sent me and I just wanna get it over with and go home as soon as I can.' The sincerity of these sentiments is considerably devalued by the repeated use of the same shot of Richard Conte running and firing a machine gun with devastating results. It was as if the government were economising on enemies as well as munitions.

As Americans approached their third wartime Christmas, the anger and concern of the early months had given way to a grumbling irritation that things were not moving faster on the military front. The Japanese had passed the zenith of their conquests and the Nazis were being pushed back along the whole of the Russian front. The initial success of the North African campaign and the invasion of Sicily in the summer of 1943 had led to the fall of Mussolini and the expected surrender of the new Italian government, headed by Marshall Badoglio.

Unfortunately, first class German troops had poured into Italy and were waiting for the Allies when they tried to disembark at Salerno. Instead of the triumphant progress up the spine of Italy they had imagined, Mark Clark's Fifth Army were confined by incessant and accurate enemy tank and artillery fire to a beachhead not more than five miles deep. Their discomfiture was in no way eased by the presence of a German loudspeaker through which every night a guttural voice bellowed, 'OK, you guys, come and give yourselves up. We got you covered.'[9]

The soft underbelly of Europe had turned into Gunfight at the OK Corral with the added incidence of trenchfoot and frostbite. As the winter of 1943 gave way to the spring of 1944 unconditional surrender looked as far away as ever.

Since They Went Away

(June 1944 — August 1945)

An American will fight for only three things —
for a woman, for himself and for a better
world.

Ben Hecht
Foreword to *China Girl*

In the wake of *The Longest Day* and all other
dramatised accounts of D Day, it would appear that
the success of the Allied invasion of Normandy was
a foregone conclusion once the weather in the
Channel had calmed sufficiently to make the
landings practicable. In reality the fate of the expedition was, unbeknownst to them, in German hands.
The massing of American troops in England had left
no one in any doubt as to the imminence of the
invasion. The only real questions to be answered
concerned the precise timing of the operation and
the location of its primary thrust. Hitler, wrongly
advised, thought the blow would land in the vicinity
of Calais and the beaches of Normandy were relatively thinly protected by German armour. Had
Hitler gambled successfully, as he had done so
many times before in the teeth of strong 'advice',
there is no doubt that the Allies would have failed
to establish their beachheads and that the price of
such failure would have been the loss of thousands
of lives. Eisenhower, in fact, had already prepared
his press release in the event of disaster.

Uncertainty, fear and hope mingled in equal
proportions that June day in 1944. In London
emotions were kept under tight control, so tight
indeed that Ed Murrow broadcast of his intense
desire to shout at people, 'Don't you realise history
is being made today?' In America, perhaps because
the population was not yet inured to such momentous events, the surface reaction was everywhere
visible. The President abandoned his traditional fireside chat in favour of a long heart-felt prayer, and
the radio networks responded by cancelling all
commercials for the day. In New York City, the
department store Lord and Taylors stopped trading
and displayed the following notice on its front
door.

> The Invasion has begun. Our only thought can be
> of the men who are fighting in it. We have closed
> our doors because we know our employees and
> customers who have loved ones in battle will
> want to give this day to hopes and prayers for
> their safety.[1]

In the event three of the four major beachheads
were captured with relative ease, but the fourth,
code-named Omaha, was taken only with the loss of
7,300 American troops. Once the bases were secure,
the last months of 1944 seemed to be nothing but
a succession of Allied victories as Patton, Montgomery and Bradley swept southwards and eastwards. In August, Paris was liberated and the way
seemed clear to the Rhine but the Nazis regrouped
for a counter-attack in the Ardennes at the turn of
the year and, like the Italian campaign fifteen
months before, the triumphant procession turned
into a grim and costly yard by yard stagger.

In the light of historical precedents, the conduct
of Americans during the Second World War was
noticeably restrained. In previous conflicts they had
filled the streets with flags, staged wild recruiting
rallies, cheered departing soldiers madly and sung
'Over There' and 'Rally Round The Flag'. Americans
in 1861, 1898 and 1917 had believed they would
all be back for Christmas if not for Thanksgiving.
In 1941 nobody was prepared to make any sober
estimate of when the war would end. Once the
anger of Pearl Harbor had worn off, any lingering hopes of an early victory were rudely dispelled
by the Axis successes in 1942. The emotional radio
reports from Occupied Europe and Britain during
the Blitz had prepared the population for the
horrors to come. In addition, the same generation
that fought the Second World War entertained very
real memories of the sickening losses of the Great
War and the disastrous diplomatic aftermath.

The new conflict offered a second chance to remake the world but the approach this time was not one of Wilsonian idealism but of stern practicality. The United Nations as an idea marched at the forefront of the Allied battle column but for the soldiers the only war aims they were prepared to acknowledge were such noble aspirations as the full tank of petrol and the resumption of the World Series. In truth, the vision of a post-war America with every husband behind the wheel of his chromium-plated automobile and every wife enthroned in a gleaming kitchen full of miracle-working gadgets seemed the greatest incentive for the winning of the war. It was certainly a good deal more accessible as a concept than the Four Freedoms.

Even the popular image of the soldier underwent a change in the Second World War. No longer was he a latter day Davy Crockett, a proud, disciplined, resourceful, dignified hero. More likely he was just a kid, frightened by the unknown and desperately homesick. The most famous advertisement of the war was called 'The Kid In Upper Four' and was a plea for civilians to make room on trains for the travelling soldier. The young soldier, lying awake in a Pullman berth, was described as remembering 'the taste of hamburger and pop . . . the feel of driving a roadster . . . a dog named Shucks or Spot or Barnacle Bill. . . . There's a lump in his throat and maybe a tear fills his eye. It doesn't matter, kid. Nobody will see . . . it's too dark.'

The other version of the solder was the battle-hardened, weary, disillusioned veteran whose only concern was to stay alive without deserting his post. As the war progressed the heroic film treatment of the fighting man yielded progressively to this approach finding its logical conclusion in William Wellman's *The Story of GI Joe*, made in the spring of 1945 but not released until after the war in Europe was officially over. The film was based on the widely syndicated articles of the war correspondent Ernie Pyle who won the Pulitzer Prize for his sympathetic and realistic accounts of the war from the viewpoint of the ordinary infantryman.

Pyle needed considerable persuasion from the independent producer Lester Cowan before he would consent to a film being made from his book *Here Is Your War* which he published after lengthy experience of the North African and Italian campaigns. Pyle's written instructions to Cowan included the specific command that the actor who impersonated him 'must weigh in the neighbourhood of

112 lbs and look anaemic. He must not be glamorized nor have any love interest.'[2] In Burgess Meredith the producer and the journalist found the perfect compromise.

The unglamorous, naturalistic treatment dominated the whole film, despite the fact that it was shot on location in Arizona and California army camps and on the back lot of the RKO Pathe studios in Culver City. Indeed, one of the best staged sequences, the grimly realistic sniping in the ruined church of San Vittorio utilised the old sets from Cecil De Mille's 1928 production of *The Godless Girl*.

The fighting in the church, as the larger engagements elsewhere in the picture, is conducted against an unseen enemy. At the very end of the picture Robert Mitchum is killed in action even though the battle itself is never glimpsed. His body is brought back to his command ignominiously strapped over the back of a donkey, an inglorious finale, presaging the death of Olivier's Richard III whose hero is borne similarly from the battlefield.

All the men talk in the same tired, slow fashion. There are no false heroics and no noble speeches. Neither Pyle, nor by implication the audience, is allowed to respond to any solider with any overt feelings of emotion. One of them asks the journalist to get him a job when the war is over. 'Yeh', says Pyle sardonically and makes no further comment, both of them knowing that that particular Pandora's Box should scarcely be mentioned let alone approached at this stage. The purest expression of emotion, in marked contrast to the self conscious speech delivered in similar circumstances in *Guadalcanal Diary* (and quoted above) is that of a footsore infantryman. 'It sounds kinda silly, but when I'm resting like this I get a kick out of just being alive.'

British audiences found *The Story of GI Joe* to be particularly objectionable in view of its singular omission of any mention of the British participation in the North African and Italian campaigns. General Clark had touched this raw nerve already when he marched into Rome in June 1944 and declaimed, 'This is a great day for the Fifth Army' to the extreme anger of the Eighth Army who had been at El Alamein when General Clark was still eating frankfurters in an army canteen four thousand miles away. This blow to British pride was redoubled when Warner Bros released *Objective Burma* in 1945 and showed to the world how Errol Flynn and his American colleagues were winning the war in the Far East. It was withdrawn from

44 *The Godless Girl* meets the Second World War. *The Story of GI Joe.*

45 Robert Mitchum demands better food for his men. Burgess Meredith gathers the information sardonically. *The Story of GI Joe.*

46 Richard Loo gives Dana Andrews a Japanese geography lesson. *The Purple Heart.*

ROBERT MITCHUM
Burgess Meredith
in
WAR
CORRESPONDENT

exhibition in British cinemas after official protests had been lodged.

The Pacific War had always been the poor relation of the global battlefields. Roosevelt, in the face of public opposition, had agreed as long ago as December 1941 that the primary objective was the destruction of Germany and that the Japanese attacks must simply be contained until the war in Europe had been won.

Although the gruelling slog of the war in the Pacific was largely unsensational, one raid provoked an enormous response at home. On 18 April 1942, in the darkest days of the defeats inflicted by the Japanese, a group of B25 bombers took off from an aircraft carrier and dropped bombs on Tokyo. The damage they caused was slight but the boost to American morale was considerable and the hopeless heroism of the act inspired the production of two excellent films, *Thirty Seconds Over Tokyo* and *The Purple Heart*. The former concentrated on the actual planning and execution of the raid, with the pilots kept ignorant of their mission until just before take-off. After the raid Van Johnson, the chief protagonist, is shot down over mainland China where he is rescued by the natives. The amputation of his leg is performed without the benefit of anaesthetic but he does not allow this to depress him unduly and manages to accept the present of a pair of slippers with good grace. In due course he is reunited with his wife (who has the thinnest pregnancy in medical history) although he falls over before he can get to her and the ending is pleasantly tearful in the best MGM tradition.

The Purple Heart on the other hand made no such concessions. Although conceived in 1943 its release was delayed until the following year because it was not until 1944 that the War Department was prepared to concede officially that the Japanese had indeed been torturing American prisoners of war. Darryl Zanuck who wrote and produced the picture was quite prepared to wait until the end of the war to release his picture so strongly did he feel about it.

Although Zanuck based his script on no hard factual evidence (none of course existed) and constructed it along traditional Hollywood melodramatic lines, it did offer Lewis Milestone a sound platform on which the director built a formidable motion picture. *The Purple Heart* supposes that the eight American flyers shot down in the Doolittle Raid were put on trial for their lives although the conventions of war state clearly that captured enemies must be accorded the privileges consistent with their status as prisoners of war. The Japanese contend that the men were trying to bomb civilian rather than military targets (even though they later try to bribe the Americans with offers of prisoner of war status in return for the information they seek). The chief officers of the Japanese armed forces need to know desperately where the planes that bombed Tokyo came from. The Americans will volunteer only their own ranks, names and serial numbers, leaving the Japanese no option but to torture the information out of the crews.

The Purple Heart was intended to strengthen public hatred of the Japanese at a time when it appeared as if the war in Europe was stealing all the headlines. Apart from their subversion of the processes of justice the Japanese are also to be found behaving in the most unseemly manner when anything untoward happens — in marked contrast to the long held Western belief in Oriental inscrutability. As Donald Barry leaps from the dock to attack an armed guard, the Clerk of the Court (who, in British films, only just manages to prop himself on his feet long enough to toss Exhibit A on the Judge's desk before sinking back exhausted) performs a wild dance of fury, brandishing his fists and screeching unintelligibly. When news of the fall of Corregidor arrives, the entire court is covered with officers performing their fanatical samurai dances with all the attendant yells and screeches.

The final scene shows the men, still refusing to reveal the vital information, marching or in some cases limping proudly to their deaths. Some films have been known to manipulate this kind of ending in order to arouse a spurious sentimentality. *The Purple Heart* makes an honest and sincere use of sentiment.

The Allied problems in the Pacific war were appreciably exacerbated by the fact that the two key military figures on the Allied side were suffering from acute megalomania. Chiang Kai-shek was only interested in using American munitions to fire at Mao Tse-tung and his Communist renegades whom Chiang clearly thought a bigger personal danger than the Japanese army of occupation. General MacArthur on the other hand had passed through megalomania and was heading for self-ordained divinity. He returned to the Philippines as it had been foretold in the holy scriptures, on 22 October 1944 but the Japanese with their own personification of divinity biting his finger nails back in Tokyo refused to accept the dogma laid down for them. They lost the naval engagement of Leyte Gulf but fought doggedly on the islands until well into July 1945.

The death toll rose alarmingly in the last months of the war. The attempt of the marines to take Iwo Jima in February 1945 provoked the bloodiest battle in marine history but in April the casualties on Okinawa surpassed even this; the Japanese lost 110,000 men and the Allies 50,000. These figures suggested appalling losses when the invasion of mainland China and the Japanese islands themselves began. Even the aid of Russia who entered the war against Japan after the Potsdam Conference only promised to substitute thousands of dead Russians for thousands of dead Americans and British. Something else was needed quickly.

The decision to drop an atomic bomb on Japan caused the new President, Harry Truman, remarkably little heart-searching. The Japanese called what they thought was a bluff and at 8.15 a.m. on 6 August 1945 a B 29 dropped the bomb on Hiroshima which killed over 70,000 people. Three days later the Russians scrambled into the war, hours before the second bomb fell on Nagasaki killing 35,000. On 2 September 1945 General MacArthur received the surrender of the Japanese Emperor aboard the USS *Missouri* with appropriate solemnity. What he didn't know at the time was that kamikaze pilots were taxiing into position on a nearby airfield ready to kill themselves and all on board the ship. It was only with some difficulty that they were restrained and Japan was spared a most terrible divine retribution.

The dropping of the bomb changed the complexion of the world let alone the war. Few people doubted its terrifying power although few people understood the principle of nuclear fission on which it was based. To most of the world it was simply a bigger and better stick of dynamite. This undoubtedly shaped the thinking of the farmer in Newport Arkansas who wrote to the non-existent 'Atomic Bomb Co.' at Oak Ridge.

> I have some stumps in my field I should like to
> blow out. Have you any atomic bombs the right
> size for the job? If you have let me know by
> return mail and let me know how much they cost.[3]

Although the conclusion of hostilities needed the intervention of the most lethal weapon ever conceived, the course of the war, certainly after D Day,

seemed inevitably headed for an Allied victory. Accordingly, the politicians of all the countries involved during the final year of the conflict had to decide once and for all what they had been fighting for and to determine the shape of the post war world.

Henry Morgenthau, US Secretary of the Treasury, devised a plan which would have meant the pastoralization of Germany, while Stalin demanded reparation payments of $20 billion from the defeated nation. Both of these ideas were abandoned in the face of reality and the mutually acceptable notion that the country be divided into four zones of occupation.

The dramatic reversal of fortune on the Eastern Front in 1943 saw the Red Army steamroller its way towards Berlin in 1944. As the Russians liberated more and more of Eastern Europe it was apparent to Churchill that since they were unlikely to want to relinquish it willingly at the end of the war, it might be as well if Allied troops shook hands with their Russian comrades as far East as possible. Roosevelt, fortified by a solid victory over Thomas E. Dewey in the 1944 Presidential Election, assured Churchill that he could handle Stalin. Roosevelt placed great reliance on his ability to charm the Russian leader even though Stalin's command of the English language was largely restricted to 'What the hell goes on here?' and 'Where's the toilet?'[4]

The presence of Soviet arms in Eastern Europe gave Stalin an unparalleled diplomatic weapon. The Russian aim had long been to establish a series of 'satellite' states on her eastern borders which would give her effective power in these regions and almost complete military security. Accordingly, when the Red Army was within ten miles of the gates of Warsaw in August 1944 it pointedly refrained from helping the uprising of the Polish underground resistance and calmly sat on its hands while the partisans were annihilated. Russian policy was best served by the installation of a government chosen by Moscow not by the resistance movement or the Polish government in exile in London. Roosevelt and Churchill insisted that the Polish government hold free elections to determine the future leaders of the country and although Stalin agreed, it became clear very rapidly that his definition of 'free' elections was not the same as the others'.

The final conference of the Big Three took place at Yalta in February 1945 when plans were laid for Russian co-operation in the war against the Japanese,

47 Three faces of Oriental inscrutability
Philip Ahn and friend

48 Keye Luke and friend

49 Anthony Quinn and friend (Hollywood
version) *China Sky*.

the constitution of the liberated Eastern European governments and the organization of the United Nations. In subsequent months Roosevelt and Churchill would be accused of 'betraying' the Allied cause at Yalta by making large scale concessions to the Russians. Poland, Rumania and China were apparently 'sold down the river', a difficult geographical feat at the best of times. However, a realistic assessment of the terms discussed there shows only that the Allies exchanged a nominal recognition of the Soviet military power for certain verbal agreements particularly with regard to the first United Nations conference in San Francisco in April.

Following the disaster of the inter-war League of Nations and the bitter memory of the American Senate's refusal to support it in 1919 great hope was laid in the new UNO as the safeguard against future wars. Hollywood found the idea congenial and references to the Organisation started to creep into scripts. In *Over 21*, which Sidney Buchman adapted from Ruth Gordon's play about Max the middle aged journalist who wants to do his bit in the armed forces, the hero discusses with a colleague, Macdougall, the complex political issues of the time.

> *Macdougall* 'A couple of bad boys started this thing and *we're* gonna finish it. And the sooner the better.'
> *Max* 'That's right. But what worries me is the bad boys of the *next* generation. The world won't survive the next war. To finally lick those bad boys of today it took about fifteen years to get the decent countries into an unbeatable team. They were too busy grinding their [own] axes. Keeping that team together now is about the only hope for the future.'

Alexander Knox who played Max in this Columbia film, had moved from Twentieth Century-Fox. Coincidentally, his part there had been the title role in the lavish biography of the inspiration behind the League of Nations, Woodrow Wilson. *Wilson* was Darryl Zanuck's most ambitious project and was in preparation during 1944 at the same time as he was trying to adapt for the screen Wendell Willkie's best-selling book, *One World*. Well aware of the unaccustomed risk he was taking on behalf of a company whose previous forays into history had been typified by *In Old Chicago* and *Alexander Graham Bell*, Zanuck declared, not entirely in jest, 'Unless these two pictures are successful from every standpoint I'll never make another film without Betty Grable.'[5]

In the event the promised screen version of *One World* never materialised but *Wilson*, despite excellent reviews, made no impact on the nation at large. The problem was principally the uneasy alliance between the worthiness of Zanuck's intentions and the screams of the producer's natural commercial instincts. The audience is thus constantly reminded that although Wilson was one of the most important Presidents in US history he was really just a plain old college professor at heart with three teenage daughters. Scenes of Wilson making political speeches

> 'I believe as Lincoln did that Democracy with all its faults and failures if properly guided and interpreted holds the future of the world.'

are interspersed with those of his daughters looking over the White House 'like any other American family moving into a new home', and the maid reporting on the wonderful democracy that apparently prevails among the White House kitchen staff. Wilson finishes a cabinet meeting and relaxes with a detective novel, while the girls discuss their prospective dates for the evening.

The film works best when indulging in vitriolic attacks on German duplicity and racial superiority, but even when committed to active participation in the war, Zanuck makes the point with a gorge-rising scene at the railway station where Mrs Wilson is handing out coffee to the doughboys and the President is there to wish them good luck. One of the boys tells the President, 'My father was German. I'm just an American' and his colleague introduces the rest of the group as 'Mike yonder's a Bohunk, this guy's Irish, Tex here claims he's just from plain Texas and my name's Vespucci, Mr President, but I'm just an American too'.

In retrospect one cannot help feeling that it might have been better if Zanuck had had the courage of his reservations and simply cast Tyrone Power as Wilson and Betty Grable as his wife and commissioned Irving Berlin to turn the more didactic speeches into popular song form.

Another of the reasons that *Wilson* fell flat was that the film-going public of the country was largely uninterested in the issues of democratic government in Poland or the composition of the Security Council of the United Nations. To them the war was a nuisance and the sooner it was over and the men were demobbed, the quicker everyone could concentrate on the crucial matters of life, namely the

50 Ruth Nelson looks suitably impressed by her father's declaration of
war on Germany. *Wilson*.

removal of wartime controls and the spending of all those wartime savings on consumer products like automobiles, steaks and nylon stockings.

Even though the men were away in the armed forces family bank deposits continued to swell as more and more women were working full time, many in industries which had never previously admitted women. The acute shortage of male workers forced the hands of reluctant managers and women were soon to be found making precision instruments, and working in blast furnaces. Between 15 per cent and 25 per cent of the workers in American shipyards in 1944 were women.[6] Because of this new trend more industrial plants were compelled to employ female counsellors as their male counterparts proved incapable of coping with the sudden incidence of problems relating to menstruation, pregnancy and abortion.

The film industry was shaken to its foundations by this profound social change. The female dancers in Hollywood decided that the hours were shorter and the pay was better at the aircraft and munitions factories of Southern California, a state of affairs which gave splitting headaches both to the studios' casting directors and their oversexed producers.

Nevertheless, as the attractive ones went out of circulation at one end of the system there was a corresponding groundswell of talent at the other. At Paramount in February 1943 more than fifty positions 'of medium importance' vacated by men were filled by women. At Warners, wrote The *Hollywood Reporter*, 'there are four women in the accountancy department holding jobs formerly done by men. Columbia's messengers and reception room clerks are nearly all be-skirted.'[7] The accolade was reserved for Ms Esther Nobles whom Monogram turned from a plain Jane of a payroll secretary into a beautiful Transportation Manager.

Just as the lack of male stars worried Hollywood front offices during the war years so the lack of male customers caused distributors and exhibitors a few problems. The latter were urged to display glamour posters of the male stars who were left to attract a new and important box office patron — the unescorted female. Previously it had been sufficient to produce a cardboard cut-out of Dorothy Lamour in a sarong or Lana Turner in a sweater to induce the male customer to part with his and his female companion's money, but since about half the women in wartime cinemas were not escorted by men, renewed market research was clearly imperative.

The changing role of women in wartime society was the basis of *Tender Comrade*, RKO's tribute to the working women of America. Ginger Rogers starred in this story of a household of girls who live and work together while their men are engaged elsewhere. Lela Rogers whose mission in life was to run an anti-Communist Geiger counter over her daughter's scripts, sniffed out a typical piece of Dalton Trumbo chicanery. Mrs Rogers picked out 'share and share alike — that's the meaning of democracy', held it up between thumb and forefinger and dropped it four years later with a wrinkled nose on the desk of the House UnAmerican Activities Committee. In 1944, however, *Tender Comrade* roused no such political controversy. Indeed *Look* magazine's review began with the immortal phrase.

> If this war has done nothing else for the women of America, it has taught them *how* and *when* to wear trousers.[8]

One of the results of wartime pressure was a startling increase in the number of marriages and a proportionate rise in the birth rate. In the hard years of the Depression the annual number of births hovered around the two million mark. By 1944 the figure had almost doubled. Many of these were known as 'goodbye' babies despite the fact that draft boards deferred the calling up of fathers. Many of these 'goodbye' babies next said 'hello' to their fathers in the divorce courts whose precincts in the immediate post-war years were jammed with couples who had made a mistake.

Romance and courtship became a lost art at a time when weddings were arranged to suit the convenience of the US Army rather than the bride's mother. A fascinating if faintly dispiriting depiction of the situation appeared in Vincente Minelli's *The Clock*. It was made during 1944 and 1945 with his new wife, Judy Garland, who meets, marries and regrets having married Robert Walker all in the space of three days. Minnelli appears to have been influenced by King Vidor's *The Crowd* (1928, also MGM) because the oppressive, hateful anonymity of the city almost destroys the relationship at a number of times in the film. Walker plays a soldier on leave, a country boy experiencing the mixed joys of New York City for the first time. The skyscrapers seem to be falling on him, no native New Yorker will talk to him, his attempts to read the newspaper are frustrated by the jostling of the crowd and he finally meets Garland when she trips over him at the foot of an escalator and travels up the staircase without her heel. Their efforts to ride on the subway end in disaster, as they are separated first by abruptly closing doors and then by a confusion over the local and express trains. The hasty wedding ceremony is performed in a squat, ugly room with the clatter from the passing trains drowning their vows. Even the loving reconciliation is tinged with distrust as the final crane shot shows Garland as just one more anonymous wife.

The strain on the family unit was enormous when the father was posted abroad and the mother had to go out to work or become one of the 27,300,000 people who moved house at some point during the war years. The incidence of juvenile delinquency climbed alarmingly. Monogram exploited the trend with such epoch-making pictures as *Where Are Your Children?* and *Are These Our Parents?* which were in fact more nearly related to the superficial treatments of the Lost Generation of the 1920s than to the specific social problem of 1944. Cinema exhibitors saw another symptom when they discovered that unaccompanied teenagers were staying in their theatre seats from 4 p.m. until the end of the last show, thus denying the box office the necessary pleasure of re-selling their seats.

The migratory hordes were motivated almost entirely by money. Blacks moved from the established rural poverty of the South to the new urban poverty of the North. In 1943 there were race riots in Detroit, unparalleled in bloodshed until the long hot summers of the Lyndon Johnson years. Men in search of government contracts descended on Washington in such numbers that the housing shortage in the capital city became an institution as well known as the Capitol itself. When Roosevelt died in April 1945, and reporters flocked to Harry Truman's flat on Connecticut Avenue, they found a queue forming downstairs outside the apartment block manager's room for a conveniently located rent-controlled flat which would shortly be coming on the market. The classic, if apocryphal, morbid story of the housing shortage concerned the crime journalist who raced round to the landlord of the latest murder victim to find he had been beaten to the door by the policeman who had got to the scene of the crime just slightly earlier. The delicious George Stevens film *The More the Merrier* did no more than justice to the idiocies which followed in the wake of the wide gulf between the demand for accommoda-

tion and the limited supply available.

The complaints about queueing and rationing dominated the home front because there were no military calamities to supersede them in importance. The efforts made by Americans to partake of the self-sacrifice of war seemed puny and trivial to Europeans. A Hollywood trade paper reported,

> Because of candy shortages several theaters in Montana are now selling hard-boiled eggs and dill pickles over their candy counters and doing a brisk trade.[9]

The film industry exhibited its desire to tone down its natural exuberance for the duration when it banned 'all lavish displays of food on the screen'. Apparently, noted *Variety* with alarm,

> An abundance of steaks, roasts and other delectable viands in pictures are causing audiences to smack their lips audibly and make other sounds that interfere with the progress of the stories.[10]

The supreme film of the home front experience was David O. Selznick's epic *Since You Went Away* which made no attempt to disguise its unashamed celebration of what the foreword called 'The Unconquerable Fortress — the American home 1943'. It was a happier choice for Selznick than the property he had been contemplating at the start of the year — a book called *Mein Kampf* by that well known Austrian artist and entertainer, Adolf Hitler. 'The material is in the public domain', said the producer defiantly, 'but formalities pertaining to the acquisition of screen rights still remain to be ironed out.'[11] Whether because Hitler turned out to be one of those obstreperous writers who refused to clock in at the studio at 9 a.m. every morning or because of contractual disputes with his agent over billing, the project was abandoned without official explanation.

Since You Went Away is a perfect example of Hollywood film-making at its best, tugging constantly at real emotions but drawing back coyly before dreaded 'realism' spoiled the poignancy of the drama. Claudette Colbert plays the wife whose husband has just been drafted. She knuckles down to the task of running her large three bedroomed detached house by resorting to such swingeing economies as trading in her car and Hattie McDaniel and taking a paying guest in the shape of the gruff ex-Colonel played by Monty Woolley. The film is composed of a series of episodes in one of which

51 Christmas Eve inside the American Fortress.

52 Claudette Colbert, Jennifer Jones and Shirley Temple wondering about Pop and whether David Selznick's extravagant shooting methods will mean overtime payments. *Since You Went Away*.

53 The film they said could never be made. George Sanders in beastly good form in *They Came to Blow Up America*.

Colbert and her two daughters, Jennifer Jones and Shirley Temple, struggle across country to New York where they just miss their father passing through on his way to an overseas posting. On the return journey Shirley falls asleep on the shoulder of a nice old granny type from Central Casting, who it appears has a daughter just about Jennifer Jones's age. 'Where is she now?' asks Colbert brightly. The old lady smiles and shakes her head. 'I don't know. You see she was at Corregidor.'

There are many pieces of consummate technical artistry pulled off by the director, John Cromwell, and his two cinematographers, Lee Garmes and Stanley Cortez. The dance at the army camp and the tearful farewell at the railway station are two of the best. The latter concludes with a long, long crane shot, echoing the classic one of Vivien Leigh picking her way through the dummies and the extras in the main street of Atlanta in *Gone With The Wind*. This time the camera pulls back to find Jennifer Jones standing alone on the deserted platform, lit by a solitary shaft of light.

More typical of Selznick, however, are the bravura emotional moments which run throughout the course of the film. On her first night alone, Colbert discovers the note left under her pillow 'Wherever I am I'll be kissing you goodnight' and she scuttles sobbing into *his* twin bed. The dreaded telegram 'YOUR HUSBAND REPORTED MISSING IN ACTION' arrives and knocks her senseless. Recovering, she flicks over their album only to find the poem he had written on the birth of their first child,

'So We Are Three
My Darling,
My Darling's Darling
And, humbly, Me.'

and she dissolves once more. (The poem was originally written by Selznick for his first wife, Irene Mayer.)

Colbert adjusts somewhat to the thought of life without her husband and even goes to work as a lady welder in a shipyard (Selznick had read the statistics too), where she meets Nazimova who recites for her the lines inscribed on the Statue of Liberty. On Christmas Eve, after the household has retired, she unwraps his present to her and sits crying in the armchair when the phone rings shrilly. 'Cable, yes, read it again', she stammers, her voice choked with tears. She dashes up the stairs towards the girls shouting, 'He's coming home, he's coming

home' and as Cromwell dissolves to a high angle exterior shot of the fortress at night, his audience dissolves also, for the umpteenth time.

Selznick, however, was not one to keep the trowel in the garden shed if it could be useful in the studio. The epilogue ('No epilogue, I pray you, for your play needs no excuse') comes up on the roller 'BE OF GOOD COURAGE AND HE SHALL STRENGTHEN YOUR HEART ALL YE THAT TRUST IN THE LORD' with a deafening crescendo that seems to drown out poor Max Steiner's four-hundred-piece orchestra.

The overtly religious ending to *Since You Went Away* raises an intriguing point about Selznick. His preoccupation with middle-class 'normality' is everywhere in evidence in the film, particularly in the scenes with Jennifer Jones (whom he married shortly after the picture was completed). One wonders whether this obsession with 'nice' girls, soda fountains, and discussions on the front porch stemmed from Selznick's own lack of experience of anything remotely like it. On most films with a Jewish producer one might ascribe it to a non-Jewish director, writer or designer, but since Selznick wrote *Since You Went Away* and made his feelings on all other matters abundantly clear in his infamous memoranda, one cannot take such refuge here.

The Second World War was eventually won not in the American home but in the American factory. The volume of munitions and supplies was simply prodigious. For every one man serving in the armed forces there were at least three civilians engaged in war related work. The Office of War Mobilisation during its life produced 80,000 tanks, 276,000 planes and 71,000 naval vessels. The expenditure for the War Office, the Navy Department and the Maritime Commission for the fiscal year 1944 was more than double the entire National Debt which caused so much controversy in the 1930s. The National Debt itself meanwhile rose from $45 billion in 1940 to $260 billion in 1945. The Gross National Product in 1940 had been $97 billion; by 1944 it was already $190 billion. It was mightily stimulated by a daily infusion of $300 from government agencies in Washington.

Personal consumer income rose proportionately of course. This was best measured by the number of new income tax payers. For every four people paying income tax in 1939 there were fifty by the end of 1942. The length of the average working week rose from forty hours in 1941 to forty-five hours in

1944 and the average gross weekly wage increased from $25.20 in 1940 to $43.39 in 1945.[12]

Few industries knew hard times during these boom years. The film industry supplying a product that had never been in higher demand benefited greatly. All the major studios turned in healthy trading figures and it needed real talent to make a flop. *Andy Hardy's Double Life*, reported MGM proudly 'in its world premiere at Loews Valentine in Toledo is outgrossing every picture ever played at popular prices at that theater. It is doing 259 per cent of normal business.'[13] Bad news from the front drove people into the cinemas for escape, while good news sent them there in celebration. The traditional lull in business that historically coincides with the last two months of a Presidential Election campaign was nowhere to be found in the autumn of 1944.

With the end of the war in sight the studios began to dust off plans for expansion which had lain mouldering in the drawer since 1940. There seemed to be no end to the public's gullibility and it was jokily asserted that it was a time when even good pictures made money.

Somewhere down in the accountancy department of one of the studios a man with frayed cuffs and terminal dandruff was discovering in 1945 that films were costing significantly more to produce than they ever had before. The million dollar budget was an everyday event and although profit margins were large they were dependent on a constantly expanding market. The studios knew they had a huge backlog of awful films to release to the unsuspecting newly liberated countries of the world and were not worried.

If anything, the heady atmosphere of the summer of 1945 was the time for re-releasing the Twentieth Century-Fox production of *They Came to Blow Up America*, starring Anna Sten and George Sanders. The film had not been an enormous success when it was made in 1943. Audiences had obviously failed to understand the foreword which earnestly assured them that the picture was NOT based on documented facts.

The Fruits of Victory

(September 1945 — September 1947)

VJ was officially announced at 7 p.m. on Tuesday 14 August 1945 but the inevitable public rejoicing smacked more of relief than exhilaration. Feelings of insecurity and fear of what the immediate future held were everywhere apparent. The post-war world lacked the nominal stability given to the Allies by the comforting presence of the Big Three war leaders. Stalin was already resuming his former role of the Red bogeyman and Churchill was now the leader of His Majesty's Opposition. The jowls sat powerless on the benches of the House of Commons darkening daily as the dreaded Labour government nationalised large sections of British industry and presided over the liquidation of the British Empire.

The death of Franklin Roosevelt in April 1945 had been a terrible blow to Americans, almost as shocking in its immediate impact as the assassination of President Kennedy was to be some years later. It took a certain amount of thought for many people in 1945 to remember a time when there had been another President in the White House. The debut of his successor, the bald-headed Senator from Missouri, was not auspicious. Truman's much quoted remark to the Press — 'Boys, I felt as though the moon, the stars and all the planets had fallen on me' — did not inspire confidence. The easy majesty of Franklin Roosevelt had been replaced by a man who threatened physical injury on a music critic who wrote slightingly of his daughter's singing and whose wife, in sharp contrast to Eleanor Roosevelt, had spent her early years perfecting the art of whistling through her teeth.

Fear of Truman's lack of presidential timbre was intensified by the devastating new power at his dis-

posal given to him by the successful accomplishment of the Manhattan Project. The spectre of 'the bomb', even if it was not publicly acknowledged, hung over the world from the day Hiroshima was devastated. MGM approached its story of the making of the bomb in its traditional glossy manner and then withdrew suddenly when it was realised just how fraught with danger the production was.

The Beginning or the End (1947), a studio fabricated account of the Manhattan project, seemed at first to be an echo of *Madame Curie* and other hygenic scientific discoveries with its fictional framework and a romantic subplot of a young scientist and his bride. However, whereas radium, the electric light bulb and other such advances had clearly been of value to mankind, the benefits of the atomic bomb were distinctly dubious. The film shrugged its shoulders and simply concluded that it was an extremely dangerous weapon, must not be taken internally and should be kept out of the reach of children. Assigning Norman Taurog to the direction of *The Beginning or the End* was presumably the result of the studio's belief that he could make the picture as successful as he had made *Young Tom Edison*. In the event the studio released it with a Red Skelton comedy as the bottom half of a double bill.

Apart from the prospect of imminent Armageddon and the incompetence of the new Administration, the major concern of Americans at VJ was the fate of the economy. Nobody needed reminding that in the last year of peace despite the accelerating build up of armament construction there had been ten million men unemployed. The drive for full employment was shared by all sections of society but it was the President who was faced with the unenviable task of reconverting the national economy from war to peace without creating a depression. With memories of The Forgotten Man still fresh in the mind predictions of eight to ten million unemployed were common in 1945.

It was to offset this that Roosevelt had initiated in 1944 the Serviceman's Readjustment Act, which became known familiarly as the GI Bill of Rights. It enabled the common soldier to be portrayed more typically as an American in Paris than as a fugitive from a chain gang. This, combined with the insatiable demand for consumer goods after the wartime hiatus, accounted for the fairly successful transition of the economy from one almost entirely dominated by the government to one in which the government hid behind private enterprise and everyone pretended that it wasn't there.

Fears in Hollywood that peace would be a disaster were not fulfilled and 1946 turned out to be, in box office terms at least, the most successful year in the history of the film industry. A synagogue in St Louis which had been a temporary House of the Lord during the war years, reconverted itself to a temple dedicated to the greater glory of Louis B. Mayer in 1946.[1] Profits for the year announced by the eight major film companies amounted to over $125 million, which compared very favourably with the average annual figure of $35 million in the 1930s.[2]

Particularly pleasing to the studios was the fate of the new independent production companies which were threatening, at the end of the war, to cream off the best talent. By the end of 1946 the big trek back had begun, started by Liberty Films, that glittering constellation populated by Frank Capra, William Wyler and George Stevens, which sold itself into Paramount bondage to the infinite regret of its leading light.

The influence of Hollywood in the world was never greater than in 1946. Mere figures alone do not tell the whole story. Perhaps the most telling tribute emerged from a tribe in Nigeria whose chief complained bitterly that Hollywood imperialism had raised the cost of a wife from £10 to well over £50. In previous times the sum offered was sufficient to ensure the marriage but since the introduction of Lana Turner and Clark Gable into their lives the girls were now looking for a love match in keeping with their romantic aspirations; all of which had forced up the price something terrible.[3]

The principal challenge to the otherwise unquestioned hegemony of American films came from a dour Yorkshireman who had made a fortune in flour milling. J. Arthur Rank who had entered the capricious world of film-making in the 1930s chose the arrival of peace to make his frontal assault on the seductive riches of the American domestic market. American exhibitors chortled when they heard the news, having for years been chastised by New York critics for not playing more British pictures only to discover from painful experience that in the history of the British film industry only *The Private Life of Henry VIII* and *In Which We Serve* had made any impact on their customers.

Rank was in deadly earnest. He started to buy important cinemas abroad in territory Hollywood had previously thought its own. He bought into the powerful Schlesinger circuit in South Africa and even began to pick up strategic North American showcases. By the end of 1946 his holdings abroad amounted to 1200 cinemas and Americans decided it was time to take positive action, especially as British films led by *Henry V* and *The Seventh Veil* were starting to make inroads into their own domestic preserves.

American distributors threatened to freeze Rank out if he didn't adopt a less hostile response. The Yorkshireman replied by vowing to build his own chain of Odeons across the country. The exhibitors rubbed their hands in glee and prayed that he would open with that spectacular dying fall *Caesar and Cleopatra* on which they had taken a terrible clubbing. Rank pointed to the fact that whereas in 1945 eight British pictures had played in America and taken $2 million, in 1946 twenty pictures had survived the Atlantic crossing and grossed $8.5 million. This trend encouraged him to sign actors and actresses (like Ann Todd and Phyllis Calvert) to seven year contracts and then loan them out to Hollywood studios in the manner so successfully accomplished by David Selznick.

The British challenge to American domination was finally ended not so much by the innate superiority of American films as by the bungling of the British government and the clammy embrace of the British economy. The overwhelming national need in 1947 was to prevent the drain on British dollar resources (few as they were and fewer as they were destined to become) and since the Americans were earning about $70 million a year the film industry became the prime target for some sound Socialist planning.

In August 1947 Hugh Dalton, the Chancellor of the Exchequer, announced the imposition of a Customs duty of 75 per cent on the value of all imported films, the sum to be prepaid. Howls of pain could plainly be heard all over Southern

California. The Motion Picture Association of America promptly responded by suspending indefinitely all further shipments of film to Britain. This took the government completely by surprise. What astonished them even more was the dawning realisation that there were enough American films already in the country to cause a considerable outflow of currency reserves and that once these were exhausted something would have to take their place.

Stafford Cripps encouraged Rank to boost his own production (in the national interest) and Harold Wilson, the President of the Board of Trade, agreed to withdraw the 75 per cent ad valorem duty but at the same time he raised the quota of British-made films to be seen on British screens from 20 per cent to 45 per cent. Rank was thus persuaded against his better judgment to sprint before he could walk. To the great surprise of nobody except His Majesty's Government the British film industry, quite unable to produce immediately a large quantity of successful commercial pictures, fell flat on its face with a crash from which it has not recovered to this day.

Ironically, at the height of the British economic crisis, known familiarly as 'the dollar gap', the American economy was going through a troubled phase that looked for all the world like the British industrial scene of the 1970s. The reconversion from war to peace time economy combined with the overwhelming number of demands from the increasingly powerful unions for massive wage increases had triggered off a bout of rampant inflation. When General Motors refused to agree to a further 30 per cent pay increase the United Automobile Workers (UAW) called a strike. In April 1946, John L. Lewis demonstrated the extent of his power by leading out 400,000 miners. When in the following month there was a national rail strike the country looked on the verge of collapse.

Truman responded to the crisis by threatening to draft all the strikers into the armed forces, a course of action that should have been predictable from a man who was prepared to resort to violence after a bad music review. The nation survived the immediate industrial crisis but the effect of the strikes was to trigger off a further round of inflation so that by December 1946 living costs were three times as much as they had been five years previously. Since the demand for such diverse consumer goods as irons, razor blades and motor cars was not matched by a corresponding supply, the black market for such items thrived as never before. In the November 1946 elections the Republican party campaigned on the simple slogan 'Had Enough?' It was sufficient to return the first Republican majority in Congress since 1920.

It was in this atmosphere of national uncertainty but local success that Hollywood approached the post-war years. Buttressed by a strong feeling that the wartime hunger for movies was insatiable, Hollywood steeled itself to investigate some of the problems of contemporary American society, none of which was more important than the plight of the returning serviceman. During the last months of the war Hollywood had steadfastly refused to have anything to do with stories which dealt with peace in general for fear of grave miscalculation. The single exception was the rehabilitation of the fighting man since this was one problem that could be accurately predicted in advance.

Acting on this assumption Sam Goldwyn commissioned MacKinlay Kantor to write a fifty page treatment which would serve as the basis for a future screenplay on the subject. Meanwhile Harry Truman, to the great delight of Goldwyn's publicity agents, started demobilizing as quickly as he could. By May 1946 over seven million men had been demobbed and by the end of the year the army was down to one and a half million and the Navy to less than 700,000.

Kantor, having spent the $12,500 Goldwyn had originally paid him, reappeared some three months later with a 268 page novel entitled *Glory for Me*, written in free verse. Goldwyn, once the full realisation of the horror dawned on him, threw a terrible rage which culminated in Kantor getting another $7,500 to write a screenplay from his novel. When this too proved to be a disaster Goldwyn tossed the entire project into the laps of his two most faithful lieutenants, Robert Sherwood and Willie Wyler, and went back to shouting down the telephone at Mac-Kinlay Kantor's lawyers.

The Best Years of Our Lives turned out to be one of the greatest films ever made in Hollywood. The various talents of Wyler, Sherwood and the cinematographer, Gregg Toland, were never seen to better advantage and the inspired casting of Myrna Loy (playing her first matronly role) and Fredric March completed an impeccable cast list.

The film is centred on the readjustment problems of three returning veterans, one a dashing young Air Force Major, Fred (played by Dana Andrews) married to an unfaithful wife (Virginia Mayo), another a sailor who lost his arms below the elbow, Homer (played by Harold Russell) and a middle aged Sergeant, Al (March) who cannot resume his former life as a stolid respectable middle-class banker without the fortification of alcohol.

Their ambitions are invariably quite modest. Fred wants only 'a decent job and a little house for my wife'. Homer worries about the inevitable pity his disability will arouse in his fiancée (Cathy O'Donnell) and Al is concerned that everyone he meets will try to rehabilitate him. As the three of them fly into their home town, Boone City, over a huge yard full of discarded bombers ('What we'd have given for those in '43,' sighs Fred), they pass evidence of a prosperous peacetime society which they find themselves mentally unable to comprehend.

All of them try to avoid the moment when they must confront their relatives, but the meeting of March and Myrna Loy is depicted by Wyler with consummate artistry. His daughter Peggy (Teresa Wright) opens the door of the apartment but her exclamation of surprise is stifled by the swift application of her father's hand to her mouth. Her mother calls out from the kitchen but getting no response turns half puzzled, half anticipating as March bursts into view.

Partly because March is on the top of his form and partly because Sherwood was most at home with this character, Al emerges as the most completely rounded creation in the film and it is his scenes that remain longest in the mind. 'Last year it was "Kill Japs". This year, it's "Make money",' he muses, encapsulating the fundamental disorientation of the bemused veteran. Al finds himself incapable of accepting traditional banking procedures in the way he had unthinkingly done before. Given the task of discharging the bank's obligation under the GI Bill of Rights he agrees on the bank's behalf to pay half of the $6,000 needed by a farmer to buy his farm. Ray Collins, the bank President, points out reprovingly that the man had no collateral. Al responds, in a positively Capraesque speech, that lending on character is probably the safest investment a bank can make. Later on, at a very pompous formal dinner given by the bank in his honour, Al makes a drunken speech, full of mixed metaphors and misused clichés, while Myrna Loy ticks off on the table cloth the number of drinks he has consumed. 'The reason for my success as a sergeant',

he slurs, 'is due to my training in the bank,' and then goes on to relate an impossible story about an order from a superior officer to take a hill held by the enemy which he turned down on the grounds that the officer possessed no collateral.

In many ways the most moving scene in the film is the moment when Peggy, having fallen in love with Fred, announces to her parents her intention of finally destroying his bad marriage. March objects that it is hardly up to her. She responds by accusing them of not understanding her situation because they've always had things too easy. Loy looks at March and replies slowly,

'How many times have I said I hated you and meant it in my heart? How many times have you said you were sick of me and that we were all washed up? How many times have we had to fall in love all over again?'

If ever anyone accuses Hollywood of being constantly escapist, of never having the courage to approach contemporary problems with sincerity and humility, *The Best Years of Our Lives* and in particular this scene from it stands a living testimony to the contrary.

The film was an instant triumph both critically and commercially, brushing aside the challenge of Capra's *It's a Wonderful Life* to sweep the year's Oscars. The only complaints came from certain left-wing quarters who seized on the evidence of Hollywoodiana to proclaim it flawed in every aspect. Abraham Polonsky, writing in the recently founded left wing journal *Hollywood Quarterly*, dug into *Glory for Me* to prove that *The Best Years of Our Lives* was a fraud. In the original novel Al left the bank to work as a poor farmer and Homer was not the reasonably well-adjusted dextrous character played by Harold Russell but a blubbering spastic.

Polonsky complained bitterly that the film concentrates on the middle-class Al rather than the working-class Fred, but at the same time condemns all the characters as 'general stereotypes of the film industry and popular fiction'. Also Polonsky, perhaps rightly this time, argues that although 'the picture exposes the fraud of America's promises to its soldiers the plot forces easy solutions on its creators. Fascism is solved with a punch; a bad marriage by the easy disappearance of the wife, the profound emotional adjustment of a handless veteran by a fine girl; the itchy conscience of a banker by too many drinks. . . . Greatness was possible for *The Best*

54 Fredric March and Myrna Loy learn that their daughter is setting out to break up Dana Andrews's marriage. *The Best Years of Our Lives.*

55 Dana Andrews in successful pursuit of a job.

56 Harold Russell in successful pursuit of Cathy O'Donnell. *The Best Years of Our Lives.*

Years of Our Lives but this meant examining Fred Derry, where society hurts hardest. It was not done.'4

It was not indeed, although one cannot help feeling that perhaps the temptation to see more of the incomparable Fredric March rather than the journeyman Dana Andrews was too strong for Sherwood and Wyler to resist. Only at the very last with Andrews and Teresa Wright committing themselves to a difficult relationship is one inclined to wonder whether the director did not indeed head for the easy option rather than disappoint his audience's expectation of a conventionally happy ending.

Nevertheless the memory of *The Best Years of Our Lives* remains sharp and clear more than three decades after it was made. It will certainly survive the inept TV re-make called *Returning Home* updated to the end of the war in Vietnam and produced by Lorimar Productions (home of *The Waltons*) for transmission in April 1975. *The Best Years of Our Lives* had less of the documentary accuracy demanded of such pictures today but its evocation of a troubled time and its capture of a particular social problem was accomplished with the wit and sensitivity of truly great artists.

The figure of the returning soldier was a common one in movies in the months following VJ. Usually he came back to find his wife unfaithful, as in *The Blue Dahlia*, and the return was invariably the prelude to activities of a distinctly illegal nature, as in *Dead Reckoning*. Few pictures, apart from *The Best Years of Our Lives*, attempted a frontal assault on the real social problems of the veteran. Among those that did was Delmer Daves' *Pride of the Marines*, although this picture seems to fit Polonsky's criticism better than Wyler's.

John Garfield plays a serviceman, justifiably bitter at the blindness sustained on behalf of his country. Fortunately he is rescued and rehabilitated by the love of a good Warner Bros contract actress (Eleanor Parker) whom he tries to abandon only to fall into the Christmas tree. Shortly afterwards he willingly agrees to receive his Navy Cross which he wears proudly, having reconciled himself to his erstwhile patriotism. Faintly discerning the red top of a taxi, he clambers in and responds to the driver's 'Where to?' with an affirmative 'Home!' as 'America The Beautiful' swells conclusively on the soundtrack.

The essence of the spate of films in the late 1940s

which purported to be critical analyses of the problems facing contemporary American society was that they all believed that the problems were soluble by legislative reform and enlightened liberal attitudes. The fundamental breach in the 1960s caused by the war in Indo-China suggested that progressive liberalism must give way to the corrective dynamism of revolution, but in the more optimistic years of 1945-7 such a thought would have been dismissed as self-indulgent defeatism.

The happy ending was still sacrosanct among Hollywood's golden rules. It would have been impossible to have admitted Ray Milland's drinking problem in Billy Wilder's *The Lost Weekend* without the firm belief that the love of Jane Wyman would cure it. Unfortunately, the very quality of the film itself, as well as the fact that this very suggestion had been dismissed at least twice during the course of the movie, played against the glibness of the final scene, leaving the solution to those not involved in the ritual as faked and unconvincing.

Nevertheless, one must see these 'problem' pictures in the context of their time. Even *Gentleman's Agreement*, in which Gregory Peck disguises himself as a Jew to find out how unpleasant the sensation is, was a bold stand for Twentieth Century-Fox to take. Interestingly enough, the film was banned in Spain on the remarkable grounds that the authorities had declared that anti-semitism was not a problem. The film was therefore not exhibited in case it created a problem which did not exist before.

Nevertheless, the difficulty with which Gregory Peck assumed a Jewish identity made the film hard to believe in 1947. One infamously anti-semitic Jew approached Darryl Zanuck after the premiere of *Gentleman's Agreement* and swore to refrain from any further anti-semitic remarks in case the Jew he was insulting turned out to be a Gentile in disguise.

In the autumn of 1947 a flock of pictures seemed to be in production in Hollywood, which starred anti-Semites, much as all the pictures in 1942 seemed to be starring either Carmen Miranda or Judy Garland. MGM was toying with Sholem Asch's novel *East River* as a vehicle for Gene Kelly and Goldwyn was busily persuading Peck to play in *Earth and High Heaven*. Even Monogram thought the new line was profitable and bought a novel by Arthur Miller called *Focus* as its contribution to the Hollywood United Jewish Appeal.

Eventually the sole survivor was RKO's *Crossfire* which worked well probably because the framework was a thriller which held the interest irrespective of the moral superstructure. The solution to the vicious murder committed by Robert Ryan in the opening sequence emerges as Ryan's pathological anti-semitism. Ironically, although it is one of the few so-called 'problem' pictures to exist as entertainment in its own right, the film was turned down for exhibition by the US Navy, the US Army overseas and the Motion Picture Export Association because it was not considered to be 'suitable entertainment'.[5]

Hollywood approached new ideas like an inexperienced swimmer who puts one toe in the pool, finds the water not too cold and then dives in head first. Similarly, once a picture with a difficult theme or a particular location was seen to be successful, the air was thick with the flailing arms of imitators. *The House on 92nd Street* was the first major studio production to shoot much of its story on actual locations in New York. The producer of the film was the former *March of Time* executive Louis de Rochemont, and the combination of his flair for the topical story and Henry Hathaway's professional reliability was sufficient to manufacture an entertaining thriller.

Its success seems to have been due more to these reasons than to the sudden appearance on the screen of genuine New York streets, when for years audiences had been accepting their studio counterparts without any evident anger. Since present day television audiences do not object to the supposedly 'realistic' *Kojak* being filmed in Universal City, one should hesitate before acclaiming location shooting as the outright gift of *The House on 92nd Street* to the American film industry. Still, location shooting in the wake of this film's success certainly became more popular and the real significance of the move lies really in the decision of West Coast production offices to sanction such a large amount of filming away from the convenience of constant supervision.

De Rochemont went on to make such pictures as *Call Northside 777* and *Boomerang*, both of which followed the location formula of *The House on 92nd Street* but at the same time they also contained solid, reliable plots. *Boomerang* was compelled to cheat somewhat, switching its location from Bridgeport Connecticut to Stamford Connecticut because the police and the City Fathers did not care to be reminded of their inability to apprehend the murderer of the Catholic priest whose death in 1924 was the basis of *Boomerang's* story. The Bridgeport Chamber of Commerce reportedly tried to influence the decision of their Stamford brethren to whom Fox next applied, but these loyal citizens clearly found the glamour of spending a few weeks with Dana Andrews to be irresistible.

The other marked trend in film-making in the late 1940s was the abundance of movies which came to be known collectively as *film noir*. *Noir* was never a *genre* in the way a Western or a musical can be reasonably labelled as such. It suggested a tone, an attitude to life that was bleak, harsh and fatalistic. The term invariably evokes the image of a murder in a city street at night but in fact a *noir* film need not necessarily be dominated by an urban or a nocturnal setting. *The Postman Always Rings Twice* is set in a small roadside café on a lonely highway, yet its tone is unmistakably *noir*.

The popularity of such films in the months following the end of the war seems to suggest that they captured a certain element in the contemporary climate. One can see in *Double Indemnity* and *Laura*, both made in 1944, very clear artistic antecedents of the *film noir* flood of 1946-7. Indeed one could arguably trace the line back to *High Sierra* or *The Maltese Falcon* both of which revelled in the irresistible fatalism of *film noir*. Nevertheless, it is the principal tenet of this book that American films were influenced more by the social and political forces acting on their makers than by the mere presence of intellectual concerns in vacuo.

The muted rejoicing of VJ, caused mainly by such fears as have already been mentioned, was aggravated by the overtly cynical and hostile attitude of the Russians. The fervent American desire for a lasting peace in no way stemmed the Russian threat. When Henry Wallace made his passionate plea for the resumption of friendly relations with Russia in the face of the Truman administration's inability to find any common ground with its erstwhile ally, it was obvious that such a man could no longer be contained in the cabinet. He was removed almost immediately. In a famous speech in Fulton, Missouri, Churchill warned that an iron curtain was about to descend across Europe from Stettin in the Baltic to the Black Sea. Truman sat in the audience and knew the truth of the former Prime Minister's words.

In February 1946 demobilisation of the Russian army was halted and the emphasis in the current five year plan was switched from consumer goods

57 John Garfield sees the light at the end of the tunnel. *Pride of the Marines.*

58 Gregory Peck standing in profile to emphasise his Jewishness. *Gentleman's Agreement.*

59 The climax of *The House on 92nd Street*. One of the first transvestite
spies to hit the screen.

back to armaments. The Cominform replaced the old Comintern and the spy system in the Western world was significantly strengthened. The attempt of the American people and their elected representatives in the Eightieth Congress to concentrate on domestic matters was constantly frustrated by the increasing dominance of foreign policy. The physical devastation caused by the war in Europe and the imminent disintegration of the British Empire created a large vacuum which the Russians were happily filling. Churchill called the European continent 'a rubble heap, a charnel house, a breeding ground for pestilence and hate'. It was obvious even to those Americans whose natural inclinations steered them towards the traditional policy of isolation that any repetition of the events of 1919 would be disastrous.

The imperative became inescapable in February 1947 when Britain withdrew her forces from Greece because of the expense of keeping them there. Greece and Turkey both looked set to go Communist unless the Americans did something positive quickly. On 12 March Truman went before Congress to ask for $400 million in military and economic aid to Greece and Turkey. 'I believe', he stated firmly, 'that it is the policy of the United States to support free peoples who are resisting attempted subjugation by armed minorities or big outside pressure.' Congress agreed. The Cold War had arrived.

Hollywood responded to the new declaration of war in its time-honoured fashion of changing the nationality of its villains. German names were struck out and Russian ones scribbled in. Nazi sadism was replaced as the motivating factor for the villainy by Communist sadism. But before the flood of explicit hard core anti-Communist pictures washed over the screen, the air was still full of war weary disillusioned anti-heroes who found the new post war world a particularly nervous, cynical time to be alive.

John Houseman found the popularity of this new hero a matter for some regret. He wrote sorrowfully,

The current 'tough' movie is no lurid Hollywood invention; its pattern and its characteristics coincide too closely with other symptoms of our national life . . . . The 'tough' movie presents a fairly accurate reflection of the neurotic personality of the United States of America in the year 1947.[6]

Houseman justifies his argument with particular reference to Howard Hawks's film *The Big Sleep*, which, at the time Houseman was writing about it, had still to acquire the cult reputation which dominates any criticism of it today. Houseman points out that while Chandler dissociated himself from Marlowe as a character, the 'heroic' quality of the film's dramatisation compelled total identification on the part of the audience. Marlowe suddenly becomes 'a hero in the tradition of Rochester, Heathcliff, Horatio Alger, Buffalo Bill and Little Caesar',[7] which seems, even for 1946 to be a catholic range of heroes to be following.

Houseman complains of Bogart's unkempt appearance and the unprepossessing nature of his apartment and office. Considerably worse however is Marlowe's lack of any discernible ideal in his pattern of life. His work is motivated neither by the supposedly honourable reasons of ambition or loyalty nor by the traditionally dishonourable ones of lust and greed. He rejects the advances of both General Sternwood's attractive daughters and at the rate of $25 a day plus expenses holds his life (relatively) cheap. The summit of his ambition seems to be a full bottle of whisky and an uninterrupted sleep.

The film is populated by a procession of chiselers, nymphomaniacs and half wits, none of them possessed of skill, brains, courage or hope. Houseman perceptively argues that it is not the violence of the film which is the basis of his objections but 'the lack of moral energy, the listless, fatalistic despair'. In comparison to the characters of *film noir*, the gangsters of the early 1930s, despite their overt anti-social activities, exhibited laudable energy and lust. Houseman concludes from his analysis of *The Big Sleep* that the American people were afraid to admit to their personal post-war problems. Their strife for a solution was fruitless and they were being denied their necessary catharsis.

Houseman is undoubtedly right to draw a distinction between the classic gangster films of the previous decade and the new variation of crime picture in 1947. Little Caesar and Scarface had wanted desperately to belong to a society to which their new-found wealth and notoriety gave them entry. Bogart in *Dead End* and Cagney in *Angels With Dirty Faces* had pointed an accusing finger at the social environment of their early years, but the illegalities of *film noir* were prompted by nothing as noble or transparent.

Significantly, the parts played by women in *film noir* were a major break with their previous relegation to roles such as the gangster's moll or the girl waiting patiently for the hero to reform or to die. Stemming from Mary Astor's seductive portrait of female duplicity in *The Maltese Falcon* there flowed a stream of evil grasping women. In particular one remembers the enchanting Barbara Stanwyck as Phyllis Dietrichson, seducing Fred MacMurray into a whirlpool of murder and corruption in Wilder's *Double Indemnity*. Stanwyck manipulates MacMurray with total control throughout the action. He first sees her coming down the stairs, the camera focusing on and panning with her ankle. MacMurray recalls later the odd mixture of stale cigar smoke and the smell of honeysuckle which presages the eventual murder. Not until MacMurray shoots her does she finally admit a genuine need for him — a confession that arrives a little too late for both of .

F was full of such women. Lana Turner in an *Always Rings Twice* also managed t ual desirability to induce a reasonably o o kill her husband for her own gain. L introduction to Garfield *via* the roll of as the camera tracks in to find her legs and pans up, is similarly sensational and her seduction of Garfield as they dance close together by the light of the neon sign outside is as erotic as anything current in 1946.

She is the one with the guts and the drive and the ambition to dispense with Cecil Kellaway and just as MacMurray works out the details after Stanwyck has planted the idea of murder, so Garfield gets drawn ever more surely into the depths of Turner's murky soul. The bitter irony of the final scene when Turner, having reconciled herself to Garfield, dies in a car crash (the symbolic lipstick rolling from her unclenched fist) thus sending Garfield to Death Row but for the wrong crime, appears to suggest that personal happiness is simply no longer a reasonable expectation.

All the contemporary female stars asked to play the role of the 'bad' woman. In the 1930s the thought of Norma Shearer or Jeanette MacDonald playing *femmes fatales* would have been inconceivable. In the mid 1940s both Ann Sheridan and Joan Bennett, long-time fully paid up members of Warners and Paramount's Nice Girls Brigade respectively, were transferred to the naughty women club. Bennet had a disastrous effect on Edward G. Robinson, who, in *Scarlet Street* and *The Woman in the Window* played classic symbols of the establishment male seduced by her into giving up his respectability for a hopeless promise of a new and more attractive life.

In *The Woman in the Window*, Robinson plays a professor of criminology whose chance meeting with Joan Bennett leads to murder, blackmail and his apparent suicide. The realisation that this is another of Fritz Lang's feebly contrived happy endings does not significantly diminish the power of the film. The sedate bourgeois existence of Robinson has been violently upset with some ease and the horror of finding the levers of the establishment, which he has long been used to operating himself, working against him, leaves the audience with only the barest illusion of security.

Some of the *femmes fatales* were given the dubious benefit of a psychological motivation for their unpleasant natures. Laraine Day destroys the lives of three men in *The Locket* before it is discovered that during the course of her childhood she was blamed for the theft of a locket she had coveted but not stolen. *The Dark Mirror* also delves into psychiatry and attractive killers. This time Olivia De Havilland plays twins, one good, one a killer, both attractive and neither under long-term contract to a major Hollywood studio.

Psychiatry, or at least its superficial image, became very popular in Hollywood for a short while. Its influence certainly spilled over into those films which, it may be roughly agreed, contained sufficient *noir* elements in them to make them *films noirs* but that was by no means its only contribution to the Hollywood canon. Hitchcock used it in *Spellbound*, Olivia De Havilland suffered from its primaeval application in *The Snake Pit* but the most famous version of it was probably in the Kurt Weill musical *Lady in the Dark*, whose translation to the screen cost Paramount a fortune and sent Mitchell Leisen's career into temporary eclipse.

On the other side of the noir valley lay the mainstream of psychotic crime pictures in which the post war years gloried. In particular one thinks of *Kiss of Death*, the Henry Hathaway picture notable mainly for its remarkable portrait of the killer played by Richard Widmark. In the 1920s audiences became used to recognising the arrival of the hero when he stopped to stroke a little dog. In *Kiss of Death* Widmark establishes his character equally succinctly by strapping an old lady to her wheelchair and pushing

60 John Garfield and Lana Turner discussing the aesthetics of *film noir*. *The Postman Always Rings Twice*.

61 The supreme ecstasy of being the star of *The Bells of St. Mary's*, which is top of *Variety's* Top Grossing Pictures of 1945, is clearly visible on Sister Ingrid Bergman's face. Father O'Crosby has seen it all before.

her down the stairs. Widmark's logical successor in such films was Cagney in *White Heat* and *Kiss Tomorrow Goodbye*.

The film in which content and form merge to make one of the masterpieces of *film noir* is *Out of the Past*, which in England was known perversely as *Build My Gallows High* (the title of the original novel). All the elements are there — the *femme fatale* (Jane Greer) whose superficial innocence allied with her sexual charms conspire to lure Robert Mitchum into betraying Greer's powerful protector (Kirk Douglas). 'You're no good and neither am I', she concludes, 'we deserve each other.' After she kills Douglas the two of them head for Mexico. But Mitchum, resigned to his own despair, tips off the police who trap them at a road block. Greer shoots him but is herself dispatched by police bullets. The world is arguably a better place without her but few people seem to be left to populate the vacuum. Jacques Tourneur's direction is brilliant throughout although his grip on the audience's attention is greatly helped by the casting of two men with dimpled chins in the major roles. The confrontation of the clefts is compulsive cinema.

Probably the bleakest view of life was expounded in *Brute Force*, Mark Hellinger's story of a prison break. Hume Cronyn plays a sadistic Captain of the Guard with a positively Hitlerian obsession. Reverence of his hero is taken as far as hanging an idealised portrait of himself in his office and, more sinisterly, beating a man with a rubber truncheon while the music of Wagner issues from the record player. Shortly afterwards he reveals to the prison doctor his Nietzschean view of *untermensch* prisoners. At the end of this thoroughly objectionable film everybody dies in the final shoot-out so at least it has the small merit of a happy ending. Bosley Crowther in his review of the picture wondered tentatively whether the export of such a film abroad would give foreigners a wrong picture of the American way of life in 1947.[8]

Problems there certainly were in 1947 and *film noir*, though it did not reflect them directly, captured a certain public dissatisfaction that made such blandishments particularly powerful. Yet one must beware in examining such a phenomenon, lest one conclude that the screen was entirely overrun by *femmes fatales*, weak and corrupted men, all dying in an orgy of unrepentant blood. A look at the top grossing pictures for the year 1947 soon dispels such a thought and proves conclusively that, on the surface at least, the Hollywood domestic audience had not changed.

The Best Years of Our Lives, although released in the autumn of 1946, justly bestrode the following year's list as Samuel Goldwyn had always foretold. Following in its wake was *Duel in the Sun* which admittedly contained certain *noir* characters in Jennifer Jones and Gregory Peck but the idea that David Selznick was also among the *noir* prophets is ridiculous and the film is plastered with the great man's unmistakable taste for the emotional overkill. Third came Harry Cohn's pride and joy, *The Jolson Story* which was followed by Fox's *Forever Amber* and De Mille's solid, reliably right-wing version of colonial times, *Unconquered. The Egg and I* and *The Yearling* squeezed *The Razor's Edge* out of the Top Ten and the Goulding picture was the only vaguely *noir* film in the top twenty money-making pictures for the year in which such pictures supposedly dominated the screens. Just to add insult to injury, *The Razor's Edge* was trailed in quick succession by *The Bachelor and the Bobbysoxer* and *Mother Wore Tights*. Strange bedfellows indeed.[9]

If the Hollywood moguls looked on the list of the top grossing pictures and saw that it was good (which they did and it was, more or less) they did not see the underlying social, political and economic forces burrowing away underneath. Bing Crosby was singing and Louis B. Mayer was in his heaven but all was not necessarily well in Fairyland. The basic audience would always turn out in numbers for the exceptionally fine film like *The Best Years of Our Lives*. They would usually turn out for the good starring vehicle like the *Road* pictures, but they were abandoning in droves the badly made A picture which had traditionally scraped into profit with the help of an attractive girl on the way up or a Norman Main on the way down. The result was that film companies were starting to play even safer in their choice of screen material. In September 1946 Fox bought Kenneth Roberts's forthcoming novel *Lydia Bailey* for $215,000 on the basis of a one and a half page synopsis and the news that it was to be a Literary Guild Selection.

More significant was the explosion in 1947 of the consumer spending bomb which had been ticking away steadily since before VJ had made its mark on the industry. In the 1930s when there was little surplus cash swilling about in the economy and during the war years when there was more of it but precious little on which to spend it, the difference between the index of American *per capita* income and the index of the domestic box office varied between one and two points. In 1946, the gap opened to four points and in 1947 it had leapt to seven. The studios took their stock precautions of firing their $50 a week secretaries and their $40 a week janitors while Louis Mayer's salary climbed ever upwards towards the $1,500,000.

The shifts that Hollywood made to counteract the post-war challenges were superficially successful but ultimately futile. The burst of films shot on location was not really an answer to increasing costs as long as the massive studio overheads remained a constant worrying factor. The growth of small successful companies such as the way that Edward Golden had put *Hitler's Children* together was the true guide to future economies not the decision of MGM to trim its staff by 25 per cent in 1947. *Film noir* was useful in that it obviated the necessity for lighting entire sets but it cannot be truthfully stated that such films were ordered by production heads because they were considered to be the films that future audiences would wish to see. Hollywood invariably reacted to shifts in public demand. Its actual creation of consumer demand was restricted principally to its costumes, wigs and art direction. The world that Hollywood depicted had vanished with the Second World War and its traditional audiences having been subject to a wide range of real emotions were no longer prepared to put up with the fake heroics and easy sentimentality they had previously devoured.

As usual it took a series of external factors operating on Hollywood to awaken the industry to a new realisation. In 1947, three deadly prongs started their journey towards the heart of the American film industry. Legal proceedings were commenced by the government under existing anti-trust legislation in an attempt to divorce film production companies from their holding of cinemas. The result was beneficial in the sense that it allowed the small independent companies the chance to have their films exhibited on the major circuits, but it induced in the studios such a terror of what the future held that the self-confidence that had been Hollywood's hallmark was replaced by grisly doubts and insecurities.

The position was not helped by the increase in the sale of television sets in 1947. The flickering joke box was now moving into a position where it could seriously threaten to keep movie audiences rooted to their armchairs. Finally, on 25 September 1947 the infamous House Committee on UnAmerican Activities renewed its investigations into the extent of the influence of Communism and other false ideologies among the urban wastelands of Beverly Hills.

The Primrose Path

(October 1947 — December 1948)

I believe that under certain circumstances a Communistic director, a Communistic writer, or a Communistic actor, even if he were under orders from the head of the studio not to inject Communism . . . into pictures, could easily subvert that order . . . by a look, by an inflection, by a change in the voice. I think it could be easily done. I have never seen it done but I think it could be done.

Adolphe Menjou
October 1947

The notorious hearings, enshrined by the passage of the years as Hollywood's time of martyrdom, should really be seen against the wider background of the political onset of the Cold War. The historiography of the hearings has, to a certain extent, obscured their real significance.

J. Parnell Thomas, with his self-righteousness, his ignorance of judicial procedure and his ironic downfall (he was sent to prison for manipulating his relatives on to the Congressional payroll) was perfect casting for the part of the principal adversary. Robert Stripling, the Chief Prosecutor, would have been played brilliantly by Henry Daniell and the array of 'friendly' witnesses ran the gamut from the monosyllabic grunts of Gary Cooper who condemned Communism because it wasn't 'on the level' to the incomparable Adolphe Menjou who, trim and debonair as ever, could also have stepped straight out of one of his own pictures.

Indeed, the extrovert drama of the hearings as a whole seemed to be its principal *raison d'être*. The Committee had been in existence since the late 1930s when Martin Dies was its Chairman, but its attempts to bask in reflected glory by investigating Hollywood had met only with scorn.

Dies announced grandly that he was 'convinced that Communist influence was responsible for the subtle but very effective propaganda which appeared in such films as *Juarez*, *Blockade* and *Fury*.' Dies's articles, 'The Reds in Hollywood' and 'Is Communism Invading the Movies?', published in *Liberty* magazine in 1940 reduced Hollywood to helpless laughter. One trade paper suggested a new Oscar be presented to Dies. 'The Classification should read "For Best Original Melodrama by a Non-Professional".' The paper then sniped at the quality of his writing — 'Whatever his status as a statesman, Dies is a third-rate magazine writer.'[1]

It should not be forgotten, however, that Dies and his committee had already demonstrated they had sufficient power to induce Franchot Tone to fly to Washington to clear a possible smear on his name, but the attempt to categorise Shirley Temple as a Communist dupe misfired badly. The Committee decided instead to concentrate its attacks on more susceptible targets such as the Federal Theater Project.

In May 1947 the Committee had made exploratory inquiries before issuing its subpoenas to the unfriendly witnesses. The ten days of investigations concluded with the interrogation of 'several film figures but failed to disclose anyone allied to Joe Stalin'. 'In toto', mocked *Variety*, 'the Hollywood hearings wound up as a "B" production.'[2]

When the scene shifted to Washington in October, the Committee decided to indulge in an orgy of publicity and their activities were endlessly photographed by a battery of newsreel cameras. The witnesses gave their testimony under the heat of the Klieg lights and could be forgiven for imagining they had not left the familiar atmosphere of the sound stage. J. Parnell Thomas, perched on a copy of the Washington telephone directory to bring his nose to the right level for the camera, wielded his gavel with the panache of a De Mille megaphone.

The performances he conjured out of his actors were impeccable. The early appearances of the friendly witnesses were laced with a sophisticated comedy Lubitsch would have admired had he been alive to have been subpoenaed. Leo McCarey evoked memories of the witty dialogue of *The Awful Truth* when he discussed mournfully why neither *Going My Way* nor *The Bells of St. Mary's* had made money in Russia. He concluded. 'we have a character in there they [the Russians] do not like.' 'Bing Crosby?' prompted Stripling. 'No, God', replied McCarey dead on cue.

Predictable interjections from the Motion Picture Alliance for the Preservation of American Ideals, as presented by Sam Wood were bolstered by the testimony of such as Lela Rogers, the redoubtable mother of Ginger, and RKO's Vice President in charge of Examining All Scripts For Possible Communistic Double Entendres. Mrs Rogers's greatest contribution to America's strategic defence was her discovery of the line 'share and share alike — that's the meaning of democracy' in *Tender Comrade*. Dalton Trumbo, one of the unfriendly witnesses and the author of the line in question, had deliberately misunderstood the real nature of democracy — which was to preserve the greatest proportion of Miss Rogers's salary from the clutches of the Internal Revenue Service and other believers in the redistribution of wealth.

Following Sam Wood, the director of *A Night at the Opera* and *A Day at the Races*, was Morrie Ryskind, the co-author of *A Night at the Opera* and other Marx Brothers vehicles. Referring to the Reds in Hollywood he declared that, 'they use techniques of character assassination and if they ever get control of the screen or of the country it won't just be characters they will assassinate.' Suddenly it became clear that the hearings bore no resemblance to a Congressional committee enquiry but that it was all part of another Marx Brothers set piece. The proceedings desperately needed the sudden appearance of Groucho sliding down a fireman's pole into the witness box, or Harpo chasing a half-naked girl across the courtroom honking his horn. J. Parnell Thomas, Stripling and the defendants would then link arms and launch into a spectacular Bert Kalmar — Harry Ruby musical number.

After the comedy of Louis B. Mayer and Jack Warner trying to justify the making of *Song of Russia* and *Mission to Moscow* without admitting anything, came the melodrama of the Unfriendly witnesses. The Ten decided, after consultations with their lawyers, that they would not be drawn into fruitless admissions of any connection with the Communist Party at all but would simply take the Fifth Amendment which exempted witnesses from giving evidence against themselves.

There is no doubt that the Ten were subject to the most appalling mistreatment. Their attorneys were denied the right to cross-examine the friendly witnesses and their statements which they wrote in self-justification were not permitted to be read into the record. Thomas took one look at Lawson's statement, read the first line and refused to admit it. Nevertheless, the Ten conducted themselves, with certain exceptions, with a noticeable lack of restraint and good judgment. The result was not only a polarisation of forces and a partial 'justification' of the Committee's attacks but the crucial alienation of a significant body of sympathetic liberal opinion.

When the hearings started the liberal community in Hollywood and other branches of the arts saw a chance to make a stand against the possible incursion of censorship into their professional lives. Over and above the question of whether or not subpoenas had been issued to members of the Communist Party was the fact that an investigative Congressional committee had decided to make it its business to attack the content and style of feature films. This distinctly unwelcome addition to the ranks of the critics was a dangerous and unhealthy trend. The Committee for the First Amendment was organised by Philip Dunne, the literate, politically conscious writer whose relationship with Darryl Zanuck had always been one of professional mutual respect. Among the 'names' that Dunne collected were Bogart, Bacall, Judy Garland and Gene Kelly, but the traditional makers of liberal opinion in Hollywood, like John Huston, Fredric March, Willie Wyler and John Garfield, also joined in. Other newcomers included Paul Henried, Thomas Mann and Helen Gahagan, the infamous 'Pink Lady' to be, who stated firmly on 24 November 1947,

'I don't know whether or not there were any Communists among those subpoenaed. But whether people are Communists, Republicans or Democrats they are entitled to decent and orderly treatment in accordance with American principles.'[3]

They didn't get it. J. Parnell Thomas, that paragon of the judicial process, declared firmly that constitutional rights didn't apply to people accused of being Communists. The proceedings thereafter degenerated into a brawl. Lawyers like Charlie Katz, the respected attorney of the Unfriendly witnesses, were physically ejected from the courtroom and the taking of testimony gave way to a series of shouting matches. The Committee for the First Amendment slipped quietly away.

Two points need to be made. First, the Hollywood trials were only a small proportion of the work of the UnAmerican Activities Committee. The members clearly felt the need for a little publicity and positively gloried in the stir these inquiries made, in contrast to their thankless investigations into the influence of Communism in the Fur Workers union. The Hollywood Ten investigations were only symptomatic of a greater malaise that was starting to sweep across America in the late 1940s. There is a tendency to take John Howard Lawson's well known statement, 'I am not on trial here, Mr Chairman. This committee is on trial before the American people' and elevate it into a latter day Patrick Henry oration — which it was not.

Following on from this, it should be stated that the much more significant parts of the testimony were those referring to the link between the New Deal and the Communist conspiracy. The various pieces of social and political legislation initiated by Franklin Roosevelt between 1933 and 1935 were known collectively as the New Deal and despite their proven necessity and value had provoked a certain amount of hysterical antagonism. Roosevelt angrily compared such reaction to a businessman who is pulled out of a river when in danger of drowning but instead of thanking his rescuer berates him for not saving his top hat as well. Chief among such Roosevelt-haters were certain members of Congress, many of whom sat on important committees. The UnAmerican Activities Committee had made its hostility to Roosevelt and the New Deal quite plain. In 1938 under the chairmanship of Martin Dies it strangled the Federal Theater Project in a welter of inflammatory statements as it denounced the helpless cumbersome offshoot of the hated WPA as an organisation virtually run by Moscow and dedicated to the dissemination of Communist ideas.

Thus when Albert Maltz, one of the Ten, admitted such crimes as supporting an anti-lynching bill, the imposition of controls by the Office of Price Administration, the legislation providing for emergency housing for veterans and the Fair Employment Practices Commission, he lined himself up on the wrong side of the political fence. J. Parnell Thomas had already declared

I just want to say this now, that it seems the New Deal is working along hand in glove with the Communist Party. The New Deal is either for the Communist Party or it is playing into the hands of the Communist Party.[4]

The real significance of the Hollywood investigations was that the public debate surrounding the measures which permitted the Federal Government an increasingly larger say in the administration of people's lives was continuing even after the death of Franklin Roosevelt. Of the Unfriendly Ten themselves Billy Wilder commented acidly that only two of them had any talent — the others were just unfriendly, and seen in terms of their overall place in the history of the American cinema the judgment was not unfair.

Much uglier than the treatment meted out to the Ten was the reaction of the industry as a whole. Before the Ten gave their evidence it was apparent that the Friendly witnesses were making idiots of themselves and the entire proceedings were likely to be withdrawn due to lack of seriousness. Criticism of Charlie Chaplin, which grew apace in the late 1940s, was still in its infancy at the start of the trials. *Variety* chortled, 'Whoever heard of a man with $10 million being a Communist?'[5]

The Hays Office, now known as the Johnston Office following the succession of Eric Johnston to the post of President of the Motion Picture Association of America, swayed predictably in the wind. At the first sign of unpopularity Johnston quickly cut the Ten free and waved them goodbye, despite the fervent assurances of continued support he had given them just before they took the stand. The Johnston Office took its cue from the New York offices of the major studios which clearly felt that the slightest whiff of scandal, especially scandal relating to trafficking in Communism, would pare their profit margins to the bone.

Johnston made frantic attempts to float above the mire and addressed various meetings in Hollywood to justify his actions and to plead for future co-operation. He told a meeting of disconcerted writers that they should write films showing Communism to be not only treasonable and subversive but also ridiculous. He followed this, somewhat confusingly, by declaring that he was in favour of a free screen, subject neither to government pressure, nor to foreign propaganda.

Over at Warner Bros, Johnston addressed the

studio calling for the removal of scenes that might stir envy and discontent in less fortunate peoples. In particular, he felt that sequences showing sybaritic eating and drinking scenes as part of the American way of life were to be kept to a minimum. He announced that he came as a messenger from the American people. Harry Warner snorted audibly at this and pointed out fiercely, 'We aren't paying you $150,000 a year for being a messenger boy'. With his finger firmly on the pulse of his Wages Department, Warner added, 'We can hire messenger boys for $100 a week — maybe less.' He then went on to press home his advantage, by asking Johnston why *Duel in the Sun* had been granted a certificate of approval. Johnston was puzzled by this and looked enquiringly at Joe Breen, his chief assistant. Breen hastily volunteered that he was away sick when the film came up for review. Harry Warner raised his eyes to heaven and despaired of his own side.[6]

Eventually it became clear that the studios were responding to pressure by removing artists of suspect political sympathies. In the early 1950s the practice was enshrined in an actual blacklist, but in the wake of the HUAC investigations of 1947 the action was negative rather than positive. *Variety* reported quite openly that Katharine Hepburn had been discarded as a possibility for the lead in Leo McCarey's *Good Sam*. McCarey told the newspaper's reporter that in view of Miss Hepburn's political sympathies he would offer the role to Ann Sheridan. Similarly, unconfirmed reports that Dalton Trumbo was working on a script for Samuel Goldwyn and John Howard Lawson for Walter Wanger were quickly denied by the respective producers.[7] In 1947-8 the atmosphere in Hollywood, as in the country at large, was fiercely anti-Communist but not yet paranoid.

Indeed, in the summer of 1948 the Cold War took an improbable turn that could have been devised by a harassed film producer on the look-out for any adventure story. As relations with Russia worsened during the early part of the year, especially following the Communist coup in Czechoslovakia in February and the suicide of Jan Masaryk, the focus of the conflict shifted to Germany.

On 1 April the Russians halted all overland traffic between the Allied controlled zones of Germany (which were shortly to be established as the Federal Republic of West Germany) and the city of Berlin. The fate of two million Berliners was held in the balance until President Truman decided to airlift massive supplies to them, if necessary supported by force. In the spring of 1949, after 277,000 flights and the air freighting of two and a half million tons of food and fuel, the Russians lifted the blockade. America had shown she was not to be coerced by a Russian bluff. More importantly, the direction of American foreign policy was swinging ever more firmly away from its traditional isolationist stance.

In this respect the crucial act was Congressional approval of Marshall Aid. The plan had not been favoured with instant approval. The Left saw in the idea of huge economic aid to the beleaguered non-Communist countries of Europe a fascist plot to break ties with Russia and initiate a new phase of American imperialism. Henry Wallace warned grimly that such 'martial' aid would lead to war. His prediction was echoed by the Right, but for different reasons. Robert Taft did not see fighting the Russians for the possession of the broken-down European continent as a sensible aim of foreign policy. Marshall Aid would either be a wasteful failure or a means of subsidising America's trading rivals at the expense of concentrating on the Asian front which was more properly the focus of American interest.

One man, Senator Arthur H. Vandenburg of Michigan converted the thinking of Congress. He himself had been a traditional isolationist until 1943 but he had supported the idea of aid for Greece and Turkey in 1947 and the following year he led the fight for the adoption of the Marshall plan. The Communist coup in Czechoslovakia made his struggle a little easier. On 1 March 1948 he rose to make a brilliant twenty minute speech in the Senate at the end of which the Bill's passage was assured. On 2 April 1948 it was law. The political and military culmination of the Marshall plan and the Berlin blockade was reached in April 1949 when America formally became the lynch pin in the formation of NATO.

In 1948, however, the Russian threat was not a major pre-occupation with the American voter as can be seen from the nature of that year's Presidential election. Harry Truman fought and won it with a campaign which replayed the old Roosevelt themes. Four years later Adlai Stevenson with policies still very much in the mainstream of the Roosevelt-Truman years lost an election to Dwight Eisenhower to a large extent because he was thought to be 'soft' on Communism.

The dominant issues in the 1948 campaign were social and economic rather than ideological.

Truman's Fair Deal was a legislative programme that promised more social security, medical aid, more money to be made available for education and agriculture and the repeal of the anti-union measure known as the Taft-Hartley Act. All of this had been voted down by Congress which gave Truman a strong base for his campaign even though it was obscured by his seemingly overwhelming superficial difficulties.

The left wing of the Democratic party broke away to form the Progressive party under the leadership of Henry Wallace and Senator Taylor of Idaho. The Civil Rights platform introduced by Hubert Humphrey, who was then the Mayor of Minneapolis, persuaded the Dixiecrats to walk out of the convention and the city bosses showed what they thought of Truman's chances of getting elected by sending delegates to win over Dwight Eisenhower. Having achieved the nomination almost by default, Harry Truman set off on his campaign with only the barest resemblance of a party behind him.

His Republican opponent was Thomas E. Dewey the man who had lost to Franklin Roosevelt in 1944. Being so far ahead of the incumbent President, Dewey felt it necessary to do only the minimum of campaigning. His 'Victory Special' train rolled smoothly across the country. Occasionally the candidate made an appearance and sometimes granted the additional bonus of a speech to the assembled mob that had gathered to touch the hem of his trim moustache. In it he would studiously avoid mentioning the name of the man he was trying to oust. Dewey campaigned for only six instead of the recognised eight weeks. The opinion polls placed him so far ahead that they stopped sampling two weeks before Election Day.

Meanwhile Truman had stumped the country in a manner reminiscent of a turn of the century politician, speaking from the platform of his train wherever two or more people were gathered together. However, his 271 speeches seemed to have made little impression on the country as a whole and in particular on the *Chicago Tribune* who celebrated Election Night with the publication of an extra edition which carried the bold headline DEWEY DEFEATS TRUMAN. The paper had been on the streets for a few hours when it became apparent to a worried editor that the results were differing greatly from the scenario he had written. Wallace was making a showing only in New York and Chicago and the Dixiecrats had taken only four

of the Southern states which had been expected to have been solid for Thurmond. Elsewhere in the traditional areas of support for the Roosevelt coalition, particularly the cities, Truman was rolling up massive majorities. By breakfast time it was all over. Truman had pulled off the most remarkable Presidential victory of the century and a replica of the *Chicago Tribune's* headline joined THE BUCK STOPS HERE on his desk.

Dewey was probably even more surprised than Truman. The Republican party had chosen him in preference to Robert Taft because the antediluvian Taft had too many enemies. But it appears in retrospect that Dewey too was tarred with the Taft isolationist brush and, in the wake of an America committed to a positive stance in foreign policy as evidenced by the Marshall plan and the Berlin Blockade, he was considered too much of a risk. In addition, with the economic panics of 1946 dispelled by the emergence of a generally more prosperous America voters clearly preferred the security and familiarity of the Square Deal to the possibility of a return to Herbert Hoover's America under the Republicans. Apart from which, the mass of voters could identify with Harry Truman where they could not identify with the urbane urbanite, Dewey. Taft implied as much when he cried at the post-election inquest,

> 'I don't care how the thing is explained. It defies all common sense for the country to send that roughneck ward politician back to the White House.'

Despite Taft's incomprehension the country had voted for more of the same which only confirmed its essential stability. More people were getting richer than ever before and the Mid-West delighted in an anecdote which told of a farmer who went into the bank to pay off his $8,000 mortgage, with a bucket full of cash. When the harassed bank clerk told the farmer he had in fact brought $10,000 the farmer replied easily, 'Oh I must have brought the wrong bucket.'[8] After the economic hiccoughs of 1946 the country seemed to have rediscovered the road to prosperity and political stability. In fact it was a mirage as the following two years were to prove.

The American film industry underwent a similar pattern of superficial profitability which served to disguise very real underlying changes. Although profits declined by 40 per cent in 1948, the absolute totals were still remarkably high and suffered

62 Forrest Tucker looks more
interested in the Coca Cola
than the result of the
election. The Republic
extras look interested in
neither.

63 Ted de Corsia sprinting
into the climax of *The
Naked City*. The woman
with the pram on the left is
pointing out the advantages
of location shooting to her
baby.

only by comparison with the boom years of 1946 and 1947. The reasons for the decline in profits were much the most interesting aspect.

From an analysis of the financial returns of the first six months of 1948 it can be seen that although the gross income was almost identical to the figures for the same time period in 1947 costs had risen so steeply that profits fell by over 25 per cent. In 1946 eighteen films had earned $4 million or more. In 1947 the figure was fifteen but in 1948 it had slumped to just seven. Even that would not have made too much difference if the run of the mill A or the staple B picture were still turning in a tidy profit. Since this was no longer true the major studios began to trim their B productions heavily thereby increasing their dependence on (and obviously the cost of) their A pictures and at the same time removing a vital training ground for talented younger directors, writers and actors.[9]

Movie-going in the 1930s and during the war was a habit and a necessity. In the more affluent later 1940s this was no longer true. In 1948, 65 per cent of the audience was under the age of thirty and it was apparent that the younger generation did not have the same worshipping attitude to the shining stars in the cinema firmament as had their parents. They would go but they would prefer to select their choices less blindly than their parents had done.

Variety analysed the top-grossing films of 1948 and concluded with a tinge of sorrow,

> The draw of star names is no more than a subordinate factor in creating an audience. The star may prove a marquee lure because of his or her performance after reviews and word of mouth get around — witness Jane Wyman in *Johnny Belinda* — but there's a mighty small handful that pull 'em in on name value alone.[10]

The handful in effect was restricted to Bing Crosby, Cary Grant, Bob Hope, Clark Gable and Lana Turner.

While the search for new stars went on Hollywood continued its attempts to give its jaded public some new sensation that was still consistent with its long cherished conventions. *Film noir* in its less Teutonic aspects managed it quite well. In 1948 Robert Siodmak directed two typical examples in *Criss Cross* and *Cry of the City*, in both of which the obsession with location shooting is apparent. *Criss Cross* tries to be slightly original in using the glare of the California sun as a backdrop to much

of its nightmare. Indeed Siodmak cleverly fashions a harsh and sinister feel to his vision of Los Angeles. *Cry of the City* is more conventional in its use of rain-washed streets and comfortless echoing churches. It is particularly memorable for the final confrontation between Victor Mature and Richard Conte, especially as Mature has discharged himself prematurely from the hospital and is wearing only a raincoat (kept discreetly buttoned).

The apogee of such pictures though was Jules Dassin's *The Naked City* which carried the name of Albert Maltz on the credits. The film opens with a helicopter shot of New York City and Mark Hellinger's voice on the sound-track declaiming, 'There is a pulse to a city that never stops beating' and his triumphant proclamation, 'This picture was *not* photographed in a studio.' The *Hollywood Reporter* was tremendously impressed by this.

> To fully appreciate the enormity of the technical contributions and the new problems surmounted it should be noted that Hellinger shot *The Naked City* right on the streets of New York and used *actual* buildings for the interiors. This is explained in the narrative which is beautifully read by Hellinger in a warm sympathetic voice, whose accent literally breathes the spirit of the city.

The *New Yorker* which clearly felt insulted by Hollywood's vision of its town responded venomously 'Mr Hellinger's remarks are about as penetrating as the spiel of a guide on a sight-seeing bus' and the *New York Times* which felt a similar instinct to protect its native city from the ravages of Hollywood found the film

> a rambling, romantic sort of picture . . . that shows a great variety of people in a number of places — but very few of them seem real.[11]

Poor Hollywood! Even its decision to shoot scenes on location produced charges of escapism. In fact, a viewing of *The Naked City* today in the hindsight of *Kojak* makes the original seem very tame stuff. The relationship between Barry Fitzgerald as the lieutenant in charge of the murder investigation and his superior as compared with that of Kojak and MacNeill makes the former seem like the polite mumblings of two civil servants. When the young policeman tracks the killer to his room, the villain merely punches the cop in the face. A modern day audience would not be content unless the policeman had been shot in the head and the murderer bled his way down the stairs.

At one point there is a neatly choreographed piece of detective trailing on and off the subway in a scene which clearly impressed the makers of *The French Connection* but the climax of the show is the chase along Brooklyn Bridge, cleverly photographed by William Daniels, Garbo's old cameraman. Again, the whole thing is done so tamely by modern standards that when Hellinger's voice announces at the end 'There are eight million stories in the naked city. This has been one of them' the natural inclination is to ask to see some of the others.

Nevertheless *The Naked City* did well at the box office and was probably a more reliable pointer to the future direction of Hollywood production than the top grossing films of the year — *The Road to Rio*, *Easter Parade*, *Red River* and *The Three Musketeers*. Certainly the failure of David Selznick's *Portrait of Jennie*, a lovingly fashioned piece of *Reader's Digest* hokum was a clear indication that something was stirring in the bowels of Hollywood.

For a start J. Arthur Rank and Alexander Korda renewed their frontal assaults but this time used the tactic of threatening to sell their pictures directly to American television unless they were granted more playing time on the major circuits than had been achieved by *The Red Shoes* or *Hamlet*. This was hitting below the belt. In 1945, 40,000 television sets were in use; by the end of 1948 there were nearly two million, and significantly, a menacing flood of $10 million in advertising revenue poured into the network coffers the following year.

Despite assurances from such prophets as Ed Sullivan that television would never catch on unless it had the full support of the show business establishment the film industry saw its casual labour force drifting ominously towards employment in television. Monogram capitulated and sold its backlog of films to CBS while William Cameron Menzies and Whitney Productions, two former associates of David Selznick in his halcyon days, started to make films directly for television.

The final prong of the fatal trident was the one which hurt the most in 1948. The studios were forced to start divesting themselves of their theatre chains in observance of the government's consent decree. Although the movie executives saw in it only the financial problems, the divorce meant the end of the instant feedback the studios used to possess when their products went on view to the public. Television with its ratings obsession was to make a vital gain. In more concrete terms the government action prodded Floyd Odlum into selling RKO studios to Howard Hughes and ultimately condemning it to death.

The bricks were slowly being worked loose from the building. The events of 1948, however, were as but the written prologue on the roller caption, compared to the disaster movie of 1949 that was still to come.

Most Disastrous Chances

(January 1949 — December 1949)

Unmarried mermaids are not permitted to have children on the American screen although they can get away with it in England. The Johnston Office has just scissored the British film *Miranda* in which Glynis Johns plays a mermaid sitting on the beach at Capri with a merminnow in her arms, though the film depicts no record of her marriage to a merman.

Variety 9 February 1949

The events of 1949, torrid as they were, had the irony of neatness about them. A decade that started with many Americans looking anxiously at the march of ideology in Europe and the rapid expansion of the military might of a European power ended with the same people feeling increasingly sure that another major war was inevitable.

While China fell to the Communists and the Russians exploded the Atomic bomb that America thought they would not have for another five years, the European allies of the USA busied themselves about their domestic affairs. With the old colonial powers vacating their imperial possessions and Communism on the march, the foreign policy which advocated the 'containment' of the Communists meant an inevitable confrontation somewhere in the world. In the event it was not to happen until the following year but 1949 was marked in America by nothing so much as mounting hysteria in all aspects of national life.

Although in retrospect, like all other historical events it looks perfectly logical, the fall of China to the Communists came as a profound shock to most Americans. In 1945 the Communists had seemed no threat as the Japanese armies on the Chinese mainland surrendered suddenly to the Nationalists. Indeed many American observers thought they were merely a set of harmless agrarian radicals who saved money on clothes, and they urged Chiang Kai-shek to ally himself with Mao. Chiang, however, had spent much of the economic and military aid sent to

him during the war for use against the Japanese invader in an attempt to eliminate Mao and his followers. Roosevelt, if he knew about it, was clearly not worried by it and he deliberately sought a powerful China to offset the might of Russia and Japan in Asia. At the Cairo and Teheran conferences Roosevelt ensured that China was accorded Big Power status.

The fact that the Japanese surrender presented the Chinese Nationalists with huge areas of territory to administer only served to increase the appalling corruption within their ranks. Madame Chiang's primary concern seemed to be the accumulation of a private fortune and her example was diligently followed by her devoted disciples. When the efficient and disciplined Communists struck at the centre of the spineless Nationalists they found almost no resistance. Chiang Kai-shek moved himself and his fortune to Formosa and the American China lobby, which had long regarded China as British Imperialists considered India, pointed hysterically at the Truman Administration in general and the State Department in particular.

Their perturbation was considerably increased when, on 23 September 1949, Russia announced that she had exploded a nuclear bomb which the American establishment insisted on calling a 'device'. The triumph of the Berlin airlift which had persuaded the Russians to call off their blockade of the city only six months before now seemed to be futile. The containment of Communism didn't appear to be working out too well in practice. Again, the State Department bore the brunt of the criticism as the fear of Communism spread like a contagion.

In the wake of the unpalatable investigations conducted by the House UnAmerican Activities Committee in 1947, the American film industry had already decided to show the cleanliness of its hands by producing anti-Communist films. The disease which gripped the country in 1949 only served to

64 The Good Old Days when the Chinese preferred the Americans to death at the hands of the Japanese and the guerillas. *China Sky.*

65 Walter Pidgeon, Peter Lawford and Angela Lansbury clarify for Janet Leigh the advantages of life in the Western democracies — like impeccable dress and coiffure. *The Red Danube.*

66 John Agar gets his first lesson in Marxist Leninism from Janice Carter. *I Married a Communist.*

strengthen its resolve.

Darryl Zanuck, not for the first time, produced the prototype of the burgeoning *genre*. *The Iron Curtain* which was made in 1948 was, ironically, written by Milton Krims, the erstwhile 'Radical', who nine years previously had co-written *Confessions of a Nazi Spy*. The mediaeval wheel of fortune rolled remorselessly on. The original writer was to have been Martin Berkeley, the Communist apostate and volunteer of damning evidence against his former brethren, but he was fated not to complete the project.

The parallel with *Confessions of a Nazi Spy* amounted to more than just the coincidence of the writer. The whole plot revolved around the true story of another foreigner who, faced with the innocence of Western democratic materialism, could only betray his evil ideology. The result of his betrayal was the smashing of an alien spy ring and the exposure of a host of fifth columnists.

Dana Andrews plays the essentially good-hearted Russian, Igor Gouzenko, a humble code clerk in the Russian Embassy in Ottawa who, along with his Russian wife Anna (the very Russian Gene Tierney) resent their compulsory attendance at Communist party meetings and would clearly prefer to live in suburbia and swap stories about their children with their neighbours. After their evidence leads to the cracking of a Russian spy network the Gouzenkos are themselves in extreme danger from which they are rescued, inevitably, by the Royal Canadian Mounted Police.

The film was not a great success. Neither Dana Andrews (who had played a Russian in *The North Star* and was hence the automatic choice for any Russian part in Hollywood) nor Gene Tierney attempted Russian accents which was on the whole understandable but their Hollywood personae clashed badly with the attempt of the producer, Sol Siegel, and the director, William Wellman, to make a film in the style of the Louis de Rochemont dramatised documentaries.

The Iron Curtain was designed, hemmed and hung in turmoil. For a start the title itself gave rise to a vicious struggle between Fox, Warners and Columbia. Jack Warner claimed he had registered the title on 7 January 1946 which would have been surprising as Churchill had not at that time coined the phrase. Although Zanuck triumphed over the other moguls he was quite unprepared for a scathing attack delivered by the Russian composers, Shosta-

kovitch, Prokofiev, Khachaturian and Miaskowsky who learnt to their horror that Fox were planning to use their music as the basis for the score to the picture. Fortunately, that paragon of judicial virtue, the New York State Supreme Court, found in favour of the studio and the composers restricted themselves to an angry letter to the Editor of *Isveztia*.[1]

The opening of *The Iron Curtain* produced violent scenes at the première in New York which was picketed by what *Time* magazine called 'Wallaceites, Communist party members, fellow travelers and troubled innocents'. The confusion was greatly intensified by the arrival of the Catholic War Veterans who were clearly there to work over the other pickets. One hundred policemen, fifteen of them on horseback, were quite unable to cope and pandemonium reigned.

> A woman shook her leaflets, shrilled with nice irrelevance at a veteran, 'I'm for Wallace'. He rumbled back, 'I'm an American'. She conked him with her handbag; a policeman moving beefily forward got it in the face on the rebound.[2]

The scene would have been a considerable asset had it been included in the picture. As it was, *The Iron Curtain* performed poorly at the box office, though it was not helped by being banned in a number of countries. The French authorities hastily withdrew their permission for the film to be exhibited after Communist pickets had attacked a cinema in Belgium where the film was showing. Presumably the potential audience did not consider that the attractions of *The Iron Curtain* outweighed the likelihood of severe physical injuries.

Despite this awkward start the anti-Communist films simply zipped off the conveyor belt in 1949. Republic's *The Red Menace* was a typical example, particularly in its reception by the *New York Times*.

> It looks as though that studio on the word of its President, Herbert J. Yates, meant it to be a solemn warning against 'insidious forces' that imperil our country from within. But the ineptitude of the plotting and the luridness with which it is played render the 'menace' unimpressive and the perpetrators oddly absurd.

The review was prefaced by the pointed observation that Republic was traditionally the home of the low budget Western, and the writer concluded that it was simply absurd to imagine 'that Republic was emerging from the Sagebrush to deal with geopolitics and more modern villains than cattle rustlers and mortgage holders.' Indeed, it would have been more accurately titled as 'Law, West of the Volga'.[3]

The film's interest to the historian lies in its use of stereotypes. Molly the temptress, the beautiful girl who lures the politically unwary into the clutches of Marxist-Leninism, is possessed of a gin-ridden Catholic mother who goes by the name of Mrs Flaherty. The good lady would clearly prefer to continue in poverty rather than accept money from her fallen daughter who assaults her ears with

'Look, ma. I don't care anythin' about that bible junk. I'm doin' all right and I b'long to a party that's gonna make the world over.'

Poor Solomon, the bespectacled Jewish poet intellecual slowly begins to realise the philistine, not to say anti-Semitic nature of his party colleagues when they condemn his poetry as 'deviationist'. In a rage Sol tears up his membership card and castigates his erstwhile friends as 'trained Red seals'.

'You pretend to fight racial discrimination but you keep reminding me that I'm a Jewish-American, that Sam down there in the office is a Negro-American, that Mollie over here is an Irish-American. We're none of us hyphens, we're just plain Americans! Go on, sneer at me! Tell me I'm waving a flag. All right, but at least that flag has three colors in it, not one . . . not one bloody one!'

Sol is finally driven to jump out of the window but he leaves a message to Molly the Temptress — 'Go back home where you belong — home to your mother and Father Leary'. (The message in its literary form is admittedly somewhat ambiguous, suggesting as it does that the poor old crone is living with the priest.) *The Red Menace* was originally supposed to close with a scene of the Statue of Liberty singing 'God Bless America' but fortunately somebody's better judgment prevailed.

Critical opinion on the film differed widely, which was in itself an indication of the changing political climate in 1949. Three years previously such piffle would have scarcely merited a second glance. Now *Variety* was moved to write

In *The Red Menace*, Republic offers a picture that is a 'must' for every exhibitor to play and for every man, woman and child in the world who value their freedom to see.

The *Hollywood Reporter*, too, thought that it rated 'the wholehearted commendation of the film industry and the public. It required vast courage and firm convictions to make this story.'[4] To a certain extent the latter was correct. R.G. Springsteen's staunch fans, who sat riveted to the screen during *Rustlers of Devil's Canyon* could not have taken too kindly to the modern dress shenanigans their hero was putting over on them.

The Red Danube, made the same year by the versatile George Sidney was a typical piece of MGM patriotic propaganda, over-produced, over-written and badly cast. It features the unlikely agnostic British officer, played by Clem Miniver, who gets involved in a pointless and vacuous theological debate with a nun (Ethel Barrymore) over the fate of a beautiful ballerina (Janet Leigh) whom the Russians are trying to recapture in Vienna. Walter Pidgeon, who is known familiarly as 'Hookey' for reasons not always apparent, has the additional difficulty of watching his second in command (the indescribable Peter Lawford, playing a character nicknamed 'Twingo') fall in love with the attractive political football. The price of Pidgeon's awakening to the evils of Communism and the dangers caused by failure to believe in God and attend His services is the cathartic death of the girl. The UN wobbles on to the scene with a belated piece of legislation that promises future protection to such displaced persons.

The most fascinating of these films was probably *I Married a Communist*, in that its history became intermingled with the bizarre obsession of RKO's current owner, Howard Hughes, who apparently closed the studio for three months while an intensive hunt started for Communists on the staff of the company. (Presumably the bedroom sets were the subject of particularly intensive scrutiny.) *I Married a Communist* used up writers and directors like paper towels. The eventual writing credits went to two screenplay writers and two story authors but the script had passed through a dozen typewriters before assuming its final shape. An estimated thirteen directors then refused to become involved with the project and Hughes began to use it as a sort of litmus paper. Anyone who turned it down was suspected of being a Commie. Among those so categorised were Nicholas Ray, John Cromwell and Joseph Losey who was shortly afterwards on his way to voluntary exile in England, having bought himself out of his RKO contract.

Hughes was forced to postpone production because of these mounting delays and Merle Oberon and Paul Lukas were eventually paid off for work they never started. The picture was finished at the end of 1949 but even then Hughes pulled it out of distribution and withheld it for a further year, at which point it was re-released under the title *The Woman on Pier Thirteen*. After all the controversy the film was only a tame, rather inept, story of trouble on the San Francisco docks. Where in the 1930s gangsters took the place of exploitative capitalist bosses, so in *The Woman on Pier Thirteen* Communists were substituted for gangsters (who might be described as vaguely American). Certainly Communists were a simple target for an industry looking for two-dimensional villains.

The rising note of national hysteria militated against any rational film criticism. John Huston's *We Were Strangers*, although made in 1949 was a faint echo of the director's contributions to the liberal Warner Bros biographical pictures of the previous decade, and it benefits not at all from its stylistic flirtation with neo-realism. Either way it was a harmless story of a group of patriots who dig a tunnel in their attempt to assasinate the Cuban dictator Machado. The explosion of critical reaction must have surprised Huston. Despite the redeeming virtue of being called 'capitalistic propaganda' by the *Daily Worker*, the film clearly aroused a cold fury in The *Hollywood Reporter*.

> *We Were Strangers* is . . . the heaviest dish of Red
> theory ever served to an audience outside the
> Soviet Union . . . . It's party line all the way
> through — the Americans are shown as nothing
> but money-grubbers and the down-trodden are
> urged to revolution to achieve their freedom. . . .
> It is a shameful handbook of Marxian dialectics.

The Los Angeles district Federation of Womens Clubs was moved to write an open letter to Harry Cohn pinning the blame squarely on the studio that provided the below the line facilities. 'It is our duty to warn our members against what we feel is the latest propaganda assistance given free to Communist adherents.'[5]

Americans have traditionally been reluctant to admit that their own brand of democracy was not the only system of government right-thinking, free-thinking people automatically wanted. It was one of the principal reasons for their involvement in Indo-China in the 1960s and it was the major cause

of the great conspiracy theory which so gripped the country in 1949. If the peoples of the world who had been liberated from Nazi barbarism were going Communist there had to be a sinister reason for it. If the thought occurred to them that perhaps not all the world wanted to be as up to date as Kansas City, it was quickly suppressed. The more the map of the world became covered in the red of evil Communism instead of the red of misguided British Imperialism, the more convinced most Americans became that the only explanation there could possibly be was a betrayal, probably in the State Department.

The focus of all this discontent was the remarkable trial of a former State Department official, Alger Hiss, who was accused of being a member of the Communist party and of an espionage ring during the 1930s. His chief accuser was a former Communist called Whittaker Chambers, a fat, brooding former editor of *Time*. It was Chambers who gave the HUAC one of its most treasured moments when he led the members to his Maryland farm, and under the glare of the newsreel lights, reached into a hollowed-out pumpkin and produced a microfilm of classified State Department documents.

Fascinating as the personal contest between Hiss and Chambers was, when a second trial followed the hung jury verdict of the first, the personalities faded into the background and the two men became simply symbols of their respective ideologies.

Alger Hiss standing in the dock, immaculately attired, became the personification of the New Deal. Hiss had been educated at Harvard, a graduate of the Class of '29, a one time member of a top law firm and the Washington *Social Register*. Chambers was a graduate of the doss houses of New Orleans, an unhappy piece of flotsam, tossed up at the unpleasant and violent end of the radical spectrum of the 1930s. Hiss had come to Washington in 1933 as part of that band of bright young men who followed Roosevelt into power. While working for the Department of Agriculture under one of Roosevelt's most radical advisers, Rexford Tugwell, Hiss had presumably flirted with Communism. Fifteen years later he was standing trial for just such an 'offence'. It comforted those who had hated the New Deal or (more commonly) outgrown the need for the New Deal to be able to pin the blame on somebody in particular.

Disillusionment with the New Deal, domestic reform that was supposed to have carried on under

Truman's Fair Deal, merged in 1949 with profound dismay at the growing force of Communism in the world and the deeply rooted belief that the country's major institutions were swarming with Communist traitors. A primary list seemed to include Roosevelt and Truman, the unions, Marshall Aid, Hiss, Dean Acheson and the State Department. The rising tide of anti-intellectualism was one useful counter to such danger. The UnAmerican Activities Committee was the most glamorous, certainly the most publicised product, but the years 1949-50 saw the mushrooming of ladies' committees like the one that wrote so urgently to Harry Cohn. Mostly they concentrated their activities on stalking local bookstores and libraries for books they considered to be pro-Communist. *The Grapes of Wrath* was one of the first books designated for burning.

Ironically in 1949 reports reached the West that the John Ford film *The Grapes of Wrath* was doing wonderful business behind the Iron Curtain. Performances were preceded by a lecturer who pointed out that the picture of dispossessed Okies was an accurate portrait of general conditions in present-day America. Darryl Zanuck modified the story somewhat when he told *Variety* that the Russians had re-dubbed and re-edited a print of *The Grapes of Wrath* to prove that the Okies were typical Americans but when the print reached Yugoslavia it had to be hastily withdrawn from distribution because the standard of living of the Joads was still better than that experienced by the Yugoslavs in 1949.[6]

The shocks of that year in America united a wide range of social and economic groups in their attacks on Communist infiltration in the State Department. The post-war prosperity had released many former New Dealers from their emotional commitment to such reformist policies. Mid-Westerners who had been persuaded to vote for Roosevelt and Truman took a good look at the creases in Alger Hiss's trousers and at Dean Acheson's moustache and returned to the fold. Capra country became solid for McCarthy. The recent immigrants, in an attempt to demonstrate the sincerity of their jingoism, wanted no part of a foreign policy that could leave them vulnerable and potential traitors.

After the war too, the Catholic Church felt freer to follow the 1937 Papal Encyclical that forbade any collaboration with Communism. (It had been conveniently ignored in 1941-5.) One priest attacked a candidate who was running for the Ohio State Senate on the grounds that the man had given his support to a motion calling for the abolition of film censorship — a clear indication of Communist sympathy. If the priest needed any support he needed only gesticulate in the general direction of Cardinal Spellman whose utterances in these years were full of references to the acute danger posed by native Communism.

The atmosphere of suspicion and fatalism conveyed itself to the film-makers in Hollywood in more ways than simply the production of anti-Communist movies. The tone of the crime pictures and the thrillers, particularly those it has been suggested may be covered by the general term *film noir*, became even blacker.

Rudolph Maté found what might be described as the perfect opening to his low budget thriller *DOA*. Edmond O'Brien wakes up one morning to discover that he is dying of a slow poison. After dutifully reporting the fact to the police station he spends his last hours on earth in a painful search for his own murderer. The film, very brutal and gory for its time, was easily surpassed by the return of James Cagney to the post-war criminal scene. In *White Heat* (also 1949) as the Oedipal Cody Jarrett and the following year in *Kiss Tomorrow Goodbye* Cagney reached heights of manic fury barely dreamt of by Tom Powers (*The Public Enemy*, 1931) or Rocky Sullivan (*Angels With Dirty Faces*, 1938). When Tom or Rocky killed it was for business. Cody does it almost for pleasure. Locking an expelled member of his gang into the boot of the car, Cody allows him 'a little air' by spraying him with machine gun bullets. The death wish which seems to be with him anyway is intensified after he learns of the death of his mother. 'Top of the world, ma!' he screams as he goes up with the oil refinery.

The self-destructive urge of the psychopathic criminal was joined by the increasing cynicism of the *femme fatale* whose position it has been noted earlier is central to any examination of *film noir*. At the end of *The Strange Love of Martha Ivers* (1946) Barbara Stanwyck and Kirk Douglas die, but some hope is reposed in Van Heflin and Lizabeth Scott who walk away from the scene of evil unharmed. At the conclusion of *The File on Thelma Jordan* (1949) not only do Stanwyck and her lover die in a car crash but Wendell Cory, whom she manipulates with cold-hearted cynicism throughout her trial for murder, is not cleared as the classic Hollywood formula would have decreed. Instead he loses both his wife and his career and departs for the sunset with nothing but his guilty conscience to keep him warm.

This blackness of tone crept into the naturalistic pictures which Hollywood produced at this time. *T-Men* was the unnatural progeny of *Call Northside 777* and *The House on 92nd Street* but whereas in the parents the forces of evil were convincingly defeated by the forces of good, in *T-Men* right and wrong are indistinguishable. In the end even that is of no consquence since everyone dies in the final shoot-out anyway. Again, whereas the earlier films contained a good deal of daytime shooting on location, Anthony Mann's *T-Men* lives almost entirely by night. Indeed, John Alton's 'lighting' for the film seems to require the coining of a new word.

The other major trend in film production during 1949 was towards a continuation of the problem or message picture which had proved so successful for *Crossfire* and *Gentleman's Agreement* but again the emphasis was on the harsher side of the problem. If 1947 had been the year Hollywood discovered the Jews, 1949 was the year the Blacks acquired a commercial significance. *Home of the Brave* was originally a play by Arthur Laurents in which a Jewish soldier who went to pieces on a South Pacific Island discovered that his breakdown was the result of ingrained resentments and a fear of anti-Semitism. In Carl Foreman's screenplay the Jew changes colour (Sammy Davis notwithstanding) in a tradition which *Crossfire* had followed by turning its victim into a Jew from the homosexual of the original novel. (The day of Gay Liberation was still many years away.)

Home of the Brave was produced by Stanley Kramer in the greatest secrecy. His production was a low budget affair, without stars, and his only hope of commercial success was to get it into release before Fox's *Pinky* and de Rochemont's production of *Lost Boundaries* for *Reader's Digest*. The actors were instructed to tell everyone (including their agents) that they were working on a Western entitled *High Noon* and the two-week rehearsal period was conducted without the benefit of costumes so that any casual studio spy would be unable to probe the deceit.[7] The plan worked in that *Home of the Brave* was received with great critical and popular acclaim even in the South, where it played to packed segregated houses. The Texas National Guard used its exhibition as an excuse to stage a parade and recruiting drive outside the Houston

cinema where it was playing. Their stands were festooned with a banner which read HOME OF THE BRAVE — LET'S KEEP IT THAT WAY — JOIN THE TEXAS NATIONAL GUARD. It all depended on your definition of the term.

Lost Boundaries was less impressive in every way, principally because it fudged the issue. The story concerns a light-skinned Negro doctor who, against his better judgment, 'passes' as a white in the small New Hampshire village where he practises. When he is refused a commission in the Navy during the war, his terrible crime is revealed to all and his son runs off to Harlem where he is confronted by a sea of hostile black faces and acute squalor. His father catches up with him and persuades him to return to the village where they face the uncertain future as a united family.

The real problem is that since the doctor (played by Mel Ferrer) looks white it is impossible to understand why the villagers are so upset. It would be perfectly possible for them to accept him as white because to all intents and purposes he is white. The film then is really about the bigotry of small-town life rather than the difficulties of racial integration.

The same objection could be applied to *Pinky*, whose heroine, Jeanne Crain, again looks white and had 'passed' as such in the North where she works as a nurse. Her white doctor fiancée comes to take her back but she becomes gradually reconciled to her black origins and stays in the poverty of the South, turning the mansion of the local landowner into a day centre and clinic for the local children.

The most forthright of this sudden rush of Negro pictures was Clarence Brown's *Intruder in the Dust* made from the William Faulkner novel. Brown had shown his masterly control of small-town life in the 1930s with *Ah Wilderness* and *Of Human Hearts*, but *Intruder in the Dust* has a bitterness and a fatalism which neither his earlier films nor his rivals in 1949 ever matched. A proud and obstinate small land-owner (Juano Fernandez) who rarely speaks, or indeed betrays any emotion at all, is falsely accused of shooting a white man in the back. His refusal to behave like the archetypal frightened black, blubbering and rolling his eyes, is particularly resented by the large collection of local bigots who are all set on a cheerful lynching, until halted by an old lady strategically placed in the doorway of the jailhouse, rocking away and knitting.

Variety made its own enquiries into the financial performance of these message pictures and con-

67 The man with one arm (Frank Lovejoy) meets the man with the wrong
colour (James Edwards). The director wasn't Jewish. *Home of the Brave*.

cluded that 'the public will buy 'em but they gotta
be good.'[8] Certainly when the definitive list of top
money-making films for the year 1949 was released,
Pinky was in second place with a highly respectable
domestic gross of $4.2 million. *The Snake Pit*,
Anatole Litvak's disturbing portrait of life in an
asylum, which brought Olivia De Havilland a second
Oscar, came in fourth though the crowds were
almost certainly attracted by the film's blatant but
effective sensationalism rather than by the intrinsic
importance of the problem of mental illness. Not
surprisingly, the Top Ten was largely composed of
musicals (*Jolson Sings Again*, *Words and Music*) and
conventional star vehicles (*I Was a Male War Bride*
and *Little Women*) but the worrying decline in box
office attendance figures continued with a drop of
9 per cent in the year.[9]

An interesting omission from the top grossing list
was William Wellman's *The Next Voice You Hear*,
produced by Dore Schary with all the bad taste of
which MGM at its best was capable. The story was
overwhelming in its banal simplicity. Every night for
six nights God talks to the world in the native language of each country over the radio. He encourages
people to be kind to each other and deliberately
refuses to show up on the seventh night because his
job is done. Everyman (James Whitmore, who looks
suspiciously as though he was being groomed by
MGM to be Spencer Tracy's substitute) realises the
error of his ways and is terribly nice to his old bat
of an aunt, the irascible boss and the officious
policeman and discovers that it works. Life is much
nicer all round. What a jolly good thing God popped
down when he did.

The film links religion to the developing American
culture of middle-class suburbia. The religion in the
film is not that of the serious Christian or Jew but
of a friendly Religion of the Month Club in which
theology is a by-product of social coffee mornings.
It is a religion of hymns and popular songs rather
than one of masses and spirituals. The Resurrection
is replaced in this version by the Easter Bunny and
Irving Berlin. The triviality of the film is neatly
encapsulated by the sequence in which Whitmore's
motor ignition works perfectly after God has made
his appearance, whereas when the face of the Lord
was turned away from Man Whitmore had to use the
cranking handle.

The Next Voice You Hear had missed the mood
of 1949. It was not a year for nice comforting
messages of the Capra variety (especially those
delivered without Capra's dazzling expertise). It was
a time of national anxiety and mounting fear as to
what new threat the next months would bring. In
January 1950 Alger Hiss was found guilty as
charged and sent to prison. Dean Acheson stated
grimly that he would not turn his back on the condemned man. Congressman Richard Nixon declared
in fury, 'Traitors in the high councils of our own
government have made sure that the deck is stacked
on the Soviet side of the diplomatic tables.'

On 31 January 1950 President Truman announced the start of work on the hydrogen bomb. Four
days later the British government revealed that Dr
Klaus Fuchs, one of their top atomic scientists, had
been spying for the Russians. On 9 February
Senator Joseph McCarthy, the junior and almost
unknown Senator from Wisconsin, delivered a
speech to the Women's Republican Club in Wheeling,
West Virginia. At last all the threads and all the
anxieties of post-war America were starting to come
together.

Cry Havoc—Again

(January 1950 — November 1952)

McCarthyism is Americanism with its sleeves rolled.

Senator Joseph McCarthy
Wisconsin 1950

The real problem with McCarthyism is that it tends to be directly correlated with the dizzying rise and equally rapid fall of Joseph McCarthy, all of which took place in the four years between 1950 and 1954. In fact the junior Senator from Wisconsin was not only another figure on the well populated anti-Communist stage but a demagogue in the long tradition of what Richard Hofstadter has called 'the paranoid style in American politics'.

Paranoia is the key to the understanding of McCarthy and his times. It became impossible to distinguish between real evidence of treason and the wildest of allegations. McCarthy was no Woodward and Bernstein. His attempts at 'investigation' were lack-lustre to say the least. He seemed to have little of the self-righteous bigotry that so marked the proceedings of the House UnAmerican Activities Committee and for all his 'success' there was never a time when the voices of opposition were not heard somewhere.

His first grand performance came after he was asked to substantiate the charges that he had a list of 205 people who were known to the Secretary of State as being members of the Communist party and were still shaping the policy of the State Department. Nobody made a record of what McCarthy actually said in Wheeling on 9 February. McCarthy's 'list' could have been a laundry list as rumour later had it (though why McCarthy should have taken his laundry list along to a meeting of the local Women's Republican Club is unclear — unless of course it was somebody else's laundry list). Since the Senator threw 'it' away, nobody had any proof. When the news agencies picked up the story, McCarthy tried desperately to find somebody who had made a true record of what had been said. He

appealed to ham radio operators in the area without success and could only gaze forlornly at his own notes for the speech which didn't help. Rarely had a national scare campaign opened on such a bumbling note.

The Senate demanded proof of the charges and McCarthy suddenly found himself on the centre of a stage he had only meant to sneak on to from the wings for a few moments. Now he was aided by the various right wing organisations who gladly welcomed a member of the Senate to their ranks. On 20 February McCarthy took the floor of the Chamber to make his formal indictments. He carefully stacked eighty-one obsolete folders on his desk, prepared for him by other hands, and declared that he had penetrated Truman's 'iron curtain of secrecy'.

There followed a grotesque parody of *Mr Smith Goes to Washington*. For twenty-three-and-a-half hours James Stewart had stood up and denounced graft and corruption, urging the Senators to 'get up there with that lady who stands for justice and take a look at this country through her eyes', reminding them of the great inheritance of liberty of which they were the trusted guardians. However brilliant and inspiring that scene had been it was, after all, only a movie, even if it was directed by Frank Capra. Now, for six hours, Joseph McCarthy stood on his feet, refusing to yield the floor (he had seen the movie, too, presumably) while the Hearst Press played Jean Arthur to his Jimmy Stewart. As he went through each of the eighty-one folders it slowly dawned on the rest of the Senate that he had never laid eyes on them before. File number 9 turned out to be the same as number 77; Numbers 15, 27, 37 and 59 did not exist; number 72 turned out to be in the Senator's own words 'a first rate chap, a democratic American who ... opposed Communism'.[1] At the end of the show nobody ran into the cloakroom to kill himself, although most of the Republicans present might well have hoped that McCarthy would follow Claude Rains's example and relieve them of an awkward embarrassment.

Yet again the parallel with *Mr Smith* was uncanny. Just as Smith's speech in the Senate about building a boys' camp had produced a cascade of envelopes with pennies and nickels in them, so McCarthy's wretched fiasco resulted in a torrent of envelopes sent from all over the country, which arrived each day in the Senator's office with loose change and bank notes of small denomination in them. The public opinion polls confirmed that McCarthy's support in the grass roots was growing ever stronger. Slowly the Republicans in Congress started to admit that McCarthy was one of them and even Robert Taft, that distinguished son of a former President and a seeker after the highest office himself, the man who had castigated Harry Truman as a 'redneck', saw the value of McCarthy and identified himself, albeit gingerly, with the son of a working-class Irishman. As Nixon became to Eisenhower so McCarthy could be to Taft.

With his support tangibly growing McCarthy acquired the confidence to start personal denunciations, however wild and however absurd. After another weird and dramatic performance he named 'the top Russian espionage agent' in the United States and 'Alger Hiss' boss in the spy ring in the State Department' as Owen Lattimore. Lattimore, a professor at Johns Hopkins University, had been a top advisor on Far Eastern policy and his realistic assessment of Chiang Kai-shek and his administration had earned him the dislike of the China lobby. Still, he was not the sort of man to be found skulking around deserted State department offices at the dead of night armed with an instamatic camera.

Once again McCarthy seemed to have overreached himself. Lattimore testified before the Tydings committee, set up in the wake of McCarthy's earlier charges, and satisfied them that his loyalty was unquestionable but in the mind of the great American public the mud that had been slung at him had been thrown for a reason, however obscure. And so it proceeded. No matter how impossible the charge was to substantiate the fact that it was made was regarded as *de facto* evidence.

In Wheeling, West Virginia where it all began, a violent controversy started when it was discovered that one of the little cards enclosed in packets of bubble gum informed the unwary child that the USSR with its population of 211 million people had its capital in Moscow and was 'the largest country in the world'. The corrupting card was removed from circulation. Yale University had to appoint a committee of distinguished alumni to protect itself against charges of Communist subversion brought against it by William F. Buckley, a recent undergraduate. Mrs Thomas J. White, a member of the Indiana State Textbook Commission charged 'there is a Communist directive now to stress the story of Robin Hood . . . because he robbed the rich and gave it to the poor. That's the Communist line. It's just a smearing of law and order.'[2] No doubt Mrs White would have been relieved to hear the Mel Brooks version of twelfth-century English history in which Robin Hood is finally revealed as a man who 'took from everyone and kept everything'. (The Communist in the woodpile was Robin's press agent, Marty, who 'wrote in scrolls he robbed from the rich and gave to the poor. He gave you such a smack in the head when he robbed you, who knew?')

The incidents piled on each other, progressing slowly from the comic and the bizarre to the sinister and the tragic. Hollywood, ever the bellwether of popular opinion, quickly wiped its hands and presented them for inspection to the UnAmerican Activities Committee. Monogram Pictures cancelled a projected film about Henry Wadsworth Longfellow on the grounds that Hiawatha's peace activities might be misconstrued as propaganda for a Communist peace initiative. The Committee, now chaired by John Wood, a Democratic Representative from Georgia was, if anything, even more iniquitous than it had been under the rule of J. Parnell Thomas.

This time the Committee headed straight for the actors and showed less interest in the writers. Sterling Hayden, Will Geer, Lee J. Cobb, John Garfield, Gale Sondergaard, Jose Ferrer, Karen Morley, Howard da Silva and Larry Parks were all subpoenaed. Some recanted and some didn't; all of them were asked for 'names'. Larry Parks begged not to be made to crawl through the mud. The Committee was not impressed. This second series of investigations, which ran parallel with McCarthy's own 'inquiries', resulted in the infamous blacklisting of all people whose views were in the slightest way suspect. The talent that was thus expelled might not have been particularly important but the climate of fear and suspicion thus engendered in the remainder of the profession led to a near-fatal creative sterility in the 1950s.

Meanwhile the anti-Communist films continued to roll off the production line. MGM sold its loveliest symbol of American virginity (Elizabeth Taylor)[3] into Communist bondage when she married Robert Taylor who, it transpired during the course of *Conspirator*, was a Soviet spy. When the Communist party orders the former star of *Song of Russia* to dispose of his lovely bride, he realises that party loyalty isn't quite what a superficial reading of Marxist doctrine had led him to believe and he commits a convenient suicide.

The Warner Bros offering was *I Was a Communist for the FBI*, again written in the style of *Confessions of a Nazi Spy* but lacking its predecessor's genuine anger. *I Was a Communist* tells the story of a man (Frank Lovejoy) who pretends to be a Communist, despite the whips and scorns of his family and close friends, in order to give the FBI vital information on the native Communist movement.

The film is typical of the patriotic chest thumping and reckless red smears that characterise the *genre* but for all its glib exploitation of Communist ideology and its one dimensional heroes (WASPS, Catholics and Schoolmarms) villains and dupes (liberals, blacks, labourers), it contains one scene of particular interest. In a luxurious hotel suite the principal Communist agents are eating caviare, guzzling champagne and toasting Soviet Russia, who made it all possible. Waving a hand a little vaguely, one of them declares, 'This is the way we're all gonna live when we take over the country.' a studio press release made it quite clear that although in the best tradition of Hollywood, genuine not imitation caviare was used for the scene, it was of the domestic variety and not imported from Russia.

The classic film of this period was undoubtedly *My Son John*, an appalling piece of anti-intellectual snobbery, conceived, co-written, produced and directed by Leo McCarey whom we last met in these pages misunderstanding the political issues of the Second World War. *My Son John* killed off Robert Walker both on screen and off and was an iniquitous waste of the rare talents of Helen Hayes. Walker plays John, the academically able son of the Jeffersons, a solid middle-class God-fearing American family. John is clearly 'not quite right i' th' ead' and, although his mother (Miss Hayes) defends him dutifully, his father (Dean Jagger) makes it quite plain that he doesn't think too much of his son's Washington job.

John arrives home and is asked by his father, 'How are things in Washington? People beginning to see things the way they are?' — a crushing indictment of the Truman administration and one to which John has no answer. Dad is active in the American Legion, boasting that attendance has recently doubled. John helpfully tries to re-write his father's speech to the Legion but the attempt is repelled with heavy casualties. 'He uses $2 words', complains Dad to Mom, which in the days when milk was less than 10c a pint was a powerful insult.

The fear of John's incipient Communism greatly distresses the household. His mother, who relies on two books alone, the Bible and her cookbook, makes John swear on the former that he is not now nor ever has been a member of the Communist party, but this is not enough and a violent quarrel which ensues when Dad returns from the Legion meeting, culminates with his clouting John on the head with the ubiquitous Bible. John falls over in the fracas and cuts his knee. His mother throws Dad out of the house and he gets healthily drunk in the time-honoured manner prescribed by the Motion Picture Alliance for the Preservation of American Ideals.

At this juncture Van Heflin appears as Steadman of the FBI, who suspects that John is involved with Ruth Carlin, the real-life spy recently convicted of being a Russian courier and sentenced to twenty years' imprisonment. When a key to Carlin's apartment is discovered in John's trousers, Mom flies after him to the capital, has a wander round the Washington Monument, the Lincoln Memorial and the Jefferson Memorial, in the face of which she realises some fundamental truths about her family. Dad, the old bigot, has 'more vision than any of us because you listen to your heart'. When John tries to get the fatal key from his mother he finds her implacably opposed to him. He threatens to have her committed to a mental institution (the implication being that this is a fairly standard Washington operating procedure for people of dissenting political views) and when he resorts to violence finds that clenched in his saintly mother's fist is not the key but — horror! — a crucifix!!!

Even at this stage his mother offers John the chance afforded to all sinners — the opportunity to repent, although she recognises that her son's refusal to play (American) football at school still presents a major obstacle. She begs him to redeem

68 Dean Jagger moments before he assaults Robert Walker with a
hardbacked version of the Bible. Helen Hayes assumes a strategic position
on the stairs. *My Son John.*

69 Van Johnson and friends in one of the best of the crop of war pictures
on release in 1950. *Battleground.*

70 John Wayne looking for Douglas MacArthur. *They Were Expendable.*

himself by 'taking the ball before the clock runs out' and she promises to cheer for him should he do so. But John makes no move, probably still trying to work out the metaphor and what he is supposed to do. 'There's the gun', sighs Mom. 'We lost. That was a tough one to lose.' The mental institution looms larger for Helen Hayes. This time on compassionate grounds.

In the face of Leo McCarey's overwhelming self-righteousness even Robert Walker cannot remain unmoved. 'The lower you sink, the higher you rise in your party, don't you John?' says Van Heflin. John slinks out of the window, recognising that his treasonable activities do not fit him to walk out through the front door like an upright believer in free enterprise. He offers to make a deal with the FBI, but before he can do so he is rubbed out by the Commies on the steps of the Lincoln Memorial. Fortunately, his last minute repentance is preserved in his speech to his Alma Mater which he just happens to have in his pocket. This is read by Van Heflin with all due solemnity.

> 'Hold fast to honour. It is sacred. I am a native American Communist spy and may God have mercy on my soul.'

The camera pans up the window of the cathedral and the music track asserts powerfully that the Republic has been saved once more but the price of freedom is eternal vigilance and a deep-seated mistrust of Washington book readers who don't play football.

Even the paranoid fears in American life so evident in the years 1949-51 and the dazzling rise of McCarthy's comet could scarcely account for such a film. The seal of approval to *My Son John* had been granted on Saturday 24 June 1950 when North Korean troops crossed the 38th Parallel and invaded the Republic of Korea. For a few days thereafter it looked as though the United States government were preparing to endorse another Munich. Dean Acheson had always held that Korea was outside the perimeters of security it would be worth America's while to maintain and was so strategically unimportant that it would be pointless to launch a military attack in its defence.

However, the refusal of the Russian representative, Jacob Malik, to attend the United Nations Security Council, meant that the Russians would not exercise their veto on any resolution. The call for a cease fire on the Sunday was ignored by the advancing North Koreans and after forty-eight anxious hours, Truman decided to send in American naval and air forces. It was a decision that produced almost unanimous support in the country. On the Thursday Seoul, the capital of the Republic of Korea, fell and General MacArthur's reports made it quite clear that unless American ground troops were committed immediately, there would be no point in the Navy's even leaving harbour. After listening to the advice of his cabinet and top military advisers, on 30 June Truman sanctioned the full use of the American forces. For a brief moment in the middle of 1950 it seemed as if the old unity of Second World War days was about to be recaptured.

There followed an entirely unexpected and undignified period of six weeks in which the American troops were utterly humiliated, after which MacArthur got to grips with the situation and started to push the North Koreans grimly towards the 38th Parallel, while another army landed at Inchon and began to squeeze the North Koreans eastwards and northwards. Soon, advance units of the UN armies were on the banks of the Yalu River which separated North Korea from Chinese Manchuria. On 24 November General MacArthur launched his final offensive designed to unite the two Koreas under UN supervision. 'The war', he told reporters confidently, 'is very definitely coming to an end shortly.'

The big danger all along had been the possibility of Chinese intervention. Truman had flown to meet MacArthur for talks on Wake Island in which MacArthur had apparently assured the President that there was no danger of the Chinese entering the war and that even if they did they would be rapidly dealt with. On 26 November Truman learned from MacArthur via the Chief of Staff, General Bradley, that 'the Chinese have come in with both feet'. The central division of the UN forces retreated and the First Marine Division were cut off forty miles from their own lines. They fought their way back but it was a pyrrhic victory. For all the experience of two world wars the belief had persisted that the boys would be home for Christmas. Now, as Seoul fell to the Communists for the second time, it was perfectly apparent that the boys were not coming home, not victorious at any rate, for a long time yet.

For the American film industry the Korean War was embarrassingly convenient. Wars were always good for business and the latest one was no exception. After six weeks the box office trend which was traditionally a downhill one in the summer months was clearly pointing upwards. In November 1950 *Business Week* commented,

> This year, the spring season, which is normally good was very bad. Exhibitors looked forward to the traditionally dull summer with little hope of relining their pockets. But then Korea broke — and for some unexplained reason unloosed a rush at the box office. Summer business was way ahead of what had been expected.[4]

The outbreak of war brought renewed hope to an industry that was watching with increasing alarm the closure of its picture palaces. Six hundred had shut their doors for the last time in the first six months of 1950. Once war had broken out, however, there was a rush to get films completed before predicted 'shortages' began. In the second half of the year 221 films were made as against 191 in the comparable period of 1949.[5]

Despite the welcome boost to cinema attendances, the industry reacted cautiously to the making of new war films. Darryl Zanuck, whose jingoism had been much in evidence during the early months of 1942, had to be persuaded by the President himself to make the short film *Why Korea?*, in which the origins of the war were badly explained to an uninterested audience. The distinction of being the first war film fell to Sam Fuller's *The Steel Helmet* which was shot in twelve days, largely in Griffith Park, at a cost of $104,000. Despite the cardboard tanks it had a certain genuine urgency about it although the Pentagon had turned down Fuller's request for combat footage because an American sergeant (played by Gene Evans) is depicted shooting an unarmed prisoner.

It had taken Hollywood six years to produce the realistic *The Story of GI Joe*. Thereafter war pictures got better and better. Lewis Milestone's *A Walk in the Sun* (1946) was followed by William Wellman's *Battleground* and Henry King's *Twelve O'Clock High* both of which deservedly finished high on the list of the Top Ten money-making pictures of 1950. Good movies about Korea though were in short supply during the course of the war. Sam Goldwyn produced the inept *I Want You* in which Farley Granger struggled to portray Dana Andrews being unsure about whether or not to get into a uniform provided by the Wardrobe Depart-

ment. *Hold Back the Night*, *Battle Circus* and *Hell's Horizons* failed to match the appeal of their titles.

Retreat Hell!, written and produced by Milton Sperling, was supposedly based on the reaction of the Marine First Division commander who, when asked if his men were retreating the forty miles to join their comrades, replied caustically, 'Retreat? Hell! We're just attacking in another direction.' The review of the film version of this epic disaster noted the incestuous nature of the Hollywood war film.

> Under Joseph H. Lewis's direction [the actors] all play their roles with the solemn authority of fellows who have seen all the right war films.[6]

The grim tidings from the front made for the same kind of fatalistic despair that gripped Britain and France during 1915 when the horrors of trench warfare became apparent. Apart from the war in the Pacific the Second World War had been fought in a way where it could be clearly seen that the Allies were appreciably winning. But as the winter of 1950-1 gave way to spring it seemed as if nothing were going to break the monotony of the war news until Harry Truman decided to fire his country's one unimpeachable godhead.

It mattered not to the nation at large that the President of the United States was, *ex officio*, the Commander in Chief of the armed forces, and as such perfectly entitled to dismiss General MacArthur, especially in view of the General's blatantly wrong and disastrous forecast of the reaction of the Chinese Communists to his North Korean exploits. What mattered, as one outraged telegram put it succinctly, 'WHEN AN EX-NATIONAL GUARD CAPTAIN FIRES A FIVE STAR GENERAL IMPEACHMENT OF THE NATIONAL GUARD CAPTAIN IS IN ORDER.' Truman, who had not been at all popular since November 1948, apart from the brief period following his decision to send the army into Korea, found himself the object of such venomous hate as was not even accorded Richard Nixon during the later stages of his career. Truman was burnt in effigy in countless towns and booed heartily when he made personal appearances at two baseball games. One popular joke proclaimed, 'This would never have happened if Harry Truman had been alive.' In Seattle a critic of MacArthur and a supporter of the President had his head shoved into a bucket of beer and held there.[7]

MacArthur flew back to America after his dismissal and aroused a massive chorus of support. Frenzied crowds besieged the front doors of the Waldorf-Astoria Towers when he took up residence in New York. The Police Department estimated that seven and a half million people lined the streets of the city to greet the hero as he rode past in his Cadillac and the Department of Sanitation announced that they had dropped sixteen and a half million pounds of litter. Even given a natural tendency to exaggeration the figures represented a lot of people and a lot of rubbish.

On 19 April 1950 just eight days after being stripped of his authority, Douglas MacArthur addressed a joint session of Congress, an honour reserved for such formidable personages as Winston Churchill in January 1942 when the links between America and Britain were never stronger. MacArthur had claimed to be 'non-political'. 'The only politics I have is contained in a single phrase known well to all of you — God Bless America!' he had confessed on his arrival, and an apolitical nation sat glued to its radio and television sets to hear what the apolitical general would say to the supreme political chamber. He made it quite clear that he regarded Truman's limited war plans as an appeasement of Communism and affirmed that in war there was no substitute for victory. His thirty-four-minute speech was interrupted thirty times by ovations and was concluded by MacArthur's recalling an old ballad that had been popular in his youth,

> 'which proclaimed most proudly that "old soldiers never die; they just fade away". And like the old soldier of that ballad I now close my military career and just fade away, an old soldier who tried to do his duty as God gave him the light to see that duty. Goodbye.'

There was hardly a dry eye in the house. Even Representative Dewey Short of Missouri, a Congressman noted for his liberal education at Harvard, Oxford and Heidelberg was moved to announce, 'We heard God speak here today; God in the flesh, the voice of God.' It was true enough that MacArthur inspired such idolatry. Thousands of New York crowds had been observed crossing themselves as MacArthur drove past them. Herbert Hoover spoke solemnly of him as 'a reincarnation of St Paul into a great General of the Army who came out of the East'. When MacArthur was late for a public appearance a journalist commented that he was probably having difficulty getting himself unnailed from his cross. The joke did not get a big laugh. After all it was probably true.

MacArthur himself did nothing to discourage the growing rumours that attested to his deification. The pipe, the trench coat and the gold-encrusted cap were outward manifestations of the new god and the General knew well enough of their value when linked to a careful and dramatic public presentation of himself. As a symbol of all that was supposedly noblest about the American army his value to Hollywood had been long recognised. His evacuation from Bataan to Australia in the dark days of 1942 is pictured in John Ford's *They Were Expendable* (MGM, 1945) as a major triumph. His appearance in Fritz Lang's *An American Guerilla in the Philippines* which was fortuitously released in the summer of 1950 was similarly brief but impressive and his presence overshadowed even that of Tyrone Power. There is an implicit belief in both the American soldiers and the natives that MacArthur will be back one day to eradicate the Japanese as forecast in his famous 'I Shall Return' proclamation which is to be found written everywhere. At the end of the picture, as the General drives through the cheering throngs, Power seems to hold back for a moment but as the figure in sunglasses approaches he draws himself erect and salutes with pride and conviction.

Although the initial MacArthur controversy fizzled out within six weeks, the reaction provoked by his dismissal, like the empty charges of McCarthy, was one more indication of the troubled state of the nation. MacArthur with his 'God Bless America' routine was calling for the re-establishment of the values cherished by an older America. He stood for a McKinley style of patriotism and a Coolidgeite approach to domestic affairs. His irresponsible recommendation to the administration that 'thirty to fifty atomic bombs [be dropped] on air bases and other sensitive points in Manchuria' showed just how immature was his grasp of the complexities of the post-war world.

Nevertheless his views were largely shared by his compatriots and by none more so than Joseph McCarthy who publicly stated that Truman had fired the General after 'a night of bourbon and benedictine' and that

> 'The Korean War is only one phase of this war between international atheistic Communism and

our free civilisation. And we've been losing that war since the shooting part of World War II ended. Losing it at an incredibly fantastic rate of one hundred million people a year.'

What was so hard for Americans to comprehend was that in addition to their losing the ideological war to the Communists, which was discussed in the previous chapter, they were now not only not winning the Korean War but the administration was seemingly content to admit that it could never be won. The Korean War was not like the Second World War where the aim of total victory was unanimously sought, and where right and wrong were clearly lined up. Truman's aim was to get a face-saving negotiated treaty as soon as possible. Meanwhile the sons of American mothers died for Osan, Yangdok and the Nakton Bulge. Senator Jenner of Indiana made the sober statement, 'This country today is in the hands of a secret inner coterie which is directed by agents of the Soviet Union'. It must have come as news to Harry Truman.

The belief that the United States was facing not only Russia as the naked enemy but a vast conspiracy of hostile anti-American Communist-inspired forces lent added grist to Hollywood's anti-Communist mill. In 1952 no fewer than twelve of them rolled off the production line. Louis de Rochemont took J. Edgar Hoover's story of how the FBI cracked an espionage ring in New England, ripped it from the pages of *Reader's Digest* and brought it to the screen as *Walk East on Beacon*. It was revealed by de Rochemont's press agents that the FBI after reading the shooting script removed '27 scenes as classified secret material'. It was not explained why such classified material had been considered inoffensive when printed in the *Reader's Digest*. The *Hollywood Reporter* thought that there was some reassurance for Americans in the sight of the latest scientific gadgets being 'intelligently utilized for the successful apprehension of traitors and spies'. The reviewer in the *New Yorker* found the greatest comfort in the depiction of the leader of the Soviet spy ring 'since I wouldn't credit him with enough ingenuity to find a stone in his shoe'.[8]

The fact that nearly every such film lost money was starting to scare producers and exhibitors even more than the threat of a box office boycott or a reawakening of interest in them by the UnAmerican Activities Committee. In March 1952, John Wayne found an interesting way of killing two birds with one press release when his production company announced that the star would appear in *Jim McLain*, a story of the adventures of a Texas cattle buyer. By the time Wayne had finished with it the title had grown to *Big Jim McLain* and the foreword quoted 'Neighbor, how stands the nation?' from Stephen Vincent Benet's *The Devil and Daniel Webster*. The question was soon answered as the film was dedicated to the Congressmen of the HUAC who continue to pursue their anti-subversive inquiries 'undaunted by the vicious campaign of slander launched against them'. Wayne, the Texas cattle buyer has now become Wayne the HUAC Commie investigator in Hawaii. Together with fellow man-mountain James Arness he pays his respects to the fallen dead at Pearl Harbor, making a clear connection between the sneaky evil Japs and the sneaky evil Commies, skulking behind the protection afforded them by the Fifth Amendment. To emphasise his red-blooded Americanism, Wayne pauses momentarily from his relentless pursuit of doctrinal dissidents to dally with Nancy Olson against the romantic background of the Pacific Ocean.

Supreme in the *genre*, however, was the remarkable *Red Planet Mars* co-written by Anthony Veiller and Myles Connolly and directed by Harry Horner. Peter Graves plays an electronics expert who makes contact with Mars. When the Martians inform him of the advanced nature of their civilisation, for some reason not too lucidly explained, the entire economy of the Western world collapses. The Russians are left to gloat in triumph.

At this point the US Secretary of Defense and a top general try to persuade the President to make war on Russia while they still have the capability. Suddenly the messages from Mars assume a spiritual nature as a result of which the West pulls its socks up and the Russian peasants are inspired to overthrow their tyrannical Soviet rulers.

This amazing collection of pseudo-scientific, religious and political mumbo-jumbo suggests that Veiller and Connolly, both former colleagues of Frank Capra, had been listening to the master with only half an ear. The religious influences on Capra's work are minimal and never insistently stated. Instead, each of his major films includes either a scene or a clear reference to the goodness of man which has a biblical origin. In *Red Planet Mars* when the Americans inquire how the Martians utilise cosmic energy without blowing themselves up, they

71 'Your're right! It *is* a Communist!' *Red Planet Mars.*

are told, 'You have been given knowledge and used it for destruction. Seventy lifetimes ago you were told to love goodness and hate evil'. An earthling wonders how to explain

'that this Authority should know what we on earth were told twenty centuries ago? Or is it possible that the Man of Nazareth and the Man of Mars are the same?'

The discovery that the first messages came not from Mars but from the radio transmitter of a fiendishly clever Nazi scientist now living in the Andes and working for the Russians is followed by confirmation that the later spiritual messages were not hoaxes but genuine Martian communications reinforces the overt religious nature of the picture. *Red Planet Mars* suggests quite vividly that the world could be clearly divided into wrong-thinking atheistic perverted Communists and right-thinking heterosexual Christian democrats. In other words the surest method of destroying Communists would be to confront them with powerful God-fearing Church-goers who would be prepared to punch them in the mouth at the slightest opportunity.

The best pictures to deal with Communist spies were those which used the villains only sparingly, as plot conveniences. Sam Fuller's *Pickup on South Street* made the right anti-Communist noises but one is never convinced that Richard Widmark's conversion from apathy to patriotism is motivated by anything other than pure self-interest. Jerry Hopper's underrated *The Atomic City*, though, was a brilliantly made thriller about the rescue of the small son of a Los Alamos physicist who has been kidnapped by Russian agents. Much of it was shot on location in New Mexico and the film benefited enormously from the decision of the Atomic Energy Commission to allow Paramount to shoot certain scenes inside the Los Alamos energy plant. The kidnappers are not the usual run-of-the-mill slant-eyed foreigners or skulking cowards, but a bull-necked American and an embittered scientist. Similarly the FBI, once they realise that the ransom for the kidnapped boy is to be the secret of the hydrogen bomb, determine on an order of priorities which places first the preservation of the bomb's secret, second the capture of the spies and third the rescue of the child.

The title of *The Atomic City* had been changed from the provisional *The Los Alamos Story* on the grounds that the great American public might think that the picture was going to be a boring documentary about a town that had suddenly reclaimed its newsworthiness. For Los Alamos in the early 1950s hummed with the activities connected with the production of thermo-nuclear weapons after the immediate post-war years had seen the dispersal of the great team brought together by the Manhattan Project. On 31 January 1950 Truman had sanctioned the request of Edward Teller that work begin on the development of a hydrogen bomb, only four months after the Russians had exploded their first atomic bomb. The announcement gave the President the fleeting illusion of popularity, but in view of the outspoken public warnings issued by Albert Einstein and J. Robert Oppenheimer and the approaching panics created by Joseph McCarthy and the North Korean People's Army, the widening of the missile gap made no appreciable difference to Truman's low rating.

At one point in 1951 less than 26 per cent of Americans approved of the manner in which the President was doing his job, a figure matched only by Richard Nixon in the very darkest days of the Watergate scandal. Truman's last two years in office, like Nixon's, were tainted with what appeared to be a succession of scandals. Although Truman's personal integrity was not in question, his judgment of people and his ability to handle them repeatedly was, and scandals with which he had nothing to do at all still further besmirched his already bedraggled administration.

Corruption was discovered on the board of the Reconstruction Finance Corporation. The Kefauver Committee set up by the Senate revealed the existence of a national crime syndicate and exposed on national television the nefarious activities of Frank Costello. Three out of five members of the much admired City College of New York champion basketball team admitted taking bribes to fix the results of their matches and West Point dismissed ninety of their candidates for cheating in examinations. Also at this time statistics revealed a large increase in the incidence of juvenile delinquency. In 1952 youngsters disenchanted with their society lacked any kind of focus. No youth culture existed to cater to their needs and no heroes with whom they could identify. Marlon Brando was still taking motor bike lessons and James Dean was standing in front of the mirror experimenting with his quiff. Even more to the point the political temper of the country was swinging safely back to the Right.

The Presidential choice facing the electorate that year was reasonably clear. Although Robert Taft, a largely unreconstructed anti-New Dealer was not carrying the Republican standard as he had been quite sure he was destined to do, his place was taken by Dwight Eisenhower whose speechwriters carefully combed his addresses looking for the fateful words 'crusade' and 'liberation' in order to eradicate them. Eisenhower himself, a self-confessed political naïf, lacked decisiveness. He steeled himself to dissociate his campaign from McCarthy by speaking glowingly of his old superior General George Marshall in Milwaukee. (McCarthy had charged Marshall in June 1951 with a 'conspiracy so immense and an infamy so black as to dwarf any previous such venture in the history of man'.) To do so would have been a major challenge to the rampant march of McCarthyism but at the last moment, on the advice of other Republican politicans, Eisenhower removed the passage about Marshall from his speech altogether.

The crisis of the Republican campaign came in mid-September when the *New York Post* headlined the existence of a 'SECRET NIXON FUND' of some $18,000.[9] Nixon's counter was the now infamous 'Checkers' speech which, despite its mawkish sentimentality, was so effective that it not only ensured that Nixon remained on the ticket, but it gave the Republican campaign the necessary impetus to carry it over the finishing line ahead of Adlai Stevenson. The loser nevertheless polled more votes than any previous Presidential winner apart from his current opponent and Franklin Roosevelt in the 1936 landslide.

In contrast to Eisenhower's unsure and fumbling start Stevenson, witty and lucid, had begun strongly. Unfortunately the 'egghead' soubriquet, tossed at him without malice by newspaper columnist Joseph Alsop, stuck fast and he became identified with the intellectuals who had followed Roosevelt to Washington in the 1930s and, even more damningly, those who had followed Dean Acheson into the State Department. McCarthy drove home the implication in an infamous televised speech in which he stated, 'Alger — I mean Adlai' and went on to castigate the candidate not only for his defence of 'that convicted traitor Hiss' but also for his disastrous choice of advisers, by whom he meant, among others, Arthur Schlesinger Jr and Archibald MacLeish. For all his eloquence Stevenson seemed to be promising more of the same — and that, in

1952, meant more corruption as well as reform in government, more juvenile delinquency as well as an increase in domestic living standards.

It was no coincidence that Eisenhower won crucially in the newly created suburbs that were mushrooming in the early 1950s. The immediate post-war years had produced a 'younger' generation who acted 'older' than their parents. University campuses swarmed with undergraduates whose ambition was to work for a big corporation that wouldn't go out of business and to live in a house furnished with tangible proof that the Depression was only a bad dream. For such as these, Eisenhower, with his pronounced lack of ideology, his professed ignorance of politics, his unimpeachable war record, his reassuring smile and his preoccupation with golf, was the perfect President.

Ironically the growth of the national economy was having a bad effect on the motion picture industry. It had boomed during the Depression because films were relatively cheap to make and they found an eager receptive audience. The prosperity of the 1950s was so widely spread that the captive audience was now no longer captive. Other entertainments competed for that share of the entertainment dollar Hollywood had formerly appropriated for itself without question. Television was not the sole reason although the effect of the 'Checkers' speech was an indication of the growing power of the medium. The net profits for the seven major film companies fell from $119.4 million in 1946 to $50.5 million in 1950.[10] The blacklisting of certain 'radicals' had deprived Hollywood not only of personnel but of anything resembling courage. The divorce of cinemas from the studios' holdings broke the link in the smooth production-distribution chain. This kind of competition was bad for Hollywood's soul.

The result of these cruel blows was the loss of Hollywood's magical elixir — self confidence. The elixir vanished soon after Louis B. Mayer was removed from the company that bore his name. No longer would MGM be playfully termed 'Mayer's Ganze Mishpocha'. His departure was coincident with the erosion of the effortless ability of the other moguls to produce with some accuracy what the public wanted. Goldwyn, Selznick and Zanuck were shadows of their former selves. Paramount drove Frank Capra to stop making movies. Warner Bros films were becoming indistinguishable from those of other studios. It was the end of an era. A writer of 'B' movies made the final pronouncement echoing the remarks of Lord Grey in 1914.

'The swimming pools are drying up all over Hollywood. I do not think I shall see them refilled in my generation.'

Notes

Chapter 1   Alarums and Excursions
1 The *Hollywood Reporter*, 14 November 1935.
2 *Variety*, 17 March 1937.
3 *New York Times*, 19 June 1937.
4 Interview with the author, 12 May 1972.
5 Interview with the author, 3 May 1972.
6 *Motion Picture Herald*, 19 November 1938.
7 Quoted in Margaret Thorp, *America at the Movies*, Yale, 1939, p. 274.
8 Jack Warner, *My First Hundred Years in Hollywood*, New York, 1964, p. 281.

Chapter 2   Over There
1 W. Manchester, *The Glory and the Dream*, Boston, 1974, p. 202.
2 The origin of the false alarm was eventually traced to a wandering reconnaissance plane.
3 *Variety*, 29 March 1939.
4 *Variety*, 17 January 1940.
5 *Variety*, 17 April 1940.
6 *Variety*, 10 April 1940.
7 *Variety*, 13 March 1940.
8 *Variety*, 29 May 1940; the *Hollywood Reporter*, 29 May 1940.
9 K. Kulik, *Alexander Korda*, London, 1975, p.232.
10 The *Hollywood Reporter*, 8 July 1940.
11 *New Masses*, 16 April 1940.

Chapter 3   Walking on Eggs
1 *Motion Picture Herald*, 18 May 1940.
2 *Motion Picture Herald*, 15 June 1940.
3 *Motion Picture Herald*, 19 October 1940.
4 *Variety*, 17 January 1940.
5 *New York Times*, 17 October 1940.
6 *Saturday Evening Post*, 6 March 1948.
7 *Variety*, 24 July 1940.

Chapter 4   No Way In
1 See the persuasive book by D. Morse, *While Six Million Died*, New York, 1975.
2 *Motion Picture Herald*, 8 March 1941.
3 *New York Times*, 27 March 1941.

4 *Motion Picture Herald*, 3 January 1942; *Variety*, 8 April 1942.
5 The script was written by Frederic Raphael and the director was Clive Donner. Peter O'Toole played the Pidgeon role with the very English John Standing replacing the bullet-headed Kraut of George Sanders.
6 F. Barker, *The Oliviers*, London, 1953, p. 179.
7 K. Kulik, *Alexander Korda*, London, 1975, p.249.
8 A. Madsen, *William Wyler*, New York, 1973, p. 215.
9 *Motion Picture Herald*, 14 June 1941.

Chapter 5   A Date Which Will Live in Infamy
1 W. Manchester, *The Glory and the Dream*, Boston, 1974, p. 259.
2 *Variety*, 10 April 1940.
3 A. Kendrick, *Prime Time*, New York, 1970, p. 271.
4 Manchester, op. cit. p. 253.
5 *Variety*, 28 January 1942.
6 *Motion Picture Herald*, 3 January 1942.
7 *Variety*, 10 December 1941.
8 *Variety*, 31 December 1941.
9 *Variety*, 14 January 1942.

Chapter 6   All Through the Night
1 *Variety*, 23 September 1942.
2 *Variety*, 18 March, 1942; 30 September 1942.
3 The *Hollywood Reporter*, 18 June 1942.
4 *Variety*, 20 May 1942.
5 *New York Times*, 26 March 1942.
6 *New York Times*, 23 March 1942.
7 The *Hollywood Reporter*, 26 May 1942.
8 *Variety*, 2 December 1942.
9 *Variety*, 11 March 1942.
10 The occasion was notable too for Greer Garson's acceptance speech which went down in history as the longest and most boring speech ever experienced in a town notable for its addiction to the sound of its own voice.
11 The *Hollywood Reporter*, 10 June 1942.

12 It was supposedly in this film that O'Brien asked Van Dyke, 'Do you want the tears to run all the way down the cheek or just half way down?'
13 *Variety*, 8 April 1942.
14 J. Goodman, *While You Were Gone*, New York, 1946, pp. 30-3.
15 *Variety*, 6 May 1942.
16 The *Hollywood Reporter*, 10 June 1942.
17 *Variety*, 18 November 1942.
18 The *Hollywood Reporter*, 1 April 1942.
19 The *Hollywood Reporter*, 20 June 1942; The *Hollywood Reporter*, 12 January 1943; The *Hollywood Reporter*, 5 February 1943.

Chapter 7   Here Is Your War
1 The *Hollywood Reporter*, 21 January 1943.
2 The *Hollywood Reporter*, 11 January 1943.
3 The *Hollywood Reporter*, 20 May 1943.
4 *Variety*, 29 December 1943.
5 The *Hollywood Reporter*, 22 February 1943.
6 *New York Times*, 5 December 1943.
7 P. French, *Westerns*, London, 1974, p. 37.
8 *New York Times*, 13 January 1944.
9 W. Manchester, *The Glory and the Dream*, Boston, 1974, p. 279.

Chapter 8   Since They Went Away
1 F.L. Allen, 'Three Years of It,' *Harpers*, December 1944.
2 *Variety*, 29 March 1944.
3 W. Manchester, *The Glory and the Dream*, Boston, 1974, p. 382.
4 E.F. Goldman, *The Crucial Decade*, New York, 1960, p. 81.
5 M. Gussow, *Don't Say Yes Until I Finish Talking*, New York, 1972, p. 107.
6 A.G. Mezerik, 'The Factory Manager Learns The Facts of Life', *Harpers*, Vol. 187, September 1943, pp. 289-90.
7 The *Hollywood Reporter*, 12 February 1943.
8 *Look*, 22 February 1944.
9 The *Hollywood Reporter*, 18 May 1943.
10 *Variety*, 31 March 1943.
11 *Variety*, 13 January 1943.
12 F. Friedel, *America in the Twentieth Century*, New York, 1965, pp. 405-11.
13 The *Hollywood Reporter*, 13 January 1943.

Chapter 9   The Fruits of Victory
1 *Variety*, 22 January 1947.
2 A.H. Dawson, 'Motion Picture Economics', *Hollywood Quarterly*, Vol. III, no. 3, pp. 217-40.
3 *Variety*, 30 June 1948.

4 A. Polonsky, 'The Best Years of Our Lives: A Review,' *Hollywood Quarterly*, Vol. II, no. 3, p. 258.
5 *Variety*, 27 August 1947.
6 J. Houseman, 'Today's Hero,' *Hollywood Quarterly*, Vol. II no. 2, p. 161.
7 Ibid., p. 162.
8 *New York Times*, 20 July 1947.
9 Details in *Variety*, 8 January 1948.

Chapter 10   The Primrose Path
1 *Variety*, 21 February 1940.
2 *Variety*, 21 May 1947.
3 Quoted in G. Kahn, *Hollywood on Trial*, New York, 1948, p. 171.
4 Ibid., p. 89.
5 *Variety*, 22 October 1947.
6 *New Republic*, 27 July 1947.
7 *Variety*, 11 June 1947; *Variety*, 12 January 1949.
8 W. Manchester, *The Glory and the Dream*, Boston, 1974, p. 348.
9 *Variety*, 14 July 1948; 26 January 1949.
10 *Variety*, 5 January 1949.
11 The *Hollywood Reporter*, 21 January 1948; *New Yorker*, 13 March 1948; *New York Times*, 13 March 1948.

Chapter 11   Most Disastrous Chances
1 *New York Times*, 18 April 1948; *Los Angeles Times*, 8 June 1948.
2 *Time*, 21 May 1948.
3 *New York Times*, 27 June 1949.
4 *Variety*, 15 May 1949; The *Hollywood Reporter*, 25 May 1949.
5 The *Hollywood Reporter*, 22 April 1949; *Los Angeles Express*, 12 May 1949.
6 *Variety*, 21 December 1949; *Variety*, 4 October 1950.
7 Mark Robson: interview with author, 10 December 1975.
8 *Variety*, 19 October 1949.
9 *Variety*, 4 January 1950.

Chapter 12   Cry Havoc — Again
1 There is an excellent account of this bizarre performance in W. Manchester *The Glory and the Dream*, Boston, 1974, pp. 523-4.
2 E.F. Goldman, *The Crucial Decade*, New York, 1960, p. 258.
3 'Symbol', already, 'symbol'.
4 *Business Week*, 25 November 1950.
5 *Variety*, 14 June 1950.

6 *New York Times*, 20 February 1952.

7 R. Rovere and A. Schlesinger, *The General And The President*, New York, 1952, p. 19.

8 The *Hollywood Reporter*, 30 April 1952; *New Yorker*, 7 June 1952.

9 *New York Post*, 18 September 1952.

10 *Variety*, 27 December 1950.

Bibliography

1   Magazines, Newspapers and Periodicals
Variety
Daily Variety
The *Hollywood Reporter*
Motion Picture Herald
New York Times

2   Books and Articles
Allen, F.L., 'Three Years of It', *Harpers*, December, 1944.
Barker, F., *The Oliviers*, London, 1953.
Baxter, J., *The Cinema of Josef von Sternberg*, London, 1971.
Baxter, J., *Sixty Years of Hollywood*, London, 1973.
Bentley, E. (ed.), *Thirty Years of Treason*, London, 1972.
Bessie, A., *Inquisition in Eden*, East Berlin, 1967.
Burns, J.M., *Roosevelt: The Lion and the Fox*, New York, 1956.
Capra, F., *The Name Above the Title*, New York, 1971.
Cooke, A., *A Generation on Trial*, London, 1950.
Crowther, B., *The Lion's Share*, New York, 1957.
Crowther, B., *Hollywood Rajah*, New York, 1961.
Davis, J., 'Notes on Warner Brothers Foreign Policy', *The Velvet Light Trap*, no. 4, Madison, Wisconsin.
Dawson, A.H., 'Motion Picture Economics', *Hollywood Quarterly*, vol. III, no. 3.
Demming, B., *Running Away From Myself*, New York, 1969.
Elkan, F., 'God, Radio and the Movies', *Hollywood Quarterly*, vol. V, no. 2.
Feis, H., *The Road to Pearl Harbor*, Princeton, 1950.
French, P., *The Movie Moguls*, London, 1969.
French, P., *Westerns*, London, 1974.
Friedel, F., *America in the Twentieth Century*, New York, 1965.
Gassner, J. and Nichols, D., *Best Film Plays of 1943-4*, New York, 1945.
Gassner, J. and Nichols, D., *Twenty Best Film Plays*, New York, 1943.
Goldman, E.F. *The Crucial Decade*, New York, 1960.

Goodman, J. (ed.), *While You Were Gone*, New York, 1946.
Goodman, W., *The Committee*, London, 1969.
Gussow, M., *Don't Say Yes Until I Finish Talking*, New York, 1972.
Halliwell, L., *The Filmgoer's Companion*, London, 1970.
Higham, C., *Hollywood At Sunset*, New York, 1972.
Higham, C. and Greenberg, J., *Hollywood in the Forties*, London, 1968.
Hofstadter, R., *The Paranoid Style in American Politics*, London, 1966.
Houseman, J., 'Today's Hero', *Hollywood Quarterly*, vol. II, no. 2.
Jacobs, L., 'World War II and The American Film', *Cinema Journal*, Winter, 1967-8.
Jones, D.B., 'The Hollywood War Film' in *Hollywood Quarterly*, vol. I, no. 1.
Kahn, G., *Hollywood On Trial*, New York, 1948.
Kendrick, A., *Prime Time*, New York, 1970.
Kulik, K., *Alexander Korda*, London, 1975.
Lawson, J.H., *Film: The Creative Process*, New York, 1963.
Leighton, I. (ed.), *The Aspirin Age*, London, 1964.
Leuchtenberg, W.E., *Franklin Roosevelt and the New Deal*, New York, 1963.
Lubell, S., *The Future of American Politics*, New York, 1956.
McCann, R., *The People's Films*, New York, 1973.
Madsen, A., *William Wyler*, New York, 1973.
Manchester, W., *The Glory and the Dream*, Boston, 1974.
Manvell, R., *Films and the Second World War*, London, 1974.
Mayer, A., 'An Exhibitor Begs for "Bs"',' *Hollywood Quarterly*, vol. III, no. 2.
Miller, M., *Plain Speaking*, New York, 1973.
Mowry, G.E., *The Urban Nation*, New York, 1968.
Perrett, G., *Days of Sadness, Years of Triumph*, New York, 1973.
Polonsky, A., 'The Best Years Of Our Lives: A Review', *Hollywood Quarterly*, vol. II, no. 3.
Richards, J., *Visions of Yesterday*, London, 1973.
Rovere, R., *Joseph McCarthy*, New York, 1973.

Rovere, R. and Schlesinger A.M., *The General And The President*, New York, 1952.

Seldes, G., 'How Dense Is The Mass?', *Atlantic Monthly*, vol. 182, no. 5.

Sherriff, R.C., *No Leading Lady*, London, 1968.

Thomas, B., *Selznick*, New York, 1972.

Truman, H.S., *Year of Decision*, New York, 1955.

Trumbo, D., *Additional Dialogue*, New York, 1972.

Warner, J., *My First Hundred Years in Hollywood*, New York, 1964.

General Index

Bold figures in both indexes refer to pages on which illustrations appear.

Index of Film Titles

Hollywood Goes to War

A historian's view of the relationship between
American history and the American film industry,
this book is a witty and perceptive account of
Hollywood and its films in the years from the outbreak
of the Second World War in Europe to the end of the
war in Korea. It describes how film makers and their
industry were shaped by and responded to the strong
political and social stimuli of wartime America.

Colin Shindler offers a fundamentally different and
entertaining way of approaching the social history of
those years, by examining the recurring question of
whether the movies were a reflection of the society in
which they were produced, or whether by virtue of
their undeniable propaganda power the films
shaped that society. Combining evidence from
literary, visual and oral sources, he covers a wide
range of movies, emphasising in particular *Casablanca,
Mrs Miniver, The Best Years of Our Lives* and
Since You Went Away.

In addition to placing the films in a social and
political context, Colin Shindler writes in the belief
that great events are rarely the result of careful and
successful planning, but more typically the product
of a mixture of misguided zeal and plain incompetence.
He shows that Hollywood is a perfect example of the
bone-headed way in which people behave when they
are dealing with large amounts of money and power.

Enjoyably nostalgic, *Hollywood Goes to War* should
appeal to all film enthusiasts, to those interested in
war and its effect on contemporary society, and to
those of us who have at any time been fascinated or
repelled by a 'war movie'.

This is the second book to be published in the series,
'Cinema and Society', edited by Jeffrey Richards.
Review extracts for the first book in the series –
Swordsmen of the Screen, by Jeffrey Richards – are
displayed on the back flap.